The Soviet Union and the Politics of Nuclear Weapons in Europe, 1969–87

CORNELL STUDIES IN SECURITY AFFAIRS

edited by Robert J. Art *and* Robert Jervis

Strategic Nuclear Targeting, edited by Desmond Ball and Jeffrey Richelson

Japan Prepares for Total War: The Search for Economic Security, 1919–1941, by Michael A. Barnhart

Citizens and Soldiers: The Dilemmas of Military Service, by Eliot A. Cohen

Great Power Politics and the Struggle over Austria, 1945–1955, by Audrey Kurth Cronin

Public Opinion and National Security in Western Europe, by Richard C. Eichenberg

Innovation and the Arms Race: How the United States and the Soviet Union Develop New Military Technologies, by Matthew Evangelista

Men, Money and Diplomacy: The Evolution of British Strategic Foreign Policy, 1919–1926 by John Robert Ferris

The Wrong War: American Policy and the Dimensions of the Korean Conflict, 1950–1953, by Rosemary Foot

The Soviet Union and the Politics of Nuclear Weapons in Europe 1969–1987, by Jonathan Haslam

The Soviet Union and the Failure of Collective Security, 1934–1938, by Jiri Hochman

The Warsaw Pact: Alliance in Transition? edited by David Holloway and Jane M. O. Sharp

The Illogic of American Nuclear Strategy, by Robert Jervis

Nuclear Crisis Management: A Dangerous Illusion, by Richard Ned Lebow

The Nuclear Future, by Michael Mandelbaum

Conventional Deterrence, by John J. Mearsheimer

Liddell Hart and the Weight of History, by John J. Mearsheimer

The Sources of Military Doctrine: France, Britain, and Germany between the World Wars, by Barry R. Posen

Israel and Conventional Deterrence: Border Warfare from 1953 to 1970, by Jonathan Shimshoni

Fighting to a Finish: The Politics of War Termination in the United States and Japan, 1945, by Leon V. Sigal

The Ideology of the Offensive: Military Decision Making and the Disasters of 1914, by Jack Snyder

The Militarization of Space: U.S. Policy, 1945–1984, by Paul B. Stares

Making the Alliance Work: The United States and Western Europe, by Gregory F. Treverton

The Origins of Alliances, by Stephen M. Walt

The Ultimate Enemy: British Intelligence and Nazi Germany, 1933–1939, by Wesley K. Wark

The Soviet Union and the Politics of Nuclear Weapons in Europe, 1969–87

JONATHAN HASLAM

Cornell University Press

ITHACA

355.033
H35s

First published in 1990 by Cornell University Press.

Printed in Great Britain

Library of Congress Cataloging-in-Publication Data
Haslam, Jonathan.
   The Soviet Union and the politics of nuclear weapons in Europe,
1969–87 / Jonathan Haslam.
      p.   cm.—(Cornell studies in security affairs)
   Bibliogaphy: p.
   Includes index.
   ISBN 0–8014–2394–5.—ISBN 0–8014–9616–0 (pbk.)
   1. Soviet Union—Military policy. 2. Nuclear weapons—Soviet
Union   3. SS–20 Missile.   4. Nuclear weapons—Europe.
5. Intermediate-range ballistic missiles. I. Title.   II. Series.
UA770.H37   1990
355'.033547—dc20   89.7273
                                                       CIP

In many ways these questions are more
of politics than of defence, and more
of will than of need.

Sir Frank Cooper,
formerly Permanent Under-Secretary,
British Ministry of Defence

Contents

Preface   ix

Abbreviations   xv

Introduction: The Roots of the Problem, 1945–69   1

1 SALT I and Nuclear Weapons in Europe, 1969–72   15
   1.1 SALT and FBS   15
   1.2 Soviet Air Defence and the Impact of Vietnam   20
   1.3 US Air Power and Soviet Air Defence in Europe   27
   1.4 The Soviet Reaction to Changes in NATO
       Strategic Doctrine   29
   1.5 SALT I and NATO Politics   30

2 The Chinese Connexion, 1969–73   35
   2.1 Fighting on the Frontier   35
   2.2 China's Impact on Soviet-American Relations   36
   2.3 Reinforcement of the Soviet Far East   38
   2.4 The Threat from China Diminshed   40

3 SALT's Side-Effects, 1973–74   42
   3.1 The Price of SALT   42
   3.2 The Impact of the Schlesinger Doctrine   44
   3.3 Dissaray Within NATO   47
   3.4 Negotiations on Arms Reductions in Central Europe   52
   3.5 The Vladivostok Summit   56

4 The SS-20 Decisions: from Testing to Deployment, 1974–77   58
   4.1 The Decision on Testing   58
   4.2 NATO Rearmament   62
   4.3 The Limits of *Détente* in Europe and the Third World   70
   4.4 US Commitment to NATO in Doubt   75
   4.5 Carter Makes Matters Worse   79

5 The Reaction in Western Europe, 1977–79   89
   5.1 The Impact of SS-20 Deployment   89
   5.2 The Neutron Bomb Fiasco   96
   5.3 The Dual-Track Decision   101

6 Negotiation from Weakness: The INF Talks, 1980–83   106
    6.1 The Road to Geneva   106
    6.2 The INF Talks Begin   112
    6.3 The Russians and the Peace Movement   115
    6.4 Back to the Talks   118
    6.5 Problems with the Soviet Military   120
    6.6 The 'Walk in the Woods'   122
    6.7 Andropov Takes Power   125
    6.8 Resistance from Eastern Europe   131
    6.9 The Deadline Approaches   138

7 Reversing from the Cul-de-Sac, 1984–87   141
    7.1 The Decision to Negotiate   141
    7.2 Renewed Negotiations at Geneva   147
    7.3 Gorbachev Takes Power   150
    7.4 New Approach to Western Europe   153
    7.5 The Reykjavik Summit   164
    7.6 The Road to Washington   168

Conclusions   175

Notes   180

Bibliography   211

Index   220

Preface

On 8 December 1987 the Soviet Union and the United States of America signed an unprecedented treaty 'on the elimination of their intermediate-range and shorter-range missiles', including the Soviet SS-20 and the US Pershing II and Ground-Launched Cruise missiles. There is still no consensus as to why the Russians agreed to such an unusual measure and there is also no agreement as to why they ever deployed the SS-20. At first sight this might seem a matter best left to history. But the story behind the deployment of the SS-20 and the subsequent volte-face also contains the key to understanding the recent dramatic shift in Soviet tactics towards Western Europe.

Deployment of the SS-20 from 1976–77 caused great alarm in Western Europe. If the Russians already had weapons targeting Western Europe, why did they need to deploy a new type of missile? Why were they then apparently indifferent to protests from Western Europe? And what finally caused them not only to cancel further deployments but also to liquidate all remaining SS-20 missiles?

In an unusual if not unprecedented display of *glasnost'* the Russians themselves have been asking such questions. Soviet journalist Alexander Bovin raised the issue in *Moscow News* on 8 March 1987 and we have yet to receive a satisfactory answer: 'The building and deployment of hundreds of new missiles in Europe must have cost a huge amount of money. And if we agree to destroy these missiles: Why then were they built? Why were they deployed? It is not only me who is asking these questions. It would be very good to have competent answers to these questions'.

The SS-20 is a Western designation for the Soviet medium-range surface-to-surface nuclear ballistic missile which the Russians designated the RSD-10.[1] We refer to it as an intermediate-range ballistic missile but the Russians have no such label. The term RSD-10 refers to *raketa srednei dal'nosti* (a missile of medium-range). It is a two-stage, mobile, solid-fuel missile which came into service in 1976. Using an inertial guidance system, it can be deployed with either a 650-kiloton nuclear warhead re-entry vehicle system or three independently targeted re-entry vehicles (MIRVs), each with a 150 kiloton yield. It has a 4000 kilometre range. The missiles were carried on transporters and therefore mobile, though the transporters were limited in range; support vehicles and large command and control centres moved in train. In time of crisis the transporters may be dispersed to protected launch sites. It is estimated that from such sites the accuracy of the missile is about 750 metres circular error probable: the circumference within which 50 per cent of the warheads are expected to land. The missile would take 15 to 20 minutes to reach targets in Britain.[2]

Deployment of the missile served as the most effective public justification for the emplacement of US Ground-Launched Cruise and Pershing II missiles in Western Europe from December 1983; a step which the Russians had good cause to regret. So why did they deploy a weapon which ultimately worsened Soviet security? Clearly Soviet leaders miscalculated or, worse still perhaps, failed to make any calculations at all. But what led to the crucial decisions to test and then to deploy the missile? Initial assumptions drawn from the Western press, Western governmental publications and the Western secondary literature (all too often interchangeable) made these questions difficult to answer. *Détente* appeared to be making steady though slow progress in Europe during the mid–1970s. The United States appeared to be holding back on weapons development. The Russians seemed responsive to West European opinion, as demonstrated by concessions on human rights at the European Security Conference in 1975. Soviet defences appeared no more vulnerable to attack than before. Why should the Russians increase the capability of their nuclear forces in Europe?

Such reasoning led some in the West to draw extravagant conclusions. Former US Secretary of Defense Caspar Weinberger condemned 'the wholly unjustified creation and subsequent rapid extension of the SS-20 missile force'.[3] William Hyland agreed. As Director of the Bureau of Intelligence and Research at the US State Department from 1971 to 1975 and Deputy Assistant to the President for National Security Affairs from 1975 to 1977, he speaks with some authority. Hyland claimed the Russians aimed 'to make West European policy subject to a Soviet veto'. In his view the Russians saw the SS-20 as 'the precise instrument of intimidation'. 'Whatever the technical motives for deployment, it also seems likely that the Soviet Union sought to change radically the European balance and the European perception of that balance'.[4] It is difficult to tell whether he was the privileged beneficiary of accurate intelligence assessments or merely the victim of a fevered imagination.

There is certainly nothing wrong with Hyland's logic. But are the premisses sound? It was because I was dissatisfied with this explanation and because it totally contradicted the explanations of others that I decided to research this subject. But what are the explanations of others and why are they also not entirely convincing? Hitherto they have come in two forms. The one emphasises the apparently inexorable progression of the weapons procurement process. The other focuses on the strategic imperative. But neither encompasses larger political considerations. Both assume that decisions on Soviet defence are divorced from the demands of foreign policy.

First, the focus on weapons procurement: in a polemical antidote to the anti-Soviet hysteria of the late 1970s, Andrew Cockburn assumes that 'the desire for the new weapon or a longer production line comes first; only afterward is the threat discovered that the weapon is supposed to meet'. He therefore deduces that the SS-20 was essentially the means by which a Soviet design bureau salvaged its reputation.[5] This is not unlike the conclusion of Björn Hagelin who also gives pride of place to the procurement process in the decision to deploy the missile.[6] This is the interpretation given by no less a figure than Deputy Foreign Minister of the Soviet Union Alexander Bessmertnykh. 'I have the feeling that some decisions were "driven" not so much by political analysis as by . . . the development of technology', he said, citing the SS-20 decision as an example.[7]

The philosophy behind this kind of interpretation is that the arms race has a life of its own. The attractiveness of the interpretation lies in its apparent neutrality. Why look for ulterior political motives? No one is really in control; but Bessmertnykh may have been scoring a point at the expense of the military because he went on to emphasise that 'state interests must determine strategy, strategy as political tactics and, to a certain extent, the technological development of the armed forces'.[8] The context of the statement appears to be that of a struggle between foreign policy-makers and the military over control of Soviet strategic requirements and in such a war any arguments are ready ammunition. Bessmertnykh's assertion may therefore be only partly true. It should certainly not be taken at face value any more than previous Soviet assertions of a very different nature.

The explanations offered by others such as Raymond Garthoff, David Holloway, Stephen Meyer, Robert Berman and John Baker do assume that there is more to the process, namely strategic requirements. Berman and Baker refer to the SS-20 as 'a long overdue follow-on' to the older generation of medium-and intermediate-range ballistic missiles, though 'a major addition to the Soviet regional capability'. In these terms deployment made sense within the framework of US-Soviet strategic competition.[9] This is also the thrust of Meyer's argument. It is outlined in more detail but with the politics left out.[10] Holloway takes us two steps further in elaborating upon Soviet concern at US forward-based systems, the growing vulnerability of older generations of medium-range weapons, the adoption by NATO of 'flexible response' which put a premium on flexible weapons with quick reaction time and, lastly, the emergence of a threat from China.[11] But it is Garthoff who has produced the most comprehensive interpretation so far:

> First, there remained a military requirement for strong regional theatre strategic forces, especially in view of the growing British, French and Chinese strategic nuclear missile forces, and powerful American and allied nuclear delivery bomber and fighter-bomber forces based in Europe (and some points on the Eurasian periphery, especially US bases in the Far East) . . . Second, Soviet intermediate-range missile forces needed modernisation . . . Third, it was not advantageous to expand, or even to retain, VRBM [variable-range ballistic missiles] such as the SS-11 and SS-N-6 in theatre strategic roles, since these systems counted against the Soviet intercontinental force levels in SALT and would prevent the Soviet Union from maintaining parity in numbers of launchers under the projected SALT II Treaty . . . Fourth, while the SS-14 and SS-15 had not proved satisfactory, the more successful SS-20 (derived from the SS-16 IRBM) was now available. It would provide mobility, solid fuel, rapid reaction and accuracy . . . The SS-20 decision was, thus, a 'natural'. Moreover it was fully compatible with the SALT negotiations . . . [12]

There is enough here to refute Weinberger's allegations. But is there enough to meet the thrust of Hyland's objections? The tendency is to focus almost entirely on what Hyland himself calls 'the technical motives for deployment' to the exclusion of larger political motivations. The strategic specialist may well respond: why search for political motives when strategic motives are available? This is a most un-Clausewitzian assumption. If war is a continuation of politics, is it not conceivable that weapons procurement and deployment are also a continuation of politics? Would we really be justified in assuming that in the era of strategic arms limitation talks and at a time of slowing economic growth in the Soviet Union the testing and deployment of new weapons systems had no political significance and were not subjected to any political scrutiny? Perhaps; but we have no right to assume this to be the case. The presumption that military decisions were made without further reference to political authority or political reasoning has to be proven and not taken as axiomatic. This would not need saying but for the blinkered strategic scholasticism in some quarters which reacts to attempts to intoduce political considerations into strategic matters with something of the same discomfort typical of the military. We are, after all, only too likely to take on the biases of those we study: foreign policy specialists disdaining military requirements in the manner of the diplomat and strategic specialists mimicking the military in their disregard for the demands of diplomacy. But whereas in the world outside both diplomats and the military answer to higher political authority with the power to fuse these conflicting elements, academics are by definition answerable to no one. In attempting to fuse the two I may therefore run into trouble from both quarters.

I have had no access to state secrets. But a work of this kind, of course, requires the help of others. Above all I must thank those who read and commented on the manuscript in its entirety: David Holloway (Stanford University), Richard Ullman (Princeton University), Sir Frank Cooper (formerly Permanent Under-Secretary at the British Ministry of Defence), Ambassador James Goodby (US State Department), Matthew Evangelista (Michigan University at Ann Arbor), Robert Davies (Birmingham University), and Lawrence Freedman (King's College, London). Others helped at earlier stages: Harold Brown (formerly US Secretary of Defense), Paul Nitze (US State Department), Lynn Davis (formerly of the US Defense Department), John Barry (currently at *Newsweek*), Raymond Garthoff (Brookings Institution), Laurence Martin (Newcastle University), Sergei Kambalov (Diplomatic Academy at the Soviet Foreign Ministry), Robert Conquest (Hoover Institution, Stanford University), Roger Hansen, the late Robert Osgood, and Robert W. Tucker (School of Advanced International Studies, The John Hopkins University). There are also a number of officials whose names cannot be mentioned. I must also thank librarians at SAIS, the Hoover Institution, Library of Congress and Stanford University who made research easier than it would otherwise have been. Alex Dallin kindly arranged for me to spend 1986–87 at Stanford with limited teaching duties, thus enabling me to complete the work; the Center for Russian and East European Studies at Stanford funded the typing of the manuscript by Helen Morales.

Jonathan Haslam
King's College, Cambridge.

Abbreviations

ALCM	Air-Launched Cruise Missile
APN	Novosti Press Agency
CSCE	Conference on Security and Co-operation in Europe
EEC	European Economic Community
FBS	Forward-Based Systems (US)
GDR	German Democratic Republic/East Germany
GLCM	Ground-Launched Cruise Missile
HLG	High-Level Group (NATO)
ICBM	Intercontinental Ballistic Missile
IMEMO	Institute of World Economy and International Relations (Soviet)
INF	Intermediate-Range Nuclear Forces
IRBM	Intermediate-Range Ballistic Missile
KGB	Committee of State Security (Soviet)
MIRV	Multiple Independently Targeted Re-entry Vehicle
MRBM	Medium-Range Ballistic Missile
NATO	North Atlantic Treaty Organisation
NPG	Nuclear Planning Group (NATO)
NSC	National Seccurity Council (US)
OSD	Office of Secretary of Defense (US)
SACEUR	Supreme Allied Commander Europe
SALT	Strategic Arms Limitation Talks
SDI	Strategic Defense Initiative (US)
SLBM	Submarine-Launched Ballistic Missile
SLCM	Sea-Launched Cruise Missile
SPD	(West) German Socialist Party
START	Strategic Arms Reduction Talks
TAC	Tactical Air Command (US)
TNF	Theatre Nuclear Forces
USAF	United States Air Force
USAFE	United States Air Force Europe
VRBM	Variable-Range Ballistic Missile
WPC	World Peace Council

Introduction: The Roots of the Problem, 1945–69

The nuclear arms race and the associated problems of arms control are at root the current symptoms of long-standing malaise in the Soviet Union's relations with the West dating back to the October revolution of 1917 when Lenin and the Bolsheviks tried to spread the revolution beyond Russian frontiers, and the subsequent allied war of intervention of 1918–19 which failed to crush the revolution and thereby left the conflict between East and West unresolved. Thereafter we have seen two worlds at war: a war fought largely by unconventional means. The quarrel is essentially ideological, though the conflict has long taken geopolitical form. Contrary to the early expectations of many in the West, these differences did not significantly diminish with time. The capitalist West, whether in its democratic or dictatorial incarnation, has long viewed Soviet 'expansionism' or 'revolutionary internationalism' (depending on your viewpoint) as inimical to its own well-being. In turn the Russians have seen the West as representative of a system in decline; but a decline never so certain as to rule out the need for a little assistance to help it on its way, nor so precipitate as to preclude the presentation of major threats to Soviet security.

For long the greatest menace to Soviet security came primarily from Europe. It was Europe that felt most at risk from the Bolshevik cause. Initially, from 1921 to 1933, the greatest challenge to the Russians came from the British and French empires at a time when Moscow had no military power worthy of the name. Later the threat came from Germany (as well as Japan) at a time when Soviet military preparations, though considerable, initially proved inadequate to the task that confronted them. As a result the Soviet regime was invariably acutely conscious of the need for military readiness. Moreover the traumatic experience of war (1941–45) long defined the world view of the Soviet leadership and goes far to explain the Soviet focus on military power, particularly in Europe.

This outlook was ably summarised by Alexander Bovin of *Izvestiya*.

Chancellor Helmut Schmidt of West Germany, he remarked, had said 'he did not believe in the aggressive intentions of the Russians, but they had clearly"overdone" things as far as the strength of their defence was concerned.' Bovin continued:

> Yes, maybe, we have 'overdone' it, maybe we have created a five-fold margin of strength where we could, speaking in an abstract way, do with a threefold one. We cannot reason in the abstract. We have here not logic, but psychology. In 1942 the Germans reached the Volga and Caucasus. Not one Soviet politician, not one military man, not one Soviet person can forget it. I am afraid that for a man with computer glimmer in his eye this is no argument. Yet a person wishing to understand our problems and our intentions would do well to pause and ponder this.[1]

More than 40 years after the war, most Russians still find it hard to escape the shadow of that traumatic experience and absorb the fact that the USSR is immeasurably more powerful than before. Indeed, in answering letters from viewers on Moscow television in 1976, veteran political journalist Yuri Zhukov argued for a more realistic vision:

> Some of you say: But can one trust the imperialists? They are ready to violate any agreement. Remember 1941, Comrade Silin from Suzdal writes. Can one now rely on the firmness of detente? You are right, comrades, imperialists remain imperialists, and the Soviet Union and the fraternal socialist countries, while dealing with them, maintain the necessary vigilance. However, Comrade Silin, it is not 1941 now, not even 1950 or 1960. It is 1976: the socialist community has become powerful and the present correlation of forces in the world arena makes it possible to confront and realistically solve the problem of maintaining and strengthening peace. It is the new correlation of forces which has brought detente into existence.[2]

To sections of the Soviet military, however, the differences between 1941 and the more recent period are less apparent than the similarities. In the 1930s the Soviet regime poured money into defence, just as it does now. 'The party and the Soviet Government in the pre-war years paid great attention to the development of the defence sectors of industry. But, unfortunately, by 1941 not everything could be accomplished. We entered the war in conditions where superiority in the basic means of struggle lay on the side of the aggressor', recalled Marshal Sergei Akhromeev, Chief of the General Staff and First Deputy Minister of Defence, in May 1985. 'We remember the steep cost of the errors and mistakes permitted on the eve of the Great Patriotic War. In contemporary conditions, faced with a multiplicity of nuclear and other weapons, it would be significantly more complicated to rectify shortcomings in the course of war . . . This is why it is necessary today to maintain the military preparedness of the Armed Forces at the highest level'.[3] 'We have the right not to put ourselves in a situation similar to the one which existed in 1941', said missile specialist General Yuri Lebedev. deputy head of the Treaty and Legal Department of the General Staff, in March 1984.[4] The development of military technology in the nuclear age has combined with the experience of surprise attack in June 1941 to highlight the lessons of the Great Patriotic War: despite talk of 'reasonable sufficiency', 'vigilance' is still very much the watchword of the Soviet military. And it is the psychology of the military which overshadowed Soviet policy towards Western Europe throughout the four decades since the war. For the end of the conflict in 1945 brought no real security to the USSR, in large part because the Russians sought a unilateral solution to their security concerns; a solution challenged by the English-speaking Powers, who attempted to impose on the Russians their own conception of Soviet security needs, which necessarily meant the withdrawal of Soviet power behind Soviet frontiers. The concern of the Western Powers was as much ideological as old-fashioned geopolitical. Like it or not Moscow was still—despite rather than because of Stalin—the citadel of world revolution; the economic and social dislocation of Western Europe resulting from the war combined with the great achievements of the Soviet war effort to bring local Communist Parties to the forefront of the political stage; and the presence of the 2 874 000-strong Red Army reaching into Central Europe threatened to tilt this precarious balance to the advantage of the Communist movement in the West. These fears were largely exaggerated and in some cases cynically fostered to serve larger ends. Nonetheless, they blended with timeless notions of the importance of the balance of power, and inspired concerted resistance to the growth of Soviet influence in Europe.

The Western response to the preponderance of Soviet military power was essentially twofold: the mobilisation of American economic resources to underpin capitalism and social reformism (as against revolution) in Western Europe (1947); and the formation of an anti-Soviet alliance buttressed by American military power (1948–49).

For our purposes we need to look more closely at the role of American military power, more particularly at the origins of American forward-based systems targeting the Soviet Union: it is these systems which became the focal point of Soviet security concerns in Europe and which eventually played a crucial role in the Soviet decisions to test and deploy the SS-20.

THE ESTABLISHMENT OF US FORWARD-BASED SYSTEMS IN EUROPE

The United States had fought its air war with Germany from bases in Britain. It had formed bridgeheads for the invasion of Southern Europe from North Africa and for the invasion of Northern Europe from the British Isles. Given the continuing limitations imposed by the technology of the period, in any future conflict American power would have to be projected into Europe via overseas bases. In this respect the rise of Soviet power acted as a catalyst hastening changes already in motion. It would be misleading to assume that the United States remained passive in the face of emerging opportunities for the extension of American power, including the acquisition of bases overseas. Well before the Russians became impossible to work with in Central Europe the US Government made loans to Britain conditional upon British co-operation in the expansion of American strategic potential at a time when the United States was still demobilising its armed services. On 7 November 1945 Secretary of State Byrnes sent Foreign Secretary Bevin a memorandum requesting British assistance in obtaining bases in Iceland, the Portuguese Azores and Cape Verde islands, and, in addition, two lists, as Bevin's biographer records: 'one of some twenty-five Pacific islands or island groups, sovereignty over which had long been disputed between the USA and the UK [including the Caroline Islands, Christmas Island and the Phoenix Islands], and the other a list of ten island bases wholly or jointly under British control on which the USA had spent considerable sums and which they wished to retain. The British were asked to cede the territories in the first list and either to give or use their good offices to obtain permission for the USA to go on using the bases on the second'.[5]

The idea that the Americans were totally uninterested in extending their power after 1945 therefore needs qualification; though the idea that this was the same as a commitment to the defence of Western Europe against potential Soviet aggression simply does not fit the facts. From 1945 to 1948 US military activity in Europe was somewhat sporadic and tentative. In 1946 and following the shooting down of two US C-47s over Yugoslav territory the US Air Force sent six B-29 nuclear-capable bombers to touch down in the Western zones of Germany and fly along the frontiers of Soviet-occupied territory to act as a warning against further such incidents.[6] The US Air Force had also reached agreement with the British on the use of bases in Britain in the event of emergency.[7] And by 1947 the United States was once more building up its air fleet for possible need against the Soviet Union.[8] All planning assumed the use of forward bases.[9] In May 1947 a Joint Chiefs of Staff assessment argued that 'Approximately 80% of the entire industry [of the USSR] is within the radius of B-29s operating from bases in the British isles or the Cairo-Suez area'.[10] Yet for all this the Americans were still far from committed to confrontation with the Russians. Indeed the European Recovery Plan inaugurated by the United States in 1947 was viewed in some quarters as a sign of disengagement rather than commitment, rather in the manner of the Dawes Plan of 1924. What eventually brought US military power in the form of B-29 bombers back into Europe on a permanent basis was the crisis precipitated by Stalin in July 1948 when the Russians closed Western access by road and rail to Berlin. In these disturbing conditions Foreign Secretary Ernest Bevin pressed for a US bomber presence in Europe and the Americans responded with the request that this include Britain. On 2 July two squadrons of the 301 Bombardment Group flew into Fürstenfeldbruck via Goose Bay, Labrador. One squadron was by chance already there. The 307 Bombardment Group then arrived in Britain on 17 July. The 28 Bombardment Group arrived on the 18th.[11] The first of what were to become many forward-based systems (FBS) were now in place; for this the Russians had only themselves to blame.

The role of the FBS was outlined in the JCS Short Range Emergency Plan 1844/13 approved on 19 May 1948 under the code name 'Half Moon'. It 'aimed at the early initiation and sustaining of an air offensive against vital elements of the Soviet war-making capability'. In the event of war what was proposed was the deployment of 'available units of the Strategic Air Command to bases in England (alternatively to Iceland) and to the Khartoum, Cairo-Suez area and

conduct operations from these bases and Okinawa utilizing available
atomic bombs [then only about 50] against selected targets'.[12]
Although President Truman initially balked at such an extensive use
of atomic bombs, under the impact of the Berlin crisis that summer
his opinion soon changed.[13]

Forward-based systems were further reinforced following the
North Korean invasion of South Korea in June 1950, an event which
caused something of a war scare in Western Europe. Two more
bomber groups and a fighter group arrived in Britain that summer;
soon there were some 180 nuclear-capable B-29s in designated RAF
bases. In January 1951 longer-range B-36s arrived,[14] the United
States Air Force in Europe (USAFE) was made a separate command
under the Joint Chiefs of Staff,[15] and in that year similar bases
were set up in France, French Morocco, Greenland, Iceland and the
Azores.[16] The Tactical Air Command (TAC) was then instructed to
deploy the 49th Air Division with the nuclear-capable B-45 light
bomber and F-84 fighter bomber wings in Britain by April 1952.[17]
A pattern was set: from then on the location of such bases and the
forces concerned might change but the systems as such remained
and remain an enduring feature on the landscape.

SOVIET STRATEGIC ROCKET FORCES: TARGETING US FORWARD-BASED SYSTEMS

At the onset of the Cold War the Russians had no nuclear weapons.
It was their conventional military power forward deployed in Central
Europe which so preoccupied the West, given the presence of the
Communist fifth column within the capitalist camp.[18] But the Soviet
Government had also been working on an atomic bomb of its own
since 1943.[19] It was developing means of delivery as well, including
a primitive imitation of the B-29,[20] the medium-range Tupolev–4
(operational from 1947). And there had long been research in the
USSR on missile technology.

After the United States dropped atomic bombs on Japan Stalin
called for the speediest completion of the Soviet atomic bomb project
and pressed for rapid attainment of a secure means of delivery.[21]
Initially only aircraft were thought suitable. But by the spring of
1946 Stalin had also been persuaded of the potential of rocketry.
Simultaneous American interest in developing the German V-2,
which had terrorised British homes in and around London, may well

have acted as a spur. Analyzing the Peenemünde facilities and output, rocket scientist Dr Tokaty Tokaev submitted a report to Politburo member and Deputy Chairman of the Council of Ministers Georgii Malenkov in March 1946. Tokaev and his colleagues had concluded that in practical rocketry the Russians were behind the Germans.[22] The capture of V-1 and V-2 rockets plus details of the A 9/10 two-stage transatlantic rocket project, as well as of German engineers, technicians and workers thus accelerated existing Soviet experimentation,[23] though Stalin was reportedly outraged that the Americans had taken the lion's share, including the leading scientists (such as von Braun) and the underground V-2 factory in the Harz mountains.[24]

Colonel-General of Artillery Mitrofan Nedelin—years later appointed chief of the Strategic Rocket Forces—was summoned to Stalin in mid-April 1946 to discuss the further application of rocket technology to warfare.[25] 'Stalin . . . assigned most missile development programs . . . to the artillery component of the ground forces and kept their development under strict scrutiny'.[26] However, not until after rocket specialist Sergei Korolev returned from supervising the collection of data and materials in Germany at the end of 1946 did work begin at his design bureau,[27] though from then on the results were not long delayed. At a meeting in the Kremlin on 14 March 1947—two days after the promulgation of the Truman Doctrine—Malenkov emphasised to Soviet rocket scientists that developing the V-2 was far from enough: 'our strategic needs are predetermined by the fact that our potential enemy is to be found thousands of miles away', he is reported to have said.[28] A day later, at a joint meeting of the Politburo and the Council of Ministers, Stalin made the same point. Referring to the A 9/10 transatlantic rocket project developed by the Germans, he stressed that such missiles 'could be an effective straightjacket for that noisy shopkeeper Harry Truman'. A special commission was thus set up for that purpose—the *PKRDD* (*Pravitel'stvennaya Komissiya po Raketam Dalnego Deistviya*), chaired by the First Deputy Minister of the NKVD, Colonel-General Serov.[29] By September of that year a draft project was presented to the government, but from then on work was paralysed by the onset of renewed terror from the secret police and the entire schedule was set back by years.[30] The V-2 programme was already underway, however. On 18 October 1947 the Russians successfully launched their first ballistic missile: the R-1. And within three years they had also successfully tested the more advanced R-

2.[31] These became the first generation of tactical ballistic missiles in the Soviet arsenal of the early 1950s.[32] Then at about five a.m. on 29 August 1949 the Russians successfully detonated an atomic device,[33] though not yet a working atomic bomb.

Thereafter progress was slow. It is not clear whether this was due to technical difficulties—there was an acute shortage of fissionable material—or because of Stalin's relative indifference now that the political impact of the Soviet detonation had made itself felt in the West. Not until 1954 did the Russians have enough effective nuclear warheads for deployment.[34] Moreover, as US Intelligence estimated that March: 'Present Soviet capabilities for air attack on continental U.S. are limited by dependence on the TU-4 bomber (B-29 equivalent), by the apparent lack of a developed inflight refueling capability [possessed by the USA], and by the relatively undeveloped character of the Chukotskoi and Kola base areas [in the Soviet Arctic]'.[35] This left the USSR without an effective intercontinental capability unless, of course, pilots flew one-way missions. But the Russians could more easily threaten US forward-based systems in Europe. The irony was that the USA further increased rather than reduced its dependence upon those systems. In part this met the needs of US allies in Western Europe, ever anxious lest the Americans turn homeward leaving an imbalance of military power to Soviet advantage. But there were—as there still are—other factors involved. The projection of American strategic power overseas also served purely unilateral aims.

After Eisenhower became President in 1953 the United States moved to deploy considerable numbers of tactical nuclear weapons in Western Europe. They were considered a logical counter to Soviet conventional military predominance in the theatre. Even though the United States had an intercontinental reach unattained by the Russians—on 26 June 1948 the nuclear-capable B-36 bomber became operational—the Americans still relied heavily on bases overseas. This represented the continuation of the philosophy underpinning the acquisition of such bases from 1945: to place US strike power as far from the American mainland as possible and as close to the likely adversary as practicable. In a National Security Council paper of 30 September 1953 it was also affirmed that:

> The effective use of U.S. strategic air power against the USSR will require overseas bases on foreign territory for some years to come. Such bases will continue indefinitely to be an important

additional element of U.S. strategic air capability and to be essential to the conduct of the military operations on the Eurasian continent in case of general war.[36]

The B-36 remained outnumbered by the medium-range B-29. And when from early 1953 the new jet-propelled B-47 medium-range bomber began to replace the B-29, there was no great incentive to cut back on foreign bases. But even when the new and far more effective intercontinental jet-propelled B-52 bomber became operational in June 1955, the USAF continued to rely on shorter-range aircraft operating from overseas positions. And when this continued dependence on what were increasingly vulnerable bases was called into question 'Air Force officers maintained that the continued use of these admittedly vulnerable bases gave additional flexibility and efficiency to the strategic attack, added complexity to the timing of a Soviet surprise attack, and permitted the B-47s to operate from ranges nearer to their targets'. The knowledge that the Strategic Air Command (SAC) is a truly global force, pointed out Lieutenant General Walter C. Sweeney, Jr., Commander of the Eighth Air Force, 'complicates Soviet targeting and dilutes his war effort'.[37] This was said in 1959. By then the Russians had not only acquired the potential for an intercontinental capability, they were also introducing ever more effective means of attacking US air bases in Western Europe which were given priority over the intercontinental mission. Whether one judges Soviet aims as primarily offensive or defensive there could be no doubt that ridding the continent of Europe—the British Isles included—of US forward-based systems was an important aim for the Soviet military. At this stage there was no prospect of doing so through negotiation. Nor was there any real likelihood of the West Europeans asking the Americans to leave (except perhaps France under De Gaulle). A nuclear arms race in Europe was therefore inevitable.

On 17 December 1959 the Soviet Politburo and Council of Ministers created the Strategic Rocket Forces as a separate and senior service. This move followed a frustrating experience of attempting to match the United States in comparable nuclear-capable aircraft. In November 1954 the Tupolev–16 (Western designation 'Badger') entered service to supersede the TU-4 as the leading medium-range bomber. Attempts at an intercontinental capability also continued. Some equivalent of the B-52 had to be found if the United States was to be deterred from contemplating a first strike. In 1954 the

Myasishchev–4 (Western designation 'Bison') emerged with a reported 10 000-kilometre range. But it fell far short in actual performance. In 1957 the Tupolev–20 (often referred to as the TU-95), Western designation 'Bear', entered service. But this was also considered ineffective; speed and altitude problems made it too vulnerable to American defences.[38] The real hope lay with missiles; and before long the resultant experimentation had a momentous impact on Soviet medium-range capability. The early fruits of that promise became apparent on 3 August 1957 with the testing of the SS-6 (a Western designation) intercontinental ballistic missile (ICBM), followed on 4 October by the successful launching into orbit of the world's first artificial satellite. This came as a shock to the United States and enabled First Secretary Nikita Khrushchev to bluff the Americans into the belief that the USSR had attained superiority in nuclear missile capability The immediate spin-off from the Soviet advance in rocketry was the expansion of the USSR's intermediate-range capability. The SS-3 (Western designation) deployed in 1956 had only an operational-tactical range.[39] But in 1959 the Russians deployed the SS-4 (R-12) medium-range ballistic missile (MRBM) and in 1961 the SS-5 (R-14) intermediate-range ballistic missile (IRBM). The Soviet Government's undoubted success appeared to justify Khrushchev's cuts in conventional forces and his belittling of aviation: 'Given the contemporary development of military technology, military aviation and the naval fleet have lost their former significance', Khrushchev told the Supreme Soviet on 14 January 1960. 'This type of weaponry will not be reduced but replaced. Military aviation will almost be completely replaced by missile technology. We have now sharply reduced and we will, it seems, carry on with the future reduction and even cease production of bombers and of other outdated technology.'[40]

There was a continuing need for bombers, however, not least because one element of American nuclear capability was too mobile and elusive to be accessible to Soviet missiles: carrier aviation—a further component in US forward-based systems and a component which the Russians later became particularly concerned about as a consequence of the Vietnam war (see pp. 20–7). The aircraft carrier had taken several years to become incorporated into American nuclear planning, in part due to inter-service rivalry. But by the end of 1951 its role as an auxiliary in the European theatre was under discussion. In February the US President was told that atomic weapons were to be allocated to naval as well as USAF aviation;

and on 5 February 1954 the Joint Chiefs of Staff finally confirmed the role of aircraft carriers as a component of the nuclear strike force.[41]

With the appearance of the first super-carrier, the *Forrestal*, in 1955 and the entry into service of the A3D Skywarrior from March 1956, the US Navy acquired a formidable capability against targets on land as well as at sea: with inflight refuelling the A3D could fly over 1700 nautical miles to deliver a 6650 lb. bomb.[42] With the development of new lightweight nuclear bombs existing fighters could also be modified to carry nuclear weapons.[43] The A3Ds were replaced by the A6s from 1963: capable of carrying a heavy load, with good all-weather, low-flying characteristics and non-radiating navigational system to outwit enemy defences.[44]

By the 1970s there would normally be 'a requirement for four carriers forward deployed—two in the 6th Fleet [Mediterranean], two in the 7th Fleet [Pacific]'. In addition there would be 'four to five carrier[s] distributed between the 2nd [Atlantic] and 3rd [East Pacific] Fleets; ready to go, ready to surge, ready to carry out any particular commitment that arises'. This would generally mean 'two or three carriers in the 2nd Fleet, which is based in the Western Atlantic'.[45] The role of the carrier air wing was to 'establish the requisite air superiority, conduct offensive long-range strike operations against surface, air and subsurface forces, shore installations and land forces' in the event of conflict, conventional or nuclear.[46] An aircraft carrier thus served as 'a floating air base'[47] unencumbered by the restrictions that confine air operations from land dependent upon sometimes unco-operative allies. All of these systems, including carrier-based aviation, found a role in the General Strike Plan of the NATO Supreme Allied Commander for Europe (SACEUR): 'Under the GSP', a Senate report noted in 1973, 'the weapons systems available to conduct nuclear strikes within the European theatre are the land based aircraft, sea-based aircraft, fleet ballistic missiles [introduced at the end of the 1950s and based in Scotland and Spain from the early 1960s] and Pershing [1] missiles which will be assigned to SACEUR by the NATO countries in times of war'.[48]

SOVIET AIR DEFENCE AND THE FBS

Soviet awareness of the effectiveness of the FBS was heightened by the great problem of defending the country's sprawling land mass against air attack issuing from almost any direction. The growth of US air bases on the periphery of the Soviet Union was thus paralleled by the development of an elaborate system of air defence on Soviet territory (later extended to cover the East European countries). As Marshal Pavel Batitsky, one-time Chief of the Air Defence Forces, stated:

> The aggressive circles of the imperialist Powers waged a 'cold war' against us and unleashed an arms race. A major place in their military preparations was given to means of air attack, which became the main means of delivering weapons of mass destruction—above all nuclear. In these conditions the Central Committee of our Party [the Politburo] and the Government judged it necessary to increase the specific contribution of the Air Defence Forces in the structure of the USSR's Armed Forces.[49]

Although primitive defences against attack from the air were established in Petrograd (now Leningrad) as early as 1918 during the most critical phase of the Allied war of intervention, and although a rudimentary air defence system had existed prior to Germany's surprise attack on 22 June 1941, the air defence forces of the Soviet Union were not formed into a separate service—the *Voiska protivo-vozdushnoi oborony*—until July 1948,[50] under the command of Deputy War Minister Marshal Leonid Govorov.[51] At this stage the Russians had plenty of short-range fighter interceptors—in 1945 there were about 3000[52]—including, from 1946, the new jet-propelled MiG-9 and Yak-15s[53]; and on 30 December 1947 the MIG-15 made its first test flight—a fighter which acquired a considerable reputation during the Korean War (1950–53).[54] There were also a considerable number of anti-aircraft batteries:[55] in 1945 there were some 9800 anti-aircraft guns of medium calibre.[56] But none of these was of much use against relatively high-flying B-29s or reconnaissance aircraft probing the 60 000 kilometre frontier with increasing persistence.[57] Moreover, the Russians were not advanced in electronics: they lacked a nationwide radar network. In 1945 they had only 230 radar installations.[58] Not until 1952 were the 'radio-technical forces' established on the basis of existing air observation, warning and communications troops,[59] amalgamating two separate and parallel early warning systems.[60]

Throughout the 1950s the Russians focused their attention on acquiring a means of shooting down the B-29, B-47, B-52 and high altitude reconnaissance aircraft (from 1956 the U-2). Successive generations of interceptors were therefore deployed—the Yak–25 (1954), the MiG-21 (1959) and the SU-9 (1961)—with the goal of high-altitude interception in all weathers.[61] Surface-to-air missiles were also developed. Supplies of the first surface-to-air missile (SAM-1) began to reach the air defence forces in 1952, leading to the formation of special units to service them.[62] These and other innovations led to further reorganisation; Marshal Govorov was formally entitled Commander-in-Chief of the air defence forces in May 1954.[63] This move was also a symptom of the growing importance of the forces as increasingly US forward-based systems hemmed in the Soviet land-mass: from 1953 to 1956 the Russians recorded 130 violations of Soviet airspace.[64]

Not until 1957 was the second surface-to-air missile system (SAM-2) put into service with 'a radar-guided high altitude reach in excess of 70,000 feet'.[65] The success of this system was demonstrated by the dramatic destruction of Gary Powers' U-2 on 1 May 1960 at the hands of a battery under the direction of First Lieutenant Bukin.[66] Yet for all that, there was a strong element of chance in this victory for the Russians. Not only were insufficient SAM-2s deployed along Soviet frontiers but 'it was not the first or second missile which brought down the U-2, but one of fourteen. Moreover, another hit . . . [had] destroyed a MiG-19 attempting to intercept'.[67] As with Sputnik in 1957, so with Soviet air defence, an isolated success on the part of the Russians was followed by a barrage of excessive boasting from Moscow which enhanced the Western tendency to exaggerate the USSR's military capabilities, defensive as well as offensive. Only with the onset of the Vietnam war and American bombing of the North in 1965 did the Russians become more aware of the deficiencies in their much-vaunted air defences against US aircraft. But by then the focus of Soviet attention and resources had shifted decisively towards the deployment of a system for defence against American missiles, leading to relative neglect of the threat from US aircraft, misleadingly viewed as a lesser problem. It was the construction of an anti-ballistic missile system around Moscow which eventually brought the United States to the negotiating table with the Russians, negotiations that eventually resulted in the strategic arms limitation talks (SALT): the starting-point of our story.

But before we proceed, certain crucial elements from the preceding account must be bourne in mind because of their importance to the narrative and analysis which follow. First, the East-West conflict dates back to 1917 and the clash of ideologies; Soviet support for social unrest beyond Russian frontiers was, and still is, eloquent testimony to the importance of ideology and has done much to nourish the conflict. Second, these ideological differences are what made the West Europeans hypersensitive to the shift in the balance of power in Europe to Soviet advantage in 1945–47. Third, and in reaction to this, it was primarily Western Europe which drew US forces onto the continent from 1948 and which has sustained their presence thereafter. Lastly, Moscow viewed the arrival and further deployment of US forces as a direct threat to the security of the homeland, which had to be countered by the development of both offensive and defensive means. These were the necessary causes of the nuclear arms race in Europe which is the legacy of the postwar era.

1 SALT I and Nuclear Weapons in Europe, 1969–72

US Assistant Secretary of Defense for International Affairs Richard Perle told the Senate Armed Services Committee on 1 March 1982 that 'the development and deployment of the newest and most capable Soviet theater nuclear system, the SS-20, is almost certainly a product of the interim agreement on offensive arms signed in 1972 . . .'[1]

1.1 SALT AND FBS

The strategic arms limitation talks (SALT), the negotiations which eventually resulted in that agreement, originated with an initiative by US Secretary of Defense Robert McNamara during the mid-1960's. McNamara was concerned lest the construction of anti-ballistic missile systems (ABM) further intensify the arms race between the USA and the USSR. The first soundings were made in Moscow by US Ambassador Llewellyn Thompson in December 1966. The Soviet response in January 1967 was cautiously positive. Indeed the Russians apparently wished to extend the agenda to include offensive as well as defensive systems. However, the Soviet military expressed strong objections, and as a consequence these early moves took some considerable time to lead to the ultimate goal. The Soviet-led invasion of Czechoslovakia in August 1968 further delayed progress, as did the US Presidential elections at the close of the year. After an abortive and futile attempt by President Richard Nixon and his Assistant for National Security Affairs Henry Kissinger to link progress on arms limitation to Soviet good behaviour elsewhere in the world, negotiations finally opened on the 24 November 1969 in Helsinki.[2]

It was not long before the Russians attempted to extend the agenda to include the issue of non-strategic nuclear weapons. On 26 November head of the Soviet delegation Deputy Foreign Minister Vladimir Semenov pointed out that any agreement had to cover all threats as seen by both parties; in this sense there was no self-evident symmetry of security concerns between the two sides. Soviet territory was menaced not only by US strategic bombers and inter-continental ballistic missiles (ICBMs) but also by what Semenov referred to as lighter delivery aircraft (LDA): a term which later gave place to the more generic 'forward-based systems' (FBS).[3] Yet the Russians were not prepared to discuss their nuclear weapons systems targeted on Western Europe.

Semenov's position on FBS 'seemed to be based on the concern and insistence' of the Soviet armed forces.[4] The military in the Soviet Union had tried to block the road to negotiations on the limitation of strategic arms. As former Soviet diplomat Arkady Shevchenko—not always a reliable witness—recalls: 'Defense Minister [Marshal Andrei] Grechko remained permanently apoplectic during SALT. His incurable distrust of, and violent opposition to, the talks, so well known to all of us involved in the negotiations, affected even the more realistic and sophisticated generals and politicians in a negative way. Grechko would repeatedly and irrelevantly launch into admonitory lectures on the aggressive nature of imperialism, which, he assured us, had not changed. There was no guarantee against a new world war except a continued buildup of Soviet armed might . . . Grechko reluctantly accepted the opening of SALT, but almost immediately began a guerrilla campaign that helped to stall the process.'[5]

Grechko's attitude would scarcely have seemed out of place in the Pentagon. Since the early 1960s, when the USA possessed strategic nuclear superiority and had made use of the threat implicit in that capability to force the withdrawal of Soviet IRBMs from Cuba during October 1962, the Russians had been straining every muscle to reach parity and, if possible, predominance. The philosophy of the Soviet military was epitomised in the following statement by Colonel M. Vetrov, writing in the restricted journal *Voennaya Mysl'* in August 1971:

> *The military power of socialism is an important factor in maintaining and consolidating peace and ensuring international security.* This is based on the fact that the struggle between socialism and

capitalism is developing according to the laws of the class struggle and, in the final analysis, the side which prevails will be the one which has the greater material power, including military power. This usually dictates the forms of the struggle as well.

The way the present contradiction between the two world systems will be resolved depends on the alignment of these forces, primarily the military.[6]

It was this attitude which bedevilled progress towards SALT from 1967 to 1968, for the military had no desire to cap the burgeoning capability of the Soviet rocket forces which, as Grechko proudly pointed out in 1969, 'have been the beneficiaries of especially high growth.'[7]

Indeed according to figures given by President Nixon in 1972 the Soviet Union possessed a mere 224 operational ICBMs in mid–1965, as against an American total of 934. By the end of 1969 the Soviet figure had risen dramatically to 1190 as against the US figure of 1054.[8] And although the Americans were still ahead in respect of bombers, the US goverment believed this lead might easily diminish at the then current rate of Soviet development. As Nixon told Congress:

Until the late 1960's, we possessed strategic forces that provided a clear margin of superiority.

In the late 1960's, however, the balance of strategic forces changed. While our forces were held at existing levels, the Soviet Union moved forward vigorously to develop powerful and sophisticated strategic forces which approached and in some categories exceeded, ours in numbers and capability.[9]

In these circumstances the Soviet military did not see why they should not continue to forge ahead unhindered.

The balance of forces was certainly changing, and the Americans were seriously interested in an accommodation. But the sources of the conflict remained the same. Kissinger's abortive attempt to link progress in arms limitation with Soviet good behaviour in the Third World showed where the shoe pinched, as Lenin used to say. With the prospect of defeat in Vietnam the goals were unchanged: to stem the spread of Communism across the globe. They simply had to be attained by other means. Given the changing balance of power—at the military level to Soviet advantage, on the political level to the advantage of revolution in the Third World, and at both levels to the disadvantage of the USA—it was unlikely that Moscow would concede on 'linkage'. The following comment in *Izvestiya* in April 1969 underlined that fact:

> The 'theory' is being put about to the effect that the USSR is more interested than the USA in putting an end to the uncontrolled arms race and that therefore, they say, the USA can in return be granted some sort of concessions in other areas. The thinking behind this is quite transparent: on the one hand, to hinder the Soviet Union's fight against the arms race (the aim here is to portray any constructive move by Soviet diplomacy as evidence of 'weakness'); on the other hand, to dampen the aspirations of Americans towards negotiations and an agreement, to prompt them to put forward the sort of diplomatic deal that would put a brake on any further progress.[10]

Furthermore, linkage could work both ways. The Soviet military were not alone in their opposition to SALT. There were those in Moscow who objected most vehemently to 'selective co-existence'. With the US Government bombing allied Vietnam, how could true Communists negotiate with the Americans on other issues? The fundamentalist position was presented unequivocally in the Communist Party journal *Kommunist* in August 1970:

> The imperialist theory of so-called 'selective co-existence', envisaging the possibility of relations of peaceful co-operation with some socialist countries and freedom to conduct aggressive wars against other countries and nations, does not meet the interests of strengthening peace and international security.[11]

This section of opinion was to voice its doubts again in the coming years. But it was the military who stood to lose most from SALT and who therefore pressed their arguments the most forcibly and consistently, particularly on US forward-based systems.

'We heard more about it than any other subject', head of the US delegation Ambassador Gerard Smith recalls.[12] To the extent that the Soviet military wished to play the 'spoiler' in the talks, FBS undoubtedly proved a useful instrument; for the US delegation resolutely refused to take FBS into account[13] and negotiations very nearly ground to a halt on this issue: 'It became the central block to progress. All Soviet-proposed solutions—withdrawal, destruction, or compensation—were equally unattractive', Ambassador Smith has noted,[14] adding that 'Any provision affecting U.S. forward-based systems was absolutely unacceptable.'[15]

However, the obduracy of the Soviet military amounted to more than wilful sabotage of the talks. The Russians saw their security in terms very different from the NATO Powers. 'As the Soviet position evolved', Smith recalls, 'it appeared that they considered FBS a real American strategic advantage. Semenov put it this way—if one looked at a map of Europe and Asia one would find many bases,air force, naval, and other military bases, each of which contained large stockpiles of American nuclear weapons; thus, in a discussion of strategic force considerations, how could one fail to take this situation into account?'[16]

The Soviet case was publicised in the military newspaper *Krasnaya Zvezda* on 13 May 1970. 'In Europe alone', Colonel Alexandrov argued, 'the United States continually maintains more than 600 fighter aircraft, of which more than 500 are equipped to carry nuclear weapons'. These LDA were based in Britain, Germany, Greece, Italy, the Netherlands, Spain and Turkey. They could be reinforced by some 200 aircraft of which 100 were nuclear capable from carriers in the Sixth Fleet in the Mediterranean in the event of 'a worsening of the situation in Europe or in the Middle East' (memories of the six-day war of June 1967 were still fresh). There were in addition 500 nuclear capable aircraft in the Seventh Fleet in Far Eastern waters. Alexandrov continued: 'about twenty per cent of airborne nuclear weapons in the United States aviational strike force are located in the European zone, playing a continuous role in the day-to-day strength of NATO's combined air forces and ready to take off to deliver a nuclear strike within fifteen minutes of receiving an order'. As far as the Russians were concerned, such weaponry was 'tactical only in name':

> the fighting capability of American tactical and carrier strike aircraft, the actual regions in which they are positioned and the constantly high state of readiness for the use of nuclear weapons indicate that, like strategic bombers, they are assigned mainly to accomplish strategic objectives by means of delivering nuclear strikes directly against targets on the territory of the Soviet Union and other socialist countries.[17]

The Soviet military 'were said to stress the ability of these aircraft to reach the Soviet Union in a short time. They were reported to consider American FBS aircraft more effective in some respects than the

B-52 bombers, because their flight time was shorter, they could fly at lower altitudes, and their bomb release was said to be more effective.'[18]

1.2   SOVIET AIR DEFENCE AND THE IMPACT OF VIETNAM

Soviet sensitivity to the role of LDA had been heightened by the Vietnam war. Through the greater part of the conflict, at least until 1969–70, the Americans were more aware of the great losses sustained in attack than of their successes in penetrating enemy defences. On 26 July 1965, in response to US bombing and after Soviet assistance, North Vietnamese surface-to-air missiles (SAMs) came into operation. As a consequence American losses rose dramatically.[19] The Americans found North Vietnamese air defences alarmingly well organised—'Soviet radar-directed antiaircraft artillery, Soviet ground control intercept and early warning radars, Soviet MiGs and Soviet surface-to-air missiles were woven into an integrated system that was, according to American pilots who had flown in both wars, far more dangerous than anything encountered in "the barrel" over Germany during World War II'.[20] The Russians, however, saw things differently. It was the speed and effectiveness with which the Americans overcame these defences which so impressed the Soviet military. In March 1967 Marshal of Aviation Krasovskii published an article on 'Trends in the Use of Aircraft in a Nuclear War', in the restricted military journal *Voennaya Mysl'*. Then commandant of the Gagarin Air Force Academy and with a point to score against the élite strategic rocket forces, Krasovskii emphasised 'the increased power of means of nuclear attack and considerably increased combat potential of aircraft'. The relevance of this to the LDA in Europe was obvious: 'Operations against strategic and operational-strategic objectives can be carried out by long-range rocket-carrying aircraft'. They could also be used in conjunction with a rocket attack as a means of overcoming the air defence system.[21] Moreover, the Russians faced not merely a technologically more advanced opponent but also a better trained opponent. An article in the Soviet air defence forces journal, *Vestnik Protivovozdushnoi Oborony*, noted as late as 1979: 'a greater part of the pilots in the Unites States Air Force in Europe has combat experience received in the course of the war in South-East Asia. This experience is widely studied and put to practical use in the course of the combat training of pilots in the air forces of other countries in NATO'.[22] A specific concern which arose directly from the Vietnam experience was the use of carrier-based aviation, which featured in a further article in *Voennaya Mysl'* in June 1967 entitled 'U.S. Aviation in the War in Vietnam'.[23] This issue had obvious implications for war in the European theatre, particularly after the battle of Khe Sanh in South Vietnam from 20 January to 31 March 1968. In an awe-inspiring effort to raise the siege of US marines near Khe Sanh, the Americans launched 'Operation Niagara', a veritable waterfall of destruction. More than a decade later, the Russians were still talking about it. 'During the battles near Khe Sanh, more than 100,000 bombs were dropped in 55 days in 25,000 sorties from aboard US aircraft carriers', Major-General Viktor Starodubov of the Soviet General Staff noted in an interview in 1981.[24] Commander of the US Military Assistance Command in Vietnam, General Westmoreland, asserted that the 'key to our success at Khe Sanh was firepower, principally aerial firepower'.[25] And President Johnson praised the operation as 'the most overwhelming, intelligent, and effective use of air power in the history of warfare'.[26] The Russians did not disagree. Thereafter the increasingly effective use by the United States of electronic counter-measures (ECMs) and low altitude flying against the North Vietnamese air defence system installed by the Russians in 1965 gave the Soviet General Staff additional pause for thought.

When the air war over North Vietnam was resumed in 1969, the United States Air Force (USAF) was 'ready with new aircraft, tactics, and training. They went Downtown with a virtual armada of airplanes, each with a specialised mission and all synchronised together in a strike package far more sophisticated than the rudimentary packages of the Rolling Thunder era. And even though the air defenses were even tougher, the USAF lost proportionately fewer aircraft and crews'.[27] The Commander of the US Tactical Air Command (TAC) dismissed as 'groundless' the hypothesis that because of the mounting sophistication of air defence systems, the days of the manned penetrator might be numbered. 'I can remember people saying at the outset of World War II that it would be impossible to penetrate the strong German AAA capabilities. I recall when I took command in Vietnam [as the Commander of the Seventh Air Force] that people told me they couldn't imagine how we could operate strike forces in North Vietnam, and predicted that we would be knocked out by the enemy's surface-to-surface missiles . . . But look at the record. The SAMs [surface-to-air missiles] have not stopped us. We have been reasonably agile in the development of equipment and tactics to counter the enemy's defensive systems'.[28]

It might be thought that the experience of the October 1973 war taught a different lesson. But successful employment of the SAM-6 (surface-to-air missile 6) by the Arabs against Israeli pilots in the war did not impress the Russians, nor leading Israelis, for that matter. Major-General Peled, acting commander of the Israeli air force in 1975, commented: 'A ground-to-air missile is actually a mechanical toy. It [appears to be] a thinking adversary, it changes course, it follows you—but actually it is a very limited robot. I would say that the emotional stresses created in Vietnam, and later in Israel, by this type of semiintelligent weapon following you were far more than was warranted by its capability'.[29] The US Department of Defense also saw the SAMs as no great threat. In a report published in 1978, Chairman of the Joint Chiefs of Staff General Brown (USAF) referred to 'the less than complete success of Soviet-supplied surface-to-air missile defenses in the Vietnam and Middle East conflicts'.[30] Furthermore, only one month after the Arab-Israeli war in November 1973 head of the air defence system Marshal Pavel Batitsky emphasised the importance of the lessons drawn from the Vietnam experience, arguing that 'Aircraft will long retain the role of the principal striking power'. In particular he pointed to American experimentation with new types of aircraft which could penetrate air defences at low altitude and at supersonic speed, to the development of electronic counter-measures (ECMs) and to low altitude flying tactics.[31] The air defence forces journal *Vestnik Protivovozdushnoi Oborony* commented that 'for the defending side the destruction of low-flying targets has . . . become a substantially complex problem'.[32] As late as 1983 these problems were still to the forefront of Soviet concerns. Even with the associated technical difficulties closer to resolution, the psychological difficulties remained. An article appeared in the air defence forces journal in November 1983 written by Captain Agapov, entitled 'Airborne—A Low-Flying Target', and dealing with the 'psychological' and 'emotional' difficulties in training the *zenitchiki* (SAM operatives) to shoot down low-flying targets:

> During the course of several years I was given the duty of commanding a surface-to-air missile battery. I may say that the most difficult task for me was to teach operators to work with confidence on low-flying targets. I recall the eagerness, I might

even say, elation and enthusiasm with which lance sergeant V.
Burov and lance corporal A. Gal'finger worked on the screens of
the display unit, when the 'enemy's' planes moved at great height.
They were in no way deflated even when various forms of jamming
were employed. But all that had to happen was that the targets
appeared at a relatively low height and lance sergeant V. Burov
began to get nervous and lance corporal A. Gal'finger, spinning
the control columns, in effect tried to extricate himself from the
exercise.[33]

Furthermore, it took a considerable period of time for the Russians
to develop weapons capable of dealing with this problem. Not until
the early 1980s with the appearance of the MiG-31 did they acquire
an interceptor aircraft with a 'lookdown shootdown' capability and
only with the development of the SAM-10, also emerging into operation in the early 1980s, did the Russians acquire missiles 'effective
against small, low-altitude targets', including low-flying aircraft.[34] As
Batitsky pointed out: 'The rivalry between "armour and shell" is
developing more rapidly now than ever. And most probably it is
advancing with the greatest ferocity between the means of air attack
and the means of air defence. And this creates no mean problem
for those who serve in our forces.'[35]

The gap between requirements and capabilities has to be set
against the background of increasing difficulties faced by the Soviet
air defence forces which arose from the rapid growth of US technology: a problem compounded by the relatively underdeveloped
infrastructure of Soviet society. 'A characteristic of recent decades
has been the explosive development of military equipment', wrote
Colonel Barabanshchikov, a professor concerned with air defence
training, in June 1974. 'This has meant that the air defence forces
specialist must, during the course of his service, master very complex
military technology in a compressed span of time. As a result a
contradiction arises between the depth and scope of the training
material and the time devoted to its assimilation, which worsens with
the reduction in the period of service of the soldiers and sergeants'.[36]
Time was also a major problem in another sense. The rapid growth
in the technology of the enemy has meant that the air defence forces
have less time to prepare for battle. At certain moments literally
an instantaneous response is required.[37] This requirement placed a
premium on efficiency, not only technical but also managerial
efficiency. It is at this point that the demands of high technology have

met with the backwardness of Soviet society. This was not merely a matter of obvious vices such as 'drunkenness', which Colonel Barabanshchikov mentioned in the article cited above.[38] There have been other problems immediately recognisable to those who have spent any time in the Soviet Union: lax discipline, the tendency of the subordinate to evade responsibility by passing decisions ever upward (*perestrakhovka*), a fear of complex machinery, and so on. All such characteristics have long been obstacles on the path to greater economic development; all such characteristics are particularly inimical to speedy and effective air defence.

Of all these characteristics the most fundamental and the most damaging has been indiscipline. Editorials on the need to 'strengthen discipline' have long been a regular feature in the air defence forces journal,[39] a problem not unknown elsewhere in the armed forces. An article by Colonel General Sozinov, Chief of Staff of the Air Defence Forces, published in April 1975, on 'Teamwork and Efficiency in the Work of Staff Officers', emphasised the importance of maintaining strict discipline in the face of an increasingly resourceful adversary:

> Combat under current conditions will be distinctive for the high degree of transience and dynamism, characterised by the widespread use of means of attack at low and comparatively low levels of altitude, by the extensive use of evasive action, by the employment of anti-missile manoeuvres and intensive jamming. The enemy will attempt to reach defence installations using the element of surprise, of unexpectedness, by taking the most favourable route after taking into account the peculiarities of ground relief— along the banks of rivers, through valleys, from the coast. This will mean that on certain routes an exceptionally complex situation will arise, which will demand from headquarters flexible control of subordinate sub-units, guaranteed safety for those in the air, and also the organization of co-ordinated action between the surface-to-air missile forces and fighter aircraft. To control forces in such a situation, . . . with the aid of the usual 'mild' methods of control, will frequently prove impossible.[40]

Given the speed and suddenness of any attack under current conditions, an important role in the effectiveness of Soviet air defence is played by what they call 'automated control systems' (*avtomatizirovannye sistemy upravleniya—ASU*). Quoting Marshal Grechko on the importance of automation in raising the efficiency of leadership in battle, Sozinov emphasised that only by means of *ASU* could officers speedily and accurately cope with the massive flow of information reaching the command post:

> However, certain staff officers sometimes mistrust *ASU*. In a number of instances this is a product of weak technical knowledge and a fear of working with them. Only this can explain why some commanders [only] irregularly conduct exercises using *ASU* . . . [41]

Sozinov stressed that contrary to popular belief the 'scientific approach' was not supposed to be the preserve of 'senior levels of leadership' (*k starshim rukovodyashchim instantsiyam*).[42] Moreover, while lacking the certainty of instructions being carried out to the letter in the face of indiscipline, the service was simultaneously too inflexible to allow for individual creativity: by the end of the 1970s Sozinov was also emphasising the need for 'officers with initiative'.[43]

Seen from the perspective of an air defence force seriously weakened by structural inefficiencies, American use of air power in South-East Asia certainly gave cause for alarm; the Russians continued to see US carrier-based aviation as a serious threat well into the 1970s. An article in *Vestnik Protivovozdushnoi Oborony* in August 1975 on 'The Tactics of the USA's Carrier-Based Aircraft' detailed the problem the Russians faced, and alerted readers to the fact that 'According to the USA's naval chiefs, thanks to the use of jamming against the air defence system's surface-to-air missile complexes they evidently succeeded in reducing the loss of aircraft in Vietnam by a factor of five'.[44] Two years later in 1977 an article by 'G. Borisov' (most probably a pseudonym) summarised the then current threat:

> Basing itself on the experience of war in South-East Asia and in the Near East, the American military leadership . . . considers that in contemporary war tactical and carrier-based aviation will play an important role in the resolution of various urgent tasks. Included in that number are the destruction of nuclear weapons and the means by which they are delivered, at their launching sites; the destruction of the enemy's aircraft in the air and on airfields; the destruction of surface-to-air missile sites and other means of anti-aircraft defence; delivering strikes from the air on military, industrial and other targets, situated on the coastline and deep within the territory of the enemy; carrying out tactical reconnaissance, [providing] air support to the military activities of ground forces, assault landing forces and much else.[45]

By this time Marshal Batitsky was sounding the tocsin. 'The massive use of manned and unmanned devices, the manoeuvrability and tremendous speed of air targets, and the use of various radar-jamming devices considerably alter the nature of air combat, imparting to it an exceptionally dynamic nature. It is important to bear in mind that in modern warfare each air target may prove to be strategically important', he stated in 1978 prior to his replacement in June by the younger and more dynamic Marshal Alexander Koldunov.[46] Furthermore, despite the much publicised emphasis in US publications on the supposed power of Soviet air defences, the Americans had in fact drawn an accurate assessment of the Soviet Union's true vulnerabilities in this area. 'A critical vulnerability . . . exists for them at low altitudes', the deputy director of scientific and technical intelligence at the US Defense Intelligence Agency pointed out in November 1979.[47] And as recently as 1983 former Secretary of Defense Harold Brown noted: 'the Soviets have had to spend four or five times as much on air defenses as the United States has spent on its air-breathing strategic forces. Yet at any time it has been a reasonable expectation that even without a prior U.S. ballistic missile strike most of the U.S. alert bomber force would succeed in penetrating'.[48] As one F-111 pilot has remarked: 'they envisioned a high-altitude threat from our intercontinental bombers [evidently the B-70 which never got off the ground]. Well, we fooled them; we're going low'.[49]

Soviet concern focused on the F-111 fighter-bomber, which received the unusual accolade of specific mention during the strategic arms limitation talks.[50] In 1971 the F-111 was introduced into the European theatre as a considerable augmentation of NATO fire-power; its twin, the FB-111, was first deployed by the Strategic Air Command in 1969. General Burchinal, then Deputy Commander-in-Chief of United States forces in Europe, described the operational advantages of the F-111 in glowing terms:

> a ground map radar system, a blind bombing capability, an automatic terrain following system which permits blind, low level penetration profiles at high speed, an internal ECM system, a highly accurate passive navigational system, and a varied and greatly increased capability . . . The superior qualities of the F-111 increase the effectiveness of air operations by reducing the number of sorties required to destroy a particular target.[51]

Even allowing for a certain degree of hyperbole the Russians had

nothing comparable to this. Despite initial teething problems with
the first model, the F-111A,[52] the plane made a tremendous impact
during the last months of the air war in North Vietnam. 'The F-111s
went Downtown, back to Hanoi and Haiphong, again and again,
alone, at night, and in the weather'. It was so effective that the
North Vietnamese nicknamed the plane 'Whispering Death'. 'The
terrain-following radar guides it automatically at altitudes, speeds,
and in weather conditions that would be suicidal in any other
airplane, and the F-111's complex navigation and threat-warning
systems allow it to deliver ordnance in the most hostile environ-
ments', one writer has pointed out. He also reports an F-111 pilot
as having remarked with respect to the Russians: 'in the worst kind
of weather we can go hit them and they can't hit us. They know
from ten years ago when the F-111s were flying over Hanoi and they
weren't able to touch them'.[53] The American publication *Air Force
Magazine* commented that with the acquisition of the F-111 the US
Air Force in Europe (USAFE) 'represented the most powerful air
commitment in the history of NATO'.[54]

1.3   US AIR POWER AND SOVIET AIR DEFENCE IN EUROPE

The United States thus possessed a clear and avowed advantage
which acquired increasing significance now that the USSR was
approaching long-sought parity with US strategic forces. For
although the Warsaw Pact possessed many more tactical aircraft in
total (if one excludes US reserves on the American continent) these
were mainly short-range interceptors, the majority of which were
unable to track low-flying aircraft. The development of the MiG-23
(Western designation Flogger) was framed to meet that need. The
MiG-23 (Flogger-B), introduced in 1976, was 'the first Soviet aircraft
with a demonstrated ability to track and engage targets flying below
its own altitude'; even so, it had only a 'rudimentary system'
according to the US Department of Defense.[55] Not until the early
1980s with the introduction of the MiG-31 (Foxhound-A) did the
world see 'the first Soviet fighter-interceptor to have lookdown-
shootdown and multiple target engagement capabilities'.[56] Whereas
NATO was used to having a long-range deep strike tactical aircraft
capability[57]—which the Russians hoped to emulate with the introduction of the Su-24 (Fencer) in December 1974—the nearest Soviet
equivalents to NATO aircraft in the early to mid–1970s, according

to the US Department of Defense, 'had limited range and payload capabilities, short-range air-intercept radars or range-only radars, little or no capability to employ precision-guided munitions, and were resticted primarily to clear-weather operations'.[58]

With few exceptions the US military were willing to acknowledge this margin of advantage over the Russians. Testifying before Congress in March 1974 Chairman of the Joint Chiefs of Staff Admiral Thomas Moorer argued: 'It is difficult to draw precise conclusions as to the relative balance between the US and the USSR in theater nuclear weapons . . . Nevertheless, I continue to believe that the US is at least the equal of the USSR in overall capability, and probably still the superior in nuclear weapons technology'.[59] Two years later Secretary of Defense Donald Rumsfeld confidently asserted that 'in practically every specific aspect of tactical aviation technology, [Warsaw] Pact capabilities remain deficient relative to their U.S. or NATO counterparts'.[60] Furthermore, the US Department of Defense estimated that Soviet 'pilot training, and flying time do not approach U.S. requirements',[61] factors which the Department referred to elsewhere as having 'a potentially far greater effect' on 'effectiveness' than 'equipment upgrades'.[62] The fact that the NATO Powers resolutely and persistently refused to negotiate any limitations in the sphere of tactical aviation throughout the 1970s is perhaps the most conclusive proof of perceived Western superiority in this sphere. Soviet concern at American lighter delivery aircraft was thus neither misplaced nor exaggerated. In an evaluation drawn up by the US Government in October 1972 calculations were made on the kind of 'worse case' assumptions only too familiar to the Soviet military. Assuming a 50 per cent attrition rate and launching on one-way missions, the 700 nuclear-capable fighter-bombers deployed by the United States in the European theatre could destroy either up to 25 per cent of the Soviet population, 90 per cent of Soviet M/IRBMs, or 20 per cent of the ICBMs and M/IRBMs combined.[63] And as a subcommittee of the Senate Foreign Relations Committee pointed out in December 1970 with respect to US forward-based systems in general: 'We must assume that the Soviets, as they view our placement of tactical nuclear weapons in countries far closer to their borders than Cuba is to ours, will seek to break out of the nuclear ring that has been drawn around them'.[64]

1.4   THE SOVIET REACTION TO CHANGES IN NATO STRATEGIC DOCTRINE

The Soviet government was reacting not merely to US advantages in FBS but also to changes in Western military doctrine concerning limited war in Europe which made their employment seem more likely. After five years of pressure from Washington, the NATO council finally accepted the doctrinal shift from 'assured destruction' to 'flexible response' in December 1967.[65] This was intended to signal to the Russians that in the event of a conventional Soviet attack on Western Europe, at a time when Soviet strategic forces were sufficient to deter a response from US strategic forces, NATO would use conventional and probably also limited nuclear forces in the European theatre. In December 1969 the NATO Council 'discussed measures required to implement the NATO strategy of forward defence based on flexibility in response'.[66] The philosophy underlying that decision had already led to the accumulation of some 7000 warheads in Western Europe by December 1966, a figure which in the censored words of a Congressional report 'did not include Strategic Air Command warhead [deleted] and warheads in ships afloat some of which [deleted]'.[67] In addition the resolute refusal of the West Europeans to contemplate any real increase in conventional forces, initially regarded as vital to the new strategy, when combined with pressures from the USA for the withdrawal of its troops from Europe accentuated NATO's dependence upon the use of tactical nuclear weapons. It was certainly not in Russian interests to permit the United States to restrict any conflict to the European theatre, where both Europeans and Russians would face certain devastation whereas the United States would remain untouched. However, the Pentagon worked with a different assumption in mind. 'No one can be certain that the use of tactical nuclear weapons will not lead to escalation to strategic attack, but no one can be certain that it will', argued General Goodpaster, the Supreme Allied Commander Europe, in 1971.[68]

The Russians rightly ascribed these changes to approaching strategic parity between the Super-Powers. In the restricted Soviet military journal *Voennaya Mysl'* of August 1967—with change already in the wind—military analyst Colonel Samorukov noted: 'In the United States they understand more and more clearly that in conditions of, in their opinion, an established balance in nuclear armament of both sides, the unleashing of war through the unlimited use of nuclear weapons constitutes an extremely great risk to the aggressor'.[69] But this did not lead to any fundamental reassessment of American intentions. As Defence Minister Andrei Grechko asserted: 'A nuclear attack with limited goals is specified by the NATO leadership as one of the variants of unleashing war in the secondary theatres of military operations . . . It is not excluded even in Europe'.[70] Moreover, and this was to become increasingly apparent as the Europeans resisted any growth in their conventional forces, the adoption of flexible response in fact lowered the nuclear threshold. To enhance deterrence NATO was shifting to more of a war-waging strategy, a strategy of limited nuclear war. In a further article which appeared in *Voennaya Mysl'* in June 1968, Major-General N. Vasendin and Colonel N. Kuznetsov noted:

> Recently the command element of the U.S. Army, evidently, does not exclude the possibility of opening military operations even in the main theaters with the use of just conventional means of destruction. Such a beginning of war [sic] can create favorable conditions for the movement of all nuclear forces to the regions of combat operations, bringing them into the highest level of combat readiness, and subsequently inflicting the first nuclear strike with the employment in it of the maximum number of missile launch sites, submarines, and aircraft at the most favorable moment.[71]

Several factors thus combined to instil into the Russians an acute awareness of the need to buttress their theatre nuclear capability in Europe: the extraordinarily impressive display of US air power in Vietnam; continuing efforts on the part of the USA to reinforce its superiority in theatre air capability, epitomised in the deployment of the F-111; the shift in NATO doctrine towards the option of limited nuclear war; as well as the American refusal to negotiate forward-based systems at the strategic arms limitation talks.

1.5   SALT I AND NATO POLITICS

The US refusal to negotiate FBS had as much to do with intra-alliance politics as with the stubborn insistence of the Pentagon. At the strategic arms limitation talks the US delegation 'stressed that US tactical aircraft deployed abroad involved political commitments to our allies'.[72] This was an important consideration. In reducing tension in relations with the Soviet Union the US Government had to take care not to weaken the allegiance of its allies in Western Europe. 'We have made clear that we would make no agreement which sacrificed their interests', President Nixon told Congress in February 1971.[73] Although relieved that the Americans and the Russians were finally resolving differences short of war, the West Europeans felt uneasy lest in trading concessions to establish *détente* the USA were tempted to sell short the interests of Western Europe. Such sentiments were most explicitly expressed by the French. In an article published by *Foreign Affairs* in April 1971 France's Foreign Minister, Michel Debré, asked several questions which other European statesmen raised only in private:

> in fixing the strategic situation in accordance with their vital interests, might not the two superpowers create new dangers in theaters that for them are secondary? In such cases, might not their confrontation, perhaps by way of intervening states, become actually less improbable, being confined within limits set in advance?
>
> Can Europeans help wondering whether their territory may not become a secondary theater of war for the superpowers?
>
> While the SALT negotiations proceed, some people raise the possibility that the United States might disengage from Europe and reduce its forces there. Such a disengagement would be part, of course, of an attempt to set up an equilibrium that would be less costly for the two superpowers.[74]

Mistrust existed on both sides of the Atlantic. West Germany's new opening to the East inaugurated in October 1969 by Chancellor Willy Brandt and resulting in the Moscow treaty of the 12 August 1970 (followed soon by other such treaties, with Poland and Czechoslovakia), relinquishing all territorial claims and recognising the inviolability of existing frontiers, in turn disturbed the United States as much as it reassured the Soviet Union. Given the crucial role of West Germany as the chief contributor to NATO's land forces in Europe and as the most powerful economic force within the European Economic Community, there was a barely suppressed note of alarm sounded in Washington. 'The West cannot afford to allow the momentum of individual approaches to the East to put allies inadvertently in the painful position of having to choose between their national concerns and responsibilities', President Nixon threatened.[75] Centrifugal forces within NATO were increasingly assertive. US economic policies, unilaterally decided but multilateral in impact, added to the problem: the Vietnam war had been funded from federal deficits, the resultant inflation weakened the dollar, and the devaluation of the dollar destabilised allied relationships. As the Americans themselves acknowledged: 'Our approach to China [negotiations on the reopening of relations] had an impact on Japan, as did our negotiations with the Soviet Union on our friends in Western Europe. Our unilateral economic measures affected both. As a result, our relations with our allies appeared for a period of several months to be somewhat out of pace with the innovations taken in our relations with our adversaries'.[76]

Faced with the problem of maintaining the cohesion of NATO while simultaneously reaching an accommodation with the Russians, the US Government could not afford to concede on FBS at the strategic arms limitation talks even when the Russians were willing to drop their initial and unreasonable position that only Western theatre nuclear weapons were subject to negotiated reductions. Neither was the US delegation in any position to accept the inclusion of British or French nuclear systems on the agenda even with Soviet weaponry up for limitation. Both London and Paris were equally determined that these forces and their projected growth would remain unconstrained by any future US-Soviet agreement. And these forces were not negligible.

The first Polaris submarine armed with nuclear missiles became fully operational in the British navy and was assigned to NATO for targeting in the spring of 1968.[77] Two more entered service in 1969 and a further vessel in 1970. In addition to some 50 Vulcan bombers armed with nuclear weapons, the British also possessed nuclear-armed strike aircraft in the fleet air arm.[78] France had 45 bombers and it was forming 18 IRBMs into two squadrons—the first to become operational in 1971; there were in addition five nuclear missile submarines coming into service between 1971 and 1979.[79] Gerard Smith, who headed the US delegation to SALT, sums up the position during the negotiations:

The British and French strategic missile force in 1970 totaled 84 SLBMs [submarine-launched ballistic missiles], with 100 to 125 more launchers to become operational in the next few years. By the Soviet definition of strategic systems, which included lighter

delivery aircraft, the two U.S. allies then had 375 strategic launchers and some 250 more under construction or planned.[80]

The United States had sold Britain the power plant and initial
blueprints for the submarines. Britain in turn built the later power
plants, though the USA provided the fuel, and the British
constructed all the hulls. The United States sold the missiles to
Britain but the British developed their own warheads. Each
submarine had 16 missiles and each missile was to be MIRVed with
three warheads.[81] The French had received their submarine guidance
system from the Americans, but their weapons—unlike those of the
British—were not targeted by NATO. To the Russians this was an
excessively subtle distinction. At this stage they consistently refused
to exclude the French from the tally of Western armaments. Their
reasons were not entirely surprising: 'France, although it has left the
NATO military structure, is still an ally of the United States and
does not conceal the fact that its nuclear arms are targeted on the
Soviet Union'.[82] 'You see, this is, so to say, one company standing,
figuratively speaking, on one side of the barricades', Foreign Minister
Andrei Gromyko pointed out.[83] 'Imagine that a ghastly tragedy
occurred: an English missile with nuclear warheads is in flight',
Gromyko remarked in 1983. 'Would it, perhaps, carry the label: "I
am English?" . . . Or a French missile is in flight. Perhaps it will
also fly bearing the label: "I am French, there is no need to count
me"?'[84]

The exclusion from SALT of the FBS and growing British and
French systems had important repercussions on the future of arms
control in Europe. The Russians had been replacing their ageing SS-
4 and SS-5 M/IRBMs targeted on Western Europe since 1959 and
1961 respectively with the variable-range ballistic missile, the SS-11.
But this was to be counted as an ICBM in the interim agreement
limiting strategic offensive arms concluded on the 26 May 1972, since
it was a missile which could be used on intercontinental missions.[85]

Thus it was not merely with respect to forward-based systems that
the first SALT agreements were unsatisfactory to the Russians. As
a consequence not only did they reserve the right to raise the issue
of FBS in further negotiations due to begin as SALT II in the autumn
of 1972; they also issued the following statement unilaterally nine
days before signing the SALT I treaties:

Taking into account that modern ballistic missile submarines are
presently in the possession of not only the U.S., but also of its

NATO allies, the Soviet Union agrees that for the period of effectiveness of the Interim 'Freeze' Agreement the U.S. and its allies
have up to 50 such submarines with a total of up to 800 ballistic
missile launchers thereon (including 41 U.S. submarines with 656
ballistic missile launchers). However, if during the period of effectiveness of the Agreement U.S. allies in NATO should increase
the number of their modern submarines they would have operational or under construction on the date of signature of the Agreement, the Soviet Union will have the right to a corresponding
increase in the number of its submarines. In the opinion of the
Soviet side, the solution of the question of modern ballistic missile
submarines provided for in the Interim Agreement only partially
compensates for the strategic imbalance in the deployment of the
nuclear-powered missile submarines of the USSR and the U.S.
Therefore, the Soviet side believes that this whole question of
liquidating the American missile submarine bases outside the U.S.,
will be appropriately resolved in the course of follow-on
negotiations.[86]

The Americans rejected this: on 24 May Smith announced that his
government did 'not accept the validity of the considerations in that
statement'.[87] The claim subsequently made that French and British
systems were thereby incorporated into the SALT I treaties is disingenuous: first because this unilateral statement was never accepted
by the other party and could therefore not form part of the agreements; and second the Russians did not in fact increase their submarines beyond the agreed limit to compensate for increases in Western
Europe. The compensation was, as we shall see, to be obtained
elsewhere.[88] There was in addition another area in which the
Russians sought and failed to obtain compensation, and that
concerned China.

2 The Chinese Connexion, 1969–73

2.1 FIGHTING ON THE FRONTIER

The sudden and unexpected emergence of an immediate threat to Russian frontiers in the Far East seemed to presage important and long-term consequences for Soviet policy with respect to both the SALT negotiations and *détente* in Europe. On 2 March 1969 Soviet and Chinese forces collided in a dispute over the possession of an island (Damansky/Chenpao) on the Sino-Soviet border. A minor border incident soon flared into open warfare and by 18 August the Russians were contemplating drastic action. On that day, former National Security adviser Henry Kissinger recalls, 'a middle-level State Department specialist in Soviet affairs . . . was having lunch with a Soviet Embassy official [who worked for the KGB] when, out of the blue, the Russian asked what the US reaction would be to a Soviet attack on Chinese nuclear facilities'.[1]

The threat was reiterated in an article which appeared in the *Evening News* (London) on 16 September by Victor Louis, an unofficial agent of the Soviet Government. Such sabre-rattling caused unease within the Soviet leadership, already divided over preparations for SALT. Chairman of the Council of Ministers Alexei Kosygin flew unexpectedly to Peking on 11 September 1969 in a desperate attempt to forestall war. There he and Chinese Premier Chou En-lai discussed proposals for a cease-fire and the opening of negotiations. The Chinese preconditions for further talks were that the ideological polemic should continue and that Chinese nuclear bases should not be attacked. Chou En-lai told the Albanian ambassador:

> Kosygin accepted these things in general, and he will present them to the leadership. These talks were held on the instructions of Mao Tsetung and Lin Piao. The Soviets asked for the talks because their internal situation is one of great crisis; Kosygin is the 'dove'

who has handed in his resignation on three occasions. Through these talks, they want to exert pressure on the United States of America and will have a reduction of tension for a time, without knowing how long it will continue, but we will not make any concessions to the Soviets.[2]

Negotiations ensued on 20 October 1969. The Chinese were eager to lower the level of tension. But Chou had correctly predicted that they would make no concessions and it was not long before further complications arose.

2.2 CHINA'S IMPACT ON SOVIET-AMERICAN RELATIONS

The United States now moved promptly towards a *rapprochement* with China as a means of exerting leverage on the Russians. Moscow had feared this from the very beginning. They had not only lost a former and valuable ally—this could be rationalised as inevitable given the high fever of the Chinese Cultural Revolution—but they had also succeeded in driving the Chinese towards the enemy camp through their insensitive handling of issues in dispute between the two sides. The problem was that from the outset there was a tendency in Moscow to regard the Chinese as already lost to the socialist camp. As *Krasnaya Zvezda* warned, somewhat prematurely, on 25 March 1969: 'The events of Damansky show that the Peking adventurers are going down the path of anti-Sovietism with the dark forces of world reaction.'[3] In April military comment went further, claiming 'The Mao group's struggle against the USSR and other socialist countries today . . . has become a second front side by side with the imperialist front directed against the community of socialist countries'.[4] But this was only an ideological and political front and not yet a military front. There was still time to forestall the creation of an alliance between the Chinese and the West. This aim soon became apparent in the SALT negotiations.

  In the summer of 1970 Semenov told Ambassador Smith that 'He saw a danger from adventurous circles in certain countries that wanted nuclear war between the U.S. and the U.S.S.R. Suppose, he suggested, such a country had a submarine which launched a "volley" of missiles against one or both countries and that one of them incorrectly identified the source of the strike . . . It would be in the interests of both countries to agree on necessary organization and technical arrangements against this possibility'.[5] In case the Americans were under any misapprehension as to what the Russians meant, 'Semenov observed that, while the United States seemed to regard it as technical, the Soviets considered it a political matter with technical aspects'.[6] Clearly the Russians envisaged a joint agreement to forestall a nuclear war as a means of obtaining an understanding at Chinese expense. 'It was all right to discuss technical measures as proposed by the United States. But it was necessary to discuss also questions of action to be taken by the U.S.S.R. and the United States in the event of an actual provocative use of nuclear weapons by a third country . . . The Soviets were convinced that such an agreement in itself would constitute a serious deterrent to those who might plan this sort of provocation.' Then one night during an intermission in a Rostropovich concert Semenov passed Smith a note suggesting a US-Soviet agreement for joint retaliation against any Power launching a nuclear attack. 'He proposed that we discuss specific actions by the U.S.S.R. and the United States in the event of such an attack. If facts about a provocation under preparation were obtained the sides should inform each other in a timely manner. If necessary, measures could be taken to prevent provocative use of nuclear weapons. Both sides would obligate themselves to take retaliatory action if a third country committed such aggression.'[7] But the Americans were loath to oblige. They saw that Soviet fears gave them additional leverage at SALT.[8] The sight of growing *détente* between Washington and Peking increasingly worried Soviet leaders, faced as they seemed to be with a fusion of two hostile fronts.

The Russians also moved to patch up relations with the Chinese. On 15 January 1971 the Soviet Government offered the Chinese Government a non-aggression pact, which the Chinese would not accept until the Russians explicitly recognised the need to renegotiate ownership of certain border regions.[9] To Moscow China's acceptance of the non-aggression pact would have relieved anxieties about Chinese intentions. But Chinese evasiveness also served the purpose of demonstrating to the world that Peking's intentions were not entirely pacific: they clearly wished to keep the wound open in order to exert pressure on the Russians for concessions. A further Soviet proposal appears to have had a similar edge to it. On 23 June the Russians offered the USA, China, France and Britain a conference on nuclear disarmament. Had the others accepted and China refused, then the Chinese would have been isolated diplomatically—the sort of public relations exercise the Soviets have often attempted.

The Russians also hoped to enlarge upon SALT negotiations, then deadlocked by the FBS and related issues (French and British systems), by drawing in the other nuclear Powers.[10]

Soviet attempts failed. Nothing came of the conference of five. Furthermore, the United States moved to recognise Communist China. Soviet anxieties were difficult to conceal, with the arrival of Kissinger in China due in early July 1971. 'Our party and state will consider all the possible consequences of Sino-American contacts', warned I. Alexandrov, a name linked to Politburo opinion, in *Pravda* on 25 June.[11] Kissinger's visit paved the way for the Presidential party. Nervously contemplating events from his new perch at the head of the new Institute of the USA and Canada, Dr. Georgii Arbatov warned that the USSR was watching events 'with great attention' and cautioned the United States about the dangers involved in these diplomatic manoeuvres.[12]

Moscow's hope was that the continuation of the Vietnam war might blacken the Americans in Chinese eyes. The Chinese were themselves divided over the issue of US recognition and the prospect of an American Presidential visit. China's Defence Minister Lin Piao is believed to have led the opposition, a stand which led to his disappearance, still unsatisfactorily explained, in September 1971.[13] The Russians were conscious of having lost a potential ally in Peking. It was not that Lin was pro-Soviet—indeed he is said to have 'given orders for the airfields to be filled with steel obstacles to prevent the Soviet aircraft from landing, and for the dykes to be breached and cities inundated to hinder the Soviet paratroops'[14] (evidently in 1969)—but he was at least as anti-American as he was anti-Russian, and the Russians naturally appreciated that fact, for it was the most they could hope for.[15]

2.3   REINFORCEMENT OF THE SOVIET FAR EAST

In October 1971 China was finally admitted to its seat at the UN Security Council and on 21 February 1972 Nixon arrived in Peking. Moscow's fears appeared justified. The Russians felt they were under pressure. The conflict with China was a drain on military resources. The border between the USSR (plus Outer Mongolia) and China is 7000 miles long. In 1969 there were some 25 divisions on the Soviet side of the frontier. By 1973 this had increased to 45. The number of tactical combat aircraft was raised from 200 to some 1200 by 1973.

The quantity of Soviet missiles in the Far Eastern theatre was also increased: by the end of the 1960s there were about 50 SS-4 MRBMs and SS-5 IRBMs. These were replaced by at least 120 SS-11 Variable-Range Ballistic Missiles (VRBMs). As specialist on Soviet strategy Raymond Garthoff has remarked: 'just as the United States was discarding a two-war strategic planning framework to shape its forces, the Soviet Union was adopting one'.[16] The journal *Kommunist Vooruzhennykh Sil* warned: 'The intention of the Maoists to establish their own nuclear missile potential complicates the international situation; it is fraught with the threat of military adventures on their part'.[17] The China factor thus inevitably played a part in the Soviet decision to proceed with a new generation of intermediate range nuclear weapons, though, as we shall see, by 1973–74 the sense of urgency had gone.

In Europe the dispute with China placed an additional burden on Moscow's unhappy relations with its allies, which were already under strain from domestic unrest in Czechoslovakia, Poland and East Germany. The East German leadership also became most uneasy at Moscow's *détente* with Bonn. Now that the Chinese were in conflict with the USSR, the Russians reportedly called on their allies to support them not merely morally but also materially—with token contingents—on the Sino-Soviet border. The proposal was apparently put forward and rejected when the Warsaw Pact Powers gathered in Budapest in March 1969.[18] The Romanians were the USSR's most difficult partners and subordinates in Eastern Europe. They had reacted to the invasion of Czechoslovakia in a manner not dissimilar to the Chinese, who had condemned the invasion as an illustration of Soviet aggressiveness. The late Albanian leader Enver Hoxha has recorded: 'A member of a Rumanian delegation told one of our comrades: At a time when Rumania was threatened with invasion by the Soviets [1968], Tito [the Yugoslav leader] met Ceaucescu [the Romanian leader] in Djerdap and signed a secret agreement, under which Tito would send the army up to Bucharest to help Rumania'. Hoxha doubted whether Tito would ever commit himself in this way, but the mere fact that Romanian officials were spreading such rumours was indicative of Bucharest's hostility to the Russians.[19] Other rumours were being circulated by the Chinese. A leading Chinese diplomat told the Albanian chargé d'affaires in Peking that China was about to sign 'a secret agreement' with the Romanians.[20] Elsewhere in Eastern Europe the Chinese found less scope for penetration but the reverberations of the dispute with the

USSR could still be felt. Moscow's most important ally, Poland, was not directly hostile to the Russians but was nevertheless extremely circumspect about backing the Russians against the Chinese. The Poles inevitably regarded the crisis in the Far East as an unwarranted distraction from the main issue: European security, including the resolution of the German problem. Publicly the Poles abused the Chinese but in private they stressed their wish to improve relations with Peking, and Poland's ambassador to China is said to have 'openly' criticised the Russians.[21]

The unresolved conflict with China thus complicated the USSR's existing security dilemmas. There were now three preoccupations: the USA (with Japan in train), Western Europe, and China. Not only was there China's vast standing army to contend with, China also had 18 nuclear-capable bombers,[22] and tested its first IRBM late in 1970, reportedly beginning deployment by April 1972.[23] By 1975 80 IRBMs were deployed; by 1980 the number had risen to 122.[24] A standing concern after 1969 was that China would be drawn into a common front with the Americans and West Europeans. American policy naturally played on these fears.

2.4   THE THREAT FROM CHINA DIMINISHED

The Agreement on the Prevention of Nuclear War signed by the USA and USSR in June 1973 committed the two Powers to consult when faced with the danger of nuclear war. But it did not forge the basis for joint action against China as the Russians had hoped.[25] The road was thus open for unilateral Chinese military action—were they so foolhardy—undeterred by the threat of US retaliation in the event of a Sino-Soviet war. But what is so striking is that the 'China card'— the threat of a firm alliance with China—was never really played by the United States; nor did the 'American card' prove of much use to the Chinese in shifting the Russians from their inflexible resistance to renegotiating the Sino-Soviet frontier line. Moreover, once the USSR had taken precautionary military measures on the Sino-Soviet border, there was no immediate fear of a Chinese attack. The reasons why the Russians felt more secure were more than military. As two commentators noted in the restricted Soviet military journal *Voennaya Mysl'* in September 1973, China's economy was in no condition to fight a war. The very Maoist extremism which had brought China to the brink of war with Russia in 1969 had also disrupted China's economic growth and social cohesion.[26] The Soviet Government was as conscious as the Chinese of the fact that Peking had little more than diplomacy to play with, and much if not all of this diplomacy ultimately proved to be of little more than symbolic significance.

In respect of Western Europe the Chinese took the initiative, showing a growing interest in the European Economic Community, which was enlarged in 1973 with the entry of Britain. The Soviet response to these pressures was ambiguous. On the one hand it could be argued that the USSR should buttress its defences in both the Far East and Europe so as to deter a combined assault from West and East. On the other hand it could be argued that the threat from the East necessitated a more conciliatory approach to the West or, indeed, that the continued tension in relations with the West required immediate settlement of relations with the East. The policy adopted appears to have been a composite of all these elements: the Russians continued to reinforce their positions in both East and West. This required modernisation of existing weapons systems in both the European and Far Eastern theatres. The Russians also attempted to normalise relations with the Chinese through negotiations and simultaneously moved to reduce tension in Europe. As Bovin pointed out in 1975 'China is really causing complications and for this reason we have redoubled [our] efforts both in conducting the policy of detente in relation to the imperialist states and the neutralisation of the line Peking is attempting to conduct in the international arena'.[27] Yet the Russians offered no serious concessions to either camp. With the United States losing ground the Soviet Union was becoming accustomed to having its own way in the world and neither the Chinese nor the West Europeans had the capability or the resolve to block them. By 1973–74 the immediacy of the threat from China had diminished. Because of its chronic internal instability and the resulting deterioration in its economy, China all but disqualified itself as a major player of any weight in the coming years. The Russians would express momentary alarm when the Americans and Chinese came together but this had no impact on policy other than to bolster Soviet defences. Thus, although China never became the crucial factor in the decision to move ahead with the SS-20, it did play a significant supporting role in the drama that unfolded.

3 SALT's Side-Effects, 1973–74

3.1 THE PRICE OF SALT

It was no mean achievement for the United States and the Soviet Union to agree upon the limitation of Anti-Ballistic Missile (ABM) systems and the limitation of nuclear missiles in May 1972. However, the West Europeans were always nervous that the US-Soviet *détente* might evolve into a US-Soviet entente and at the expense of their own security. Indeed these fears were taken sufficiently seriously in Washington for the US Government to take measures to reassert the unalterability of the US commitment to the common defence. The means by which this was done necessarily exacerbated differences with the Russians over the negotiating agenda at SALT II. For the United States sought to reassure its West European allies by focusing on the utility of US forward-based systems which so much concerned the Soviet military. The renewed focus on this US capability naturally reinforced the concern of the Soviet military to reduce this asset through negotiation or, if this proved impossible, to negate the value of this capability through the deployment of countervailing forces by the Soviet Union.

The SALT process had already caused dissent within the Soviet military and within the political leadership. In April 1972, just prior to the Nixon-Brezhnev summit, the United States responded to a major North Vietnamese offensive by mining Haiphong harbour; an action which reportedly caused great discontent within the Politburo. An echo of the dispute could still be heard a decade later when one Soviet commentator argued that 'if we resorted to linkage, then as you recall, in 1972 when the United States established a blockade of Vietnam, there would have been no SALT agreement, let alone solutions to other problems.'[1] Politburo divisions over SALT apparently reached the Central Committee plenum held immediately prior to Nixon's arrival in Moscow, on 19 May. Ukrainian Party leader and Politburo member Shelest, who had earlier been a vehement

42

advocate of military intervention in Czechoslovakia (1968) and had opposed *détente* with West Germany, is said to have spoken out against the line of accommodation with the USA. Not until nearly a year later did Brezhnev succeed in removing Shelest from the Politburo. However, on the eve of Nixon's arrival—he was due on 22 May—Shelest was demoted *de facto* by being appointed a Deputy Chairman of the Council of Ministers, under Kosygin, which effectively removed him from his fiefdom in the Ukraine.[2] Shelest's dissent was matched by discontent within the military. Mention has already been made of Grechko's opposition to the SALT process (see pp. 16–17). *Krasnaya Zvezda* maintained a stubborn silence on the agreements signed. Instead of a eulogy on SALT, an editorial on the anniversary of the German invasion emphasised that 'We will never forget the day on 22 June 1941, when the peaceful work of the country was interrupted by the treacherous assault of the Hitlerite aggressors'.[3] The Party newspaper *Pravda* was sober but more sanguine. Interestingly no editorial on SALT was published, but an article on 22 June appeared entitled 'An Important Step Towards Controlling the Arms Race'. However, along with the congratulations there were also reassurances for SALT's opponents:

> the limitation of strategic arms still does not remove the danger of nuclear war, although it does go in that direction. Until such time as this danger is liquidated, the Soviet Union has taken and will take every measure needed to guarantee its security and the security of its allies. This position has been taken into account by the Moscow agreements. They do not in any way weaken the defence capability of the Soviet Union and our allies.[4]

It was to the second round of strategic arms limitation talks that the Soviet armed forces now looked for restrictions on or the withdrawal of American forward-based systems. The talks opened in November 1972 and were intended to produce a comprehensive agreement to complement the interim agreement on the limitation of offensive arms reached in May. The Soviets immediately proposed 'the withdrawal of American ballistic missile submarines from forward bases'.[5] And when in March 1973 Ambassador Alexis Johnson arrived in Geneva to replace Gerard Smith at the head of the US delegation, he faced Soviet proposals to include American forward-based systems in the total of US strategic forces. 'FBS was a major Soviet focus', Johnson recalls.[6] This was also a matter Ambassador Dobrynin raised with Kissinger in Washington that

April, but to no effect.[7] The Russians persisted and tabled the matter again that autumn—also to no result. Once more NATO concerns were uppermost in American minds. 'The NAC [North Atlantic Council] was quite content with whatever approach we wanted to take on central systems as long as we promised not to touch our European FBS . . . as long as I emphasized we had no intention of withdrawing our FBS or even debating the subject, they would nod and smile appreciatively', Johnson recalls.[9]

The Americans considered they needed a margin of advantage over the Soviet Union in order to extend deterrence to cover their NATO and other allies. The Russians naturally viewed this margin of advantage—symbolised in the FBS—as detrimental to their interests, not necessarily because they hoped to invade Western Europe but because this advantage gave the USA extra leverage over the USSR in time of crisis and enabled the US Government to plan on the basis of limited nuclear war in Europe. The Soviet advance towards strategic parity *vis-à-vis* the Americans, temporarily delayed by the addition of multiple independently-targeted re-entry vehicles (MIRVs) to augment the warheads on US missiles, enhanced the importance of that margin of advantage. Naturally both the West Europeans and the American military now became concerned lest that margin be eroded. 'The dynamic equilibrium now existing between the United States strategic forces and those of the Soviet Union increases significantly the importance of US general purpose forces (including theater nuclear forces)', Admiral Moorer, Chairman of the US Joint Chiefs of Staff, stated on 5 March 1974.[10] A related point was made by the British Ministry of Defence in its *Statement on the Defence Estimates 1975*: 'The strategic nuclear forces of the West are the ultimate deterrent against strategic nuclear attack. But in a period of strategic parity they do not necessarily constitute a credible deterrent against lower levels of aggression'.[11]

3.2   THE IMPACT OF THE SCHLESINGER DOCTRINE

These concerns coincided with a larger anxiety among the US military: that the negation of American nuclear superiority would deprive the USA of leverage *vis-à-vis* the USSR, which the Americans undoubtedly had during the Cuban missile crisis of 1962. It was to rectify the likely consequences of this reduction in American power as well as to reassure the West Europeans that Secretary of

Defense James Schlesinger introduced into US strategic doctrine the notion of 'limited nuclear options'. This carried with it greater emphasis on 'counterforce' (striking the enemy's forces) as against 'countervalue' (striking population centres). It was explicitly designed to make more credible the US nuclear deterrent during the era of parity between the US and the USSR by raising the threat against the Russians in order to induce greater restraint on their part in seeking to displace US power and influence across the globe. Schlesinger said:

> It has the benefit, from my standpoint, at least, of forcing upon the Soviet Union recognition of the choice that I think we will insist that they make, to wit, whether they will come to an accommodation with the United States, or whether the process of detente will come to be viewed by the Soviets as simply a means to shift the balance of power in their favor.[12]

The Secretary of Defense was undoubtedly correct in seeing Soviet policy predicated on the assumption that *détente* would facilitate the world revolutionary process, thereby shifting the correlation of forces to US disadvantage; though the implication that this could in some way be forestalled by a more effective US nuclear posture was fundamentally mistaken. Without the prospect of increases in Soviet influence resulting from Marxist-Leninist revolutions in the Third World it is doubtful Brezhnev would have been able to sell *détente* as a policy to the hardliners within the Party and thereby isolate the disgruntled military. It is not hard to find evidence for the gains the Russians hoped to reap from *détente* in the Third World. On Moscow radio at the end of December 1973 member of the *Za Rubezhom* editorial board Yevgeny Korshunov said:

> The relaxation of international tension is in the interests of all the world's peoples, including the interests of the third world countries. Even today we can see how blocs knocked together by the imperialists for fighting the national liberation movements—blocs such as SEATO, CENTO, ASPAC— are falling apart, becoming obsolete and losing their facilities . . . the Soviet Union has never put its efforts for detente in opposition to aid to national liberation movements or support for developing countries. On the contrary, it has endeavored to use the new opportunities opened up by detente to expand mutually advantageous cooperation with the countries of Asia, Africa . . . [13]

And as Boris Ponomarev, then candidate member of the Politburo and *de facto* head of the Central Committee International Department pointed out: 'Under conditions of *détente* the class struggle . . . has begun to develop more freely and broadly.'[14]

Alerted to the fact that some were interpreting the Schlesinger doctrine as an attempt to acquire a 'first-strike' capability given the 'greater operational counter-force capabilities' in the hands of the United States,[15] Schlesinger argued that the priority was to ensure that the Soviet Union did not acquire an advantage of its own in this sphere; this 'could lead to a weakening of resolve and a dissolution of our alliances overseas'.[16] The Secretary of Defense also argued that 'there has been a declining credibility, as the Europeans see it, in the relationship of U.S. strategic forces to European security.'[17] In his report to the Senate Foreign Relations Committee outlining the case for selective nuclear targeting Schlesinger therefore emphasised its role in buttressing the Atlantic alliance.[18] When asked what type of Soviet targets the allies wished to see targeted, Schlesinger replied: 'IRBM . . . sites, to take one example. Conceivably—underscoring the conceivably—we might be talking about certain hardened command and control facilities or weapons storage sites, these kind of targets'.[19] In response it certainly made sense for the Russians to develop a mobile and therefore less vulnerable IRBM system with which to target Western Europe. By the time these changes in US military doctrine were announced to Congress the President had already approved them, as NSDM-242, in January 1974.

The Soviet reaction was a mixture of bewilderment and acute discomfort. Schlesinger himself acknowledged:

> their [the Russian] reaction to our position has been something of this sort—concern and surprise. The reason for surprise, as expressed to some of our own people [deleted] is that they always assumed that we would target this way, therefore, why do we now say so, what is the purpose of all this fanfare?[20]

Comments by Chairman of the Joint Chiefs of Staff General Jones can only have added to Soviet mystification and consequent suspicion. He told the Senate Armed Services Committee: 'we have always targeted military targets. There has been a lot of discussion—it is interesting when I was out in the field, in Washington you would hear a lot of rhetoric about different strategies. We followed orders, but basically, the strategy stayed the same in implementation of targeting'.[21] The Russians could be forgiven for interpreting all this as a signal that the United States intended to enhance its theatre nuclear counter-force capability against Soviet missile sites.

The true purpose of all this fanfare was in large part to reassure US allies in Europe. The need for reassurances arose from growing friction between the United States and its partners in Europe, friction the Russians were certain to exploit. There were a number of problems, not least the backwash from the Vietnam war and the accompanying sense of impotence on the part of the Americans. The position was ably summarised by Principal Assistant Secretary of Defense for International Affairs Amos Jordan:

> the thing that is troubling our European allies in particular . . . is not our military capability but what they perceive to be shaky coherence and national unity which may make it impossible to use those military capabilities. It is the credibility of our commitment, not the existence of our commitments, or the strength of our forces that is in doubt in their minds.[22]

3.3 DISARRAY WITHIN NATO

This judgment followed the Watergate scandal of 1973–74, which resulted in Nixon's enforced resignation. Further problems had by then accumulated to heighten doubts in Europe about the steadfastness of the US-European relationship. One problem arose from the chronic balance of payments deficit which resulted from the costly war in Vietnam, which had itself led to a renewal of isolationist sentiment within the United States. A report of a House Armed Services Committee subcommittee in August 1972 pointed out that: 'The desire for fundamental changes in the U.S. position in the world, growing out of national anxieties not generated by our NATO involvement, has brought about considerable questioning and debate over the U.S. military presence on the European continent and the U.S. contribution to NATO'.[23] Pressure to withdraw American troops from Europe then led to renewed attempts by the Nixon administration to silence criticism through engaging other NATO powers 'in sharing the financial burden of maintaining U.S. forces in Europe' and by negotiations with the Warsaw Pact on mutual reductions (see below, pp. 52–6).[24]

The attempt to spread the US financial burden eventually succeeded, but at a political cost. Tension had also arisen from separate European overtures to the East, particularly on the part of West Germany. On 23 April 1973 Kissinger delivered a speech declaring this would be 'The Year of Europe'. But his aim was to draw recalcitrant Europeans into line with US plans and policies: 'We sought to discourage the Europeans from unilateral initiatives to Moscow by demonstrating that in any competition for better relations with Moscow, America had the stronger hand'.[25] The European counterpart to Kissinger's grievance was the fear of a growing US-Soviet condominium, alternating with an equally strong fear lest the USA jeopardise peace in Europe in pursuit of policies elsewhere in the world which were not harmonised with European interests. Both concerns were magnified by American behaviour in 1973.

On 22 June 1973, anniversary of the German invasion of Russia, the USA and the USSR signed an agreement on the prevention of nuclear war.[26] Although Britain, France and West Germany had all been forewarned of the agreement and a senior British official had even helped draft it, the document nevertheless caused unpleasant repercussions within NATO, for the alliance depended upon the threat of nuclear reprisal as a deterrent against an attack by Soviet conventional forces.[27] A Senate Foreign Relations Committee subcommittee toured NATO in September 1973, interviewing senior officials in the various capitals. It reported in October on 'the growing belief among Europeans that the United States is prepared to deal over their heads on security matters with the Soviet Union. Officials in every country we visited cited the sudden announcement of the Nixon-Brezhnev decision on the prevention of nuclear war as evidence to support their fears'. The report continued: 'one German official said to us that anything that appears to "decouple" the U.S. strategic deterrent from tactical deterrence (either nuclear or conventional) undermines the overall concept of NATO security. Another high official recently put the same idea by stating that the key strategic issue in the alliance has been and remains the control and employment of nuclear weapons'.[28]

The subcommittee delivered its report in October—the month in which war in the Middle East, in the words of Supreme Allied Commander Europe General Goodpaster, 'brought to the fore . . . the threat to Allied solidarity'.[29] Not only were the West Europeans opposed to Israel's continued occupation of Arab territory since the June 1967 war, they were also heavily dependent on the Arabs for their oil supplies. When the USA backed Israel in the war and the Russians backed the Egyptians, the West Europeans refused refuelling of US aircraft and flights across their territory. The West Germans also complained at the United States taking military stocks out of Central Europe. The Arab oil embargo imposed on 20 October exacerbated differences, and the crowning point came on 24–25 October when Washington raised the readiness of US nuclear forces (including forward-based systems) without previously consulting the allies in Europe: the excuse that the alert had to be called early in the morning scarcely held water.[30]

The oil embargo, and the dramatic rise in oil prices which followed, exacerbated the international economic situation and led directly to the recession of 1974–75. The recession created social tensions within the countries of Western Europe which ultimately threatened to jeopardise the political cohesion of the North Atlantic alliance. The unusual combination of rising inflation and a fall in production caused social democratic governments to cut defence expenditure in an effort to maintain the fabric of the welfare state. The simultaneous drift to the Left on the continent caused additional concern in Washington. Always uneasy about leftist and pro-Soviet tendencies in social democracy, Nixon and Kissinger were alarmed by the socialist wave on their side of Europe. In 1972 the French Communist Party and the newly revived Socialist Party formed a coalition in opposition: a sign that the Left was becoming more agile and thereby more effective electorally. Then in September 1973, after the overthrow of the *Unidad Popular* Government in Chile by forces of the Right, the recently elected General Secretary of the Italian Communist Party, Enrico Berlinguer, announced a new slogan for reaching power through a broader consensus: this was the *compromesso storico* (the historic compromise), which eased the party's path towards 33.8 per cent of the vote in the national elections of June 1976 in the face of ominous American threats of sanctions should the party attain power, even partially. If Italy were a potential problem, the 'revolution of the roses' of the 25 April 1974 in Portugal really threw NATO into disarray when that summer the Left took power and drew Communists into the administration. 'The problem in Portugal . . . is very serious, because it could be taken as a test case for possible evolutions in other countries, and not only if the Communists take over', Kissinger argued. 'It could also be the case if the Communists become the sinews of non-Communist government, and perhaps especially so.'[31] 'The worst scenario', he foresaw, 'is one which will show a gradual disintegration of the domestic stability of all of our friendly countries, accompanied by a growing

sense of impotence and less self-confidence by the United States,
which will sooner or later trigger a series of more aggressive actions
by hostile powers and increasing confrontations with the less
developed world'.[32]

All of this represented an unexpected windfall for the Russians.
At the very least they sought to exploit frictions between the capitalist Powers. At most they welcomed Communist revolutions in the
capitalist camp provided, of course, they in no way jeopardised
Soviet security by demanding direct military aid from Moscow and
thereby precipitating a crisis with the United States. The dislocation
of the Atlantic alliance, whether due to separate overtures to the
East or because of the October war, the Greco-Turkish conflict over
Cyprus in 1974 or the revolution in Portugal fed hopes that under
détente the global correlation of forces at the socio-political level
would continue to shift to the disadvantage of the West. 'The developing cooperation between the states of East and West and the
prospect of there being established an entirely new basis for interstate
relations . . . cannot fail to aggravate the contradictions within
NATO', one Soviet commentator observed.[33] 'The energy crisis
is . . . leaving its mark on mutual relations between . . . West
Europe and the United States', first deputy chief editor of *Izvestiya*
Nikolai Polyanov pointed out on Moscow radio.[34] And when the
Netherlands, Britain, Belgium and Denmark announced their intention of reducing military expenditure in the spring of 1975, Polyanov
commented *in extenso* on the problems facing NATO: 'the alliance
is no longer what it was twenty or even five years ago. The readiness
of the West Europeans to support the risky undertakings of the
senior partner in this or that corner of the globe is rapidly declining'.
And speaking of NATO Secretary-General Luns' call for greater
rearmament, Polyanov noted that 'as time goes on it becomes ever
more difficult to convince partners of the necessity to make sacrifices
at the NATO altar'; 'as time goes on it is becoming increasingly
impossible to keep the Atlantic team in harness and under control'.[35]
The louder the protestations from NATO, the greater the sense of
progress in Moscow: 'everybody knows that the Soviet Union has
no need at all to make any effort to "demoralise the West" since it
is splendidly accomplishing this on its own. The catastrophic economic crisis speaks for itself'.[36]

One major contributory cause of alliance instability was renewed
uncertainty in Western Europe as to the constancy of the US commitment to its defence in the event of a Russian attack. In the crucial

Central European sector of the European theatre America's allies faced a predominance of Soviet firepower at the conventional level. Although the Russians were working hard to build up a tactical nuclear weapons capability to match and thereby nullify NATO's advantage at the theatre nuclear level, what emerges from NATO communiqués during the greater part of the 1970s is an overwhelming preoccupation with the need to bolster the alliance's conventional capability *vis-à-vis* the Warsaw Pact. An assessment of the problem in the mid–1970s was given by Chairman of the US Joint Chiefs of Staff General Brown in 1975:

> Improvements in US and NATO forces during the past several years have increased capabilities considerably, with particular emphasis on conventional warfare. The thrust is to avoid being forced into nuclear war as the only alternative to unacceptable losses in a conventional battle. Strengthening conventional capability will raise the nuclear threshold, but this requires a tailored force with capabilities adequate to both initial and sustained combat . . . In all 3 NATO regions, national ground forces amount to 1.78 million, while Warsaw pact forces amount to 1.62 million in the East European Pact countries and the 3 Western USSR military districts abutting NATO territory. Pact forces, however, have increased by over 120,000 since late 1971, while NATO forces have remained relatively static. Pact increases appear to be related to upgrading of weapons systems . . . NATO tanks, while outnumbered by a factor of 2½ to 1 or 3 to 1, are, in general, superior to those of the Warsaw pact, particularly in first-shot kill probability. Pact artillery, however, outnumbers that of NATO by a factor of 2 to 1 and the larger caliber weapons have greater range. With respect to available tactical aircraft, at the beginning of hostilities, Pact outnumbers NATO by a factor of about 2 to 1; but in general, NATO aircraft have greater range and payload capability, with crews that have better night and all-weather training. NATO's ground air defence provides an effective high- and medium-altitude air defense capability. In addition to conventional strength, NATO maintains an ability to carry out tactical nuclear operations in conjunction with the strategy of flexible response.

The focus of NATO concern was the Central European theatre. The Russians held no particular advantage in Scandinavia and the Baltic, and in the southern region NATO outnumbered Pact ground forces 'almost 2 to 1' though the Greco-Turkish conflict over Cyprus (1974) raised serious questions about NATO's cohesion in the region. But in Central Europe the Russians held a significant advantage in tanks and artillery. 'In the Central Region, Warsaw Pact M-Day ground forces significantly outnumber NATO-assigned and earmarked forces', Brown reported, adding the qualification that, 'Counting all the forces of the NATO Central Region nations, together with the in-place forces of Canada, the United Kingdom, and the United States, Pact superiority is reduced'.[37]

Undoubtedly this 'worst-case' analysis overstated Soviet advantages and correspondingly understated Western advantages. But no less important from the NATO viewpoint was the perception of a renewed emphasis on the strategic offensive in Soviet military doctrine. In his memoirs former British Prime Minister James Callaghan remarks: 'a belief was growing in Western circles that the Soviet Union was revising its military doctrine about the most effective means of launching an attack on Western Europe. It would thrust its conventional forces forward rapidly in the early stages of a war to interpenetrate with Allied forces, so that the Allies, whose conventional forces are fewer, could not use their nuclear weapons without endangering their own armies'.[38]

3.4   NEGOTIATIONS ON ARMS REDUCTIONS IN CENTRAL EUROPE

In this uncertain situation pressures from Congress for the withdrawal of US forces from Europe heightened allied anxieties. Negotiations with the Warsaw Pact on force reductions were seen as a means of alleviating these fears—at the very least a stop-gap which would delay a unilateral American withdrawal;[39] and at most as a means of reducing Soviet conventional forces without simultaneously reducing NATO'S overwhelming advantage in tactical nuclear weapons. Initially the Russians were not receptive. They were too insecure. They had led the invasion of Czechoslovakia in August 1968 in order to prevent Prague's drift towards social democracy and neutralism or, worse still, integration into the Western camp. At that time West Germany still sought to revise the postwar frontiers of Europe in its favour. Not until Bonn had committed itself to maintain the territorial status quo in Central and Eastern Europe would the Russians contemplate any negotiations on arms limitation or reduction. As a result of the formation of a Social Democrat-Free Democrat coalition in West Germany in September 1969 the new government under Chancellor Brandt abandoned the irredentist claims of all preceding administrations. Having acceded to the Treaty on the Non-Proliferation of Nuclear Weapons—thereby relieving Eastern Europe of a long-standing nightmare—on 12 August 1970 the Bonn Government signed a treaty in Moscow relinquishing all territorial claims and recognising the inviolability of existing frontiers (the Russians would have preferred a tighter restriction precluding even peaceful change),[40] an agreement soon followed by similar arrangements with Poland (7 December 1970),[41] East Germany (11 December 1972),[42] and Czechoslovakia (11 December 1973).[43] It was not until the 24th Party Congress on 30 March 1971 that Brezhnev finally announced the USSR's interest in 'the reduction of armed forces and armaments in regions where military confrontation is particularly dangerous, above all in Central Europe'.[44]

In Moscow this was a controversial issue, however, as were all Brezhnev's early moves in the direction of arms control, not least the SALT process. Whereas at future congresses—the 25th in 1976 and the 26th in 1981—his report on domestic and foreign policies was accepted with a perfunctory few words,[45] the resolution on foreign policy at the 24th Party congress took up more than six pages of text, mostly emphasising solidarity with the national liberation movement in the Third World and Western hostility towards the USSR. No mention was made of disarmament.[46] Indeed, on 11 June Brezhnev felt obliged to deliver a vigorous defence of this policy. Disarmament was, he asserted, 'an inalienable constituent part' of Soviet foreign policy. He justified this position by claiming that the global correlation of forces had altered to Soviet advantage. Russia was not negotiating from weakness. The military should therefore not object:

As little as several years ago the imperialists, and above all the Americans, seriously banked on strengthening their positions in the world arena and simultaneously weakening the economy of the USSR and other countries of socialism, on confounding our plans for peaceful construction, with the aid of the arms race. Now the failure of such calculations on the part of our adversaries has become completely obvious. Now everyone can see that socialism is sufficiently powerful to secure both guaranteed defence and the development of the economy, although, of course, without large defence expenditure we would be able to drive our economy forward even faster . . .

He went on to argue that the 'imperialists' were suffering more and more from the 'negative economic and political consequences of an unrestrained arms race'. Not only was there an anti-war movement in the West, but 'even among part of the ruling circles of Western states the arms race is ceasing to be viewed as a mixed blessing'.[47]

What Brezhnev said was certainly true and not merely with respect to nuclear weapons. These factors in turn gave the Russians additional leverage in arms limitation talks. The NATO Powers sought to open talks limiting armaments in Central Europe in order to forestall a unilateral withdrawal of American conventional forces.[48] Moscow made agreement to the talks conditional upon a European Security Conference which would formally recognise the division of Germany and the postwar frontiers in Eastern Europe.[49] The NATO Powers duly tried to turn the position to their advantage by making recognition of the *pax sovietica* in Central and Eastern Europe conditional upon Soviet acceptance of undertakings to liberalise rigid state control over access to information from the West; a condition which fell under the rubric of 'basket three'. [50] Ambassador Mendelevich was a member of the Soviet delegation to the conference which opened in Helsinki on 3 July 1973. He recalls that 'In principle there could be no objection to this [the inclusion of provisions on human rights and the free flow of information], but to a certain extent what caught the eye was the intention of Western countries . . . to make questions of humanitarian co-operation all but the centre of gravity of the work of the conference.' [51] The Russians thus knew perfectly well what was going on and ultimately decided to accept the obligations but to honour them in the breach.

Given that the West appeared to need talks on limiting conventional arms in Europe more than did the Russians, the Soviet Government clearly felt it had the leverage to force reductions in US forward-based aircraft at this new forum, which opened in Vienna on 31 October 1973. The Soviet position was outlined by head of the delegation Oleg Khlestov in an interview with Novosti:

> It would be dangerous to limit the reduction to land forces only. The preservation, in its present-day form, of the colossal nuclear arsenal in Europe represents a constant and real threat to the peoples of this continent. Contemporary armed forces—land forces, air force and corresponding armaments, including units and

sub-units equipped with nuclear weapons—are inter-related. They are a single military complex. Consequently the reduction of land forces only, made on the basis of different starting-point levels and not covering nuclear weapons, would immediately violate the necessary equivalence of the reduction . . . The reduction of land forces alone could lead to a build-up of other fighting services— air force and units equipped with nuclear weapons.[52]

The Russians thus protested that 'The exclusion of nuclear weapons from the future agreement would not only lead to an increase in [their] specific gravity within the overall complex of military forces and armaments but would also facilitate their future expansion'.[53]

Blocked in Vienna, the Russians continued to press the issue of US FBS at the strategic arms limitations talks. Concern to limit US forward-based aircraft was, as has been noted, related not merely to US capabilities but also to the recent evolution of NATO military doctrine. NATO's shift towards 'flexible response' was paralleled by a shift in Soviet military doctrine. Schlesinger's enunciation of 'limited nuclear options' confirmed in Soviet minds the real prospect of limited nuclear war in Europe, which by 1968 was treated as a practical possibility. And this in turn altered weapons requirements.[54] The process was aptly outlined by senior US analyst Lt. Col. John Hines: 'An absolute requirement . . . was the continued development of nuclear forces to match at least, if not exceed, NATO's nuclear capability at the global, theater, and tactical levels. The development of such a capability would enable the Soviets to restrain further NATO's incentives for initial use and perhaps even in response to Soviet selective use, as well as better enable them to prevail in the event of escalation to a theater-wide or even global nuclear conflict'.[55] For the first time since the late 1950s the Russians had to examine their theatre nuclear capability with a view to the possibility of a war confined to Europe. And whereas the Americans had consistently been modernising their theatre nuclear capability, the Russians had not. If the Americans were willing to negotiate away that capability to attain a SALT II treaty or an agreement limiting conventional arms, then the problem might well be manageable. If, however, they refused, then the Russians would see the need to modernise their theatre nuclear capability; and this is precisely what happened.

Whether the Soviet political leadership fully accepted such reasoning is not known. What was certain to Brezhnev was that the military were unhappy at the price of SALT and that trade-offs to the military would be required if he was to secure another SALT agreement with their co-operation. Throughout this period Defence Minister Grechko continued to stress the need for 'intense vigilance' as 'an important factor . . . in improving the international atmosphere'.[56] He warned publicly that the Soviet Union had to guard against 'the most unexpected reversals, dangerous provocations and adventures on the part of the enemies of socialism and peace'.[57] Similarly head of the political administration of the armed forces General Yepishev advised against 'conscious or unconscious under-estimation of the military danger from imperialism'.[58] The military newspaper *Krasnaya Zvezda* warned:

> Despite the relaxation of tension achieved, the international situation remains complex. And it would be extremely dangerous if the opinion were to be reinforced among the public that everything is now fully in order, that the threat of war has become illusory and that the task of ensuring peace is retreating, as it were, to the middle ground and even to the background.[59]

An article in *Pravda* at the beginning of August 1974 written by Lt. General Zhilin, the Soviet military historian, also emphasised that 'it would be incorrect and even dangerous to think that the cause of peace is now "automatically" guaranteed by the very fact that the correlation of forces in the world arena has changed in favour of socialism.'[60] These public statements are not the only evidence. Earlier in 1974 Kissinger had told head of the US SALT delegation Ambassador Johnson that 'He did not want me to press Semenov too hard now, thinking that it might take time before Brezhnev could build up enough strength to override his generals and conclude a SALT treaty'.[61] This was scarcely a favourable atmosphere within which Brezhnev could make significant concessions on FBS in order to reach another strategic arms limitation agreement with the USA.

3.5   THE VLADIVOSTOK SUMMIT

During meetings with Kissinger from 25 to 27 March 1974 Brezhnev rejected his suggestion that SALT I was unequal from the US position. In retaliation Brezhnev 'produced a map showing areas of the Soviet Union that could be reached from our forward-based systems in Europe or in the Mediterranean. It was', Kissinger recalls, 'reasonably accurate if one assumed one-way missions for our fighter bombers, which Soviet planners—applying their own version of the "worst case" scenario—were bound to do.'[62] At the third US-Soviet summit in Moscow in late June nothing had changed. Grechko took the opportunity to emphasise Soviet concern at US forward-based systems. [63] There was evidently a fierce debate in Moscow as to the way to respond to the American position. An echo of the debate can be heard in a *Novoe Vremya* commentary on the Schlesinger doctrine a year later. 'Unwittingly the impression is created that one more calculation lies behind all the arguments of the USA's Defence Minister; to provoke the other side into some steps in the military field and then use them to justify new military programmes.'[64]

Nixon's replacement by Vice-President Ford on 9 August 1974 changed nothing in the US negotiating position. At Geneva the Soviet position was as insistent on FBS as before:

> Semenov . . . kept insisting that we include FBS in the nego-
> tiations, implying that they were not going to agree to equal aggre-
> gates in central systems unless we withdrew our Sixth and Seventh
> Fleet aircraft carriers from the Mediterranean and Pacific. He also
> insisted that 'allowance be made' for British and French nuclear
> missile submarines as well as China's nuclear capabilities.[65]

Brezhnev was in a difficult position. As 'the great architect of *détente*', he desperately wanted an understanding at SALT II with the United States, but his own military were still insistent upon the impossible precondition of a concession on FBS. And when the fourth summit took place, this time with Ford, at Okeanskaya near Vladivostok, Brezhnev warned the Americans 'that some members of his Politburo didn't believe detente was a good idea. If he made too many concessions in his attempt to reach an accord, he would lose their support and be in trouble at home'.[66]

But the need for an agreement triumphed. At Okeanskaya on 23–24 November 1974 the two sides agreed to an equal aggregate level of launchers, including heavy bombers, and an equal sub-ceiling on MIRVed missiles. To secure this understanding, seen as crucial to *détente*, Brezhnev had been forced to drop the issue of forward-based systems. But to make this crucial concession in the face of strong Soviet military opposition, he also had to make crucial concessions, including the decision to test the SS-20 missile.

4 The SS-20 Decisions: from Testing to Deployment, 1974–77

4.1 THE DECISION ON TESTING

The withdrawal of Soviet demands on forward-based systems at Vladivostok seemed to indicate that the Pentagon and NATO Europe had won the argument: the principle of extended deterrence had been preserved. But this illusion did not last long. Brezhnev could not afford to drop forward-based systems—a subject of great concern to the Soviet military—without also seeking compensation elsewhere. He had little choice now but to proceed with weapons programmes hitherto delayed, including the testing of the SS-20.

In the Soviet Union decisions on new weapons systems are proposed by the General Staff and presented to the Defence Council which is chaired by the General Secretary of the Party, in this case Brezhnev. Once accepted at this level the decisions are then placed on the agenda of the full Politburo for formal approval. The process by which the decision was taken to test the SS-20 is thus not difficult to retrace, neither is the approximate timing of the decision, nor the thinking which underlay the decision.

To look for a single cause, whether it be the natural flow of the military procurement process or some other factor, would be unwise. As the Russians themselves have said: 'SS-20 missiles were developed and deployed for a number of reasons'.[1] By the end of November 1974, when the decision on testing was apparently reached, a range of factors had accumulated to justify the case for a new medium-range ballistic missile. At SALT I the Russians had been obliged to leave US forward-based systems out of the count in order to obtain an agreement limiting intercontinental missiles. It had proved impossible for them to reduce or gain compensation for these systems during the SALT II negotiations; they also failed to put them on the agenda at the conference on conventional arms limitation in Vienna.

The importance of these, and of the overall balance at the theatre level had apparently increased now that the balance at the intercontinental level had been stabilised. The impressive display of US airpower in Vietnam by the aircraft which constituted the longer-range FBS in Europe highlighted their importance. The experience in Vietnam also made the Russians only too conscious of the structural flaws in their air defences, particularly when faced with low-flying targets. And the Americans were not the only threat on the horizon. There were new additions to the NATO inventory with the simultaneous modernisation and extension of British and French nuclear capabilities. In the Far East the Chinese were also emerging as a nuclear-capable adversary. Not only had capabilities grown but Western military doctrine had also shifted towards provision for limited nuclear war, a prospect pointed to by Schlesinger's advocacy of 'limited nuclear options' in planning for war with the Soviet Union. Soviet military doctrine duly followed suit and this in turn had repercussions on Soviet weapons acquisition. Attention to Soviet theatre nuclear capabilities underlined the fact that substitutes were needed for the USSR's ageing theatre nuclear bombers, and Soviet theatre nuclear missiles were not only extremely vulnerable to first strike from US forward-based aircraft, they were also in dire need of modernisation. Modernisation was made possible by new technological developments (see below). And, last but not least, there was a further and vital political factor related to these considerations. New systems were needed as a bargaining chip to force US FBS onto the negotiating agenda at SALT III. There is evidence for this. A book published in 1984 by the Foreign Ministry's publishing house points out:

> The need to modernise medium-range weapons systems which the Soviet Union faced also arose from certain political reasons. The fact is that the Soviet side more than once took the initiative to include Western medium-range capability within the process of the negotiations on the limitation of nuclear armaments. If this had happened, if this problem had been resolved by means of an appropriate agreement, then it is perfectly reasonable to suggest that the USSR would not have had any motive to modernise its weapons counterbalancing analogous systems in the West.[2]

In this respect the timing of the decision on testing the SS-20 is significant. With the SALT I interim agreement due to expire in October 1977 and in the expectation of the conclusion of SALT II by that time, the Russians would need successful test results, if not deployment, by the time SALT III opened soon thereafter if the SS-20 was to serve as a bargaining counter. It is said that Foreign Minister Andrei Gromyko argued for the SS-20. If indeed he did, it would have been for these very reasons; a mistake similar to that made by Kissinger who once saw MIRVs as bargaining chips for SALT I and Cruise missiles as bargaining chips for SALT II. But when the time came to put them on the negotiating table, the Pentagon did not want them traded in. In all this the West Europeans were a peripheral consideration. The SALT process had the unintended effect in Moscow of making Soviet foreign policy almost exclusively Americocentric. A long-serving Americanist—indeed since taking charge of the Foreign Commissariat's American Department in 1939—Gromyko naturally tended to see the world in bipolar terms and with his elevation to the Politburo in 1973 this outlook tended to reinforce Brezhnev's own new enthusiasm for a Soviet-American entente.

Diplomats might see a new medium-range missile as a bargaining chip but the military saw it as a value in its own right. 'Within a few years, the Soviet Union would have been facing NATO naked had it not modernized its medium-range nuclear weapons', argued Major-General Viktor Starodubov with typical hyperbole. 'Our earlier generations of missiles—the SS-4's and SS-5's—were produced twenty years ago. They are completely obsolete with regard to both design and material . . . The old missiles were multipurpose, all-target weapons, so to speak. For current demands they are too heavy and their warheads unnecessarily powerful'.[3] Raymond Garthoff notes that these were liquid-fuelled missiles 'with very slow reaction times (they required several hours to prepare for firing)'. In addition 'two-thirds of the launchers were on unprotected open pads, deployed in close groups of four, and even the 135 underground silos were grouped in close groups of three. A modern missile or air attack could thus in many cases deliver strikes with sufficient accuracy and payload to destroy three or four SS-4 or SS-5 launchers with one shot'.[4]

The problem of relative obsolescence was evident also in respect of theatre-range Tu–16 ('Badger') and Tu–22 ('Blinder') bombers, introduced in 1955 and 1963 respectively.[5] It is estimated that between 1973 and 1977 the Russians reduced their theatre bomber force by 225 units net.[6] Although they introduced a new bomber, the Tu–22M ('Backfire') in 1974, 'with a greater combat range and payload capability' than its predecessors, as well as 'better capability to penetrate modern air defenses,'[7] during these early years only relatively small numbers were deployed (25 in 1975, 30 in 1976, 35 in 1977, and so on) and their primary role appeared to be that of targeting US sea-based systems, including aircraft carriers in the Second and Sixth Fleets. The new medium-range missile thus represented not only a shift towards the modernisation of the Soviet theatre missile force but also a shift away from aircraft towards greater dependence upon missiles.

One of the most striking features of the SS-20 was its mobility. Since the mid-1960s the Nadiradze design bureau had been trying to develop a mobile ICBM which might survive a counterforce attack from the United States. The Russians had also been experimenting with two mobile medium-range missiles, the SS-14 and SS-15. The final product of all this effort was an intercontinental ballistic missile, the SS-16 (Soviet designation RS-14),[8] which ran into serious technical problems during testing from 1972.[9] The SS-20 is generally thought to have been formed from the upper two stages of the aborted SS-16.[10] Information on this question is still uncertain but one informed source claims this was the idea of Colonel-General of Engineering Vitaly Shabanov,[11] then (1972–74) the general director of one of the first scientific-production associations (NPOs) and later Deputy Minister of Defence for armaments.[12] NPOs in the field of arms production first appeared in 1972, though formally established only in 1973; they were formed to incorporate research institutes, design bureaux and prototype production facilities in an attempt to overcome delays in weapons development resulting from the bureaucratic separation of research institutes from design bureaux.[13] Production of the missile began at Votkinsk in Udmurtiya, just west of the Ural mountain range.[14] Testing of the missile began early in 1975.[15]

Confirmation of the need to proceed could be found in NATO planning. Quite apart from the publicity given to NATO activities, the Russians also had at least one spy in the NATO secretariat reporting on progress towards a new generation of theatre nuclear forces.[16] 'A new course of building of its own armaments was implemented by the NATO bloc as far back as 1975', Colonel-General Nikolai Chervov, head of the Disarmament and Security Affairs Department of the Soviet General Staff, has since argued. 'At that time the Americans confirmed a program of development and manufacture of Pershing II missiles . . . precisely at this time

the United States once again avoided talks on forward-based armaments not wishing possible agreements to be extended to their
medium-range systems.'[17]

Chervov's assertion is not inaccurate. But the picture was more
complex than he implies. There were contradictory forces in play in
US decisions, and Soviet weapons acquisition played a role in the
outcome of those decisions. First, there were advances in nuclear
weapons technology which found enthusiastic support within the US
defence establishment and also within NATO Europe. Second, there
was pressure from Congress on the US administration to reduce its
arsenal in Europe; a pressure which was seen by the Europeans as
further evidence of a waning US commitment to America's allies
during the era of *détente*. But instead of focusing on the anxieties
within NATO Europe which gave the crucial impulse to the campaign
for the modernisation of NATO's theatre nuclear weaponry, the
Soviet military—intent on the elimination of NATO nuclear superiority at the theatre level—focused instead on the campaign for
Western rearmament as evidence of growing dangers from the
Western alliance and they used the existence of this campaign to
justify continued efforts to modernise the Soviet theatre arsenal.

4.2 NATO REARMAMENT

The campaign to refurbish NATO's theatre nuclear arsenal took
some time to get under way. In 1971, shortly before his retirement,
NATO Secretary General Manlio Brosio circulated a personal
memorandum on 'unresolved problems' in nuclear defence, drawing
attention to the prospects offered by the growth of new technologies
in this area. Nothing concrete resulted from these reflections. The
debate did not really open until an article appeared in *The Times* on
'Miniature Nuclear Arms Developed by Pentagon for Battlefield
Use' (7 May 1973). Fears arose that the USA was moving to lower
the nuclear threshold by introducing 'mini-nukes'. This inevitably
alarmed the West Germans, whose country was the future battlefield
in any 'limited' war confined to Europe. Defence Minister Georg
Leber raised the matter at NATO's Nuclear Planning Group (NPG)
later that month. As a result, at a further meeting of the NPG in
November 1973 Allied Defence Ministers set up a study on the
impact of the new technology upon alliance nuclear policy, under
US direction: one group entitled the Military Implications Team

(MIT) under British chairmanship; the other, entitled the Political Implications Team (PIT), under West German direction.[18] As part of this process in 1974 the US Government began reporting regularly to the NPG on programmes concerning 'The Improvements of the Effectiveness of NATO's Theatre Nuclear Forces (TNF)'.[19] All of this was regarded as only a sub-theme: the 'major emphasis' was still 'placed on maintaining and improving Allied conventional forces'.[20] This order of priorities reflected the evident disparity between NATO and the Warsaw Pact in conventional armaments to the advantage of the East, and the equally evident disparity in theatre nuclear forces to the advantage of the West. However, the emergence of a strong Soviet challenge to NATO superiority in theatre nuclear weapons began to feed growing concern in Western Europe that this advantage might be eroded without continued modernisation. Thus in 1975 NATO's Director of Nuclear Planning Richard Shearer wrote:

> Improvements to the theatre nuclear force which are now under review are improved survivability of nuclear forces and weapons under conventional and nuclear attack and the idea of committing more Poseidons to NATO, recognising the unique survival characteristics of the submerged weapons system. A variety of other measures are being considered or initiated to modernise NATO's theatre nuclear force to enhance and maintain the deterrent and war termination capabilities of the force under all foreseeable operational conditions.[21]

In his report to Congress that year on 'The Theater Nuclear Force Posture in Europe' Secretary of Defense James Schlesinger spoke of the 'modernization of the theater nuclear forces to enhance and maintain the deterrent and war termination capabilities' of the alliance. In listing improvements he mentioned inter alia the 'Commitment of more Poseidon RV's (re-entry vehicles) to NATO'. He also followed up his declaration on counterforce strategy with advocacy of 'theater nuclear forces for deep interdiction' (attacks well behind enemy battle lines): 'Such threats against East European countries may also diminish their willingness to cooperate with the Soviets, thus weakening WP [Warsaw Pact] solidarity'.[22]

Aside from lighter delivery aircraft and Poseidon—the latter accounted for in SALT—the main weapon deployed for deep interdiction was the Pershing missile stationed in West Germany in 1962: a mobile tactical weapons system carrying a nuclear warhead with a range of up to 400 nautical miles.[23] An improved model—the Pershing 1A—was developed from 1969 to 1971 with a similar range.[24] But the US Army was still dissatisfied. The weapon would produce too much collateral damage (it would destroy much more than the target). In line with NATO's strategy of 'flexible response' the Americans now sought a more accurate and less destructive warhead for precision attacks on hardened targets, including command and control centres. In February 1969 the original contractor, Martin Marietta's Orlando Division, received a further contract to investigate the possibilities, and by the early 1970s work was well underway.[25] In April 1974 Assistant Secretary of the Army Augustine, reporting on the initiation of the programme, told Congress that: 'The Pershing II will have a new nose section with guidance in it so you can internally radar guide the missile. That will reduce the CEP' (circular error probable) of the weapon.[26]

By the summer of 1975 plans for the missile were being integrated into Schlesinger's plans for selected military options. On 2 June 1975 the American journal *Aviation Week and Space Technology* reported:

> The development and European co-production of Pershing 2 would provide NATO with a non-nuclear warhead for the missile as well as the present stock of tactical nuclear warheads. The non-nuclear systems would have a precision seeker and dispense penetrators to destroy aircraft runways, covered aircraft shelters and other hard targets. The Pershing 2 would be used for deep interdiction in heavily defended areas.[27]

This was one line of development, which came under army auspices. The US Air Force was also continually looking for further means to give Tactical Air Command (TAC) the ability to conduct defence suppression against heavily defended targets without risking manned aircraft. On 11 November 1974 *Aviation Week and Space Technology* reported:

> Possibility of using miniature remotely piloted vehicles to harass hostile air defences and draw missile and gunfire before launching manned aircraft strikes is under study by USAF Tactical Air Command. TAC would use large numbers of vehicles, either under remote or internal control. Some would be simple traffic decoys, others would have radar jammers, and a few would be armed and capable of homing on defense radars or weapons.[28]

The development of Cruise missiles stemmed from the same technology, though initially conceived as a strategic rather than as a
theatre nuclear weapon. After the signature of the SALT I accords
the US Government proceeded with the development of Cruise as
a bargaining chip for future negotiations with the Russians. Initially
unenthusiastic about the weapon, the Pentagon before long became
so attached to it that estrangement became unthinkable. The
Russians were concerned about the missile for the very reasons that
the Pentagon was so enamoured with it. At this stage launched from
the sea or from aircraft, these small missiles were being developed
to hug the ground in flight, using a terrain contour guidance system
to reach their targets with great precision. They therefore presented
the Russians with a problem similar to that of low-flying aircraft;
worse still, on the radar screen their cross-section was so small as to
be barely distinguishable from that of a seagull. Its limitation, or
better still, its prohibition was thus a high priority for Soviet negotiators, even before the appearance of a Ground-Launched Cruise
Missile as a potential addition to the theatre nuclear arsenal in
Europe.[29] The advent of Cruise as a theatre nuclear weapon was
facilitated by the activities of a lobby called the European-American
Workshop: a group of strategic thinkers, Atlanticist and to varying
degrees anti-Soviet in outlook. Chaired by Albert Wohlstetter, who
had consistently over-estimated Soviet military capabilities (the
'bomber gap' and the 'missile gap'), the group encompassed Johan
Holst (Norway), Uwe Nerlich (West Germany), Laurence Martin
(Britain) and Richard Burt (USA). Their major concern was to
negate Soviet efforts to nullify NATO's superiority in theatre nuclear
weapons which would, they feared, render extended deterrence
completely unworkable. To them the Cruise missile provided the
answer: some looked to it as a conventional weapon, others as a
nuclear weapon. In the conferences held by the group, influential
defence figures were drawn in to be persuaded of the case for Cruise,
including director of planning at the West German Ministry of
Defence Walter Stutzle, a man close to Chancellor Helmut Schmidt,
and Major-General Peter Tandecki, later German military delegate
to NATO's High-Level Group (for the role of the HLG, see p. 89).[30]
The influence of this lobby is somewhat uncertain, but it soon found
common cause with the Pentagon in both preventing the sacrifice of
Cruise within the strategic arms limitation talks and securing the role
of Cruise as a theatre nuclear weapon.

The Vladivostok summit at the end of November 1974 had not

resolved the issue of Cruise missile limitation. After the summit the two sides attempted to settle the text of an *aide-mémoire* detailing the understanding. The Soviet draft included Cruise missiles launched from aircraft (ALCMs) with a range of more than 600 kilometres as part of the aggregate of delivery vehicles. The Americans in turn wanted Cruise missiles excluded and would allow only ballistic missiles to be specified. Finally on 10 December 1974—with the administration anxious about the presentation of the summit's results to the Senate—the US Government conceded on the omission of the word 'ballistic' but continued to argue that this was what was intended. To cover their position, the Americans put this in a note to Gromyko.[31] However, this clumsy compromise solved nothing. It merely gave the illusion of an understanding where there was none.

The Cruise missile had fast become a prize to the American military. 'The Pentagon fought hard against the proposed restrictions on US forces', recalls James Thomson, then working in the Office of the Secretary of Defense (OSD).[32] As it became clear that long-range Cruise missiles were the main block to agreement, pressure mounted within the Ford administration to concede to Soviet demands. When Kissinger met Soviet leaders in Moscow from 20 to 23 January 1976, he proposed limits on ALCMs—which the Russians had pressed for at Vladivostok—but simultaneously pressed for limits on the Tu–22M ('Backfire') which the Americans now insisted should be counted as a strategic bomber (though they consistently refused to count their own FB-111 in that category). The US position on this issue was influenced by a faulty Defense Intelligence Agency (DIA) assessment of the range of the Tu–22M, a mistake uncorrected until nearly a decade later.[33]

The Russians were, of course, interested in the inclusion of the ACLM, but unhappy at the inclusion of the Tu–22M, which they correctly stated was only a theatre nuclear system. They were also disturbed at the US refusal to accept a 600 kilometre limit on sea-launched and ground-launched Cruise missiles (SLCMs and GLCMs, known by their acronyms as 'Slickums' and 'Glickums').[34] Thus no agreement resulted, and the Pentagon was determined that there should be no further compromise at the expense of Cruise. The battle was still on, however. It is said that in February 1976 the Americans made the Russians an offer which they rejected—to limit the deployment of SLCMs and GLCMs to 600 kilometres, with no restrictions on flight-testing up to 2500 kilometres; the catch was that the Russians accept limitations on the Tu–22M.[35] This offer was also unpopular with the Department of Defense. It is at this stage that the Department adopted the same position as the European-American Workshop. Thomson, then at the OSD, recalls: 'In the course of attempts to justify within the US government the country's right to deploy long-range GLCM, Pentagon civilians posited a theatre nuclear mission for the system, which at that time was not even in development'.[36] Early in 1976 they discreetly reclassified the SLCM and evidently also the projected GLCM as theatre nuclear weapons. The GLCM was essentially the SLCM adjusted to land use. Its rationale was spelt out in public only later, in 1977:

> The primary need for the land-attack TOMAHAWK is in a theater role where its single warhead, high accuracy capability with resultant low collateral damage, penetrability and survivability make it ideal for use in limited nuclear attacks as a theater weapon.[37]

On 18 January 1977 the Department of Defense finally instructed the USAF to develop the GLCM. On 9 February Director of Programs at USAF headquarters, Major-General Abbott Greenleaf, told a subcommittee of the House Committee on Appropriations:

> The postulation for the ground-launched Cruise missile is that it could be an effective replacement for aircraft, for example, on quick reaction alert in NATO, thereby freeing up those aircraft committed for conventional or other tasks.[38]

The International Defense Review reported:

> It has been estimated in the Pentagon that because of their accuracy and seagull-sized radar signature, an unspecified number of conventionally-armed Cruise missiles would be able, with a high degree of certainty, to destroy in one hour 75% of all airfields, bridges, supply depots etc. needed by the Warsaw Pact to sustain a blitzkrieg offensive into Western Europe, thus releasing hundreds of NATO aircraft for other tasks.[39]

The Cruise missile had fast acquired symbolic status well before its deployment in the field: as the focus of Soviet anxieties, as the Pentagon's bright hope, and, to those governments in Western Europe ever-suspicious of Kissinger's urge to come to terms with the Russians, it was an unfortunate indication of American eagerness to trade in weapons systems of potential value to the security of NATO. Not all in Western Europe were equally preoccupied; not all were equally vulnerable. The Dutch, for example, were very much in favour of a deal at the talks in Vienna, offering to trade some tactical nuclear weapons in exchange for a reduction in Soviet tanks. Georg Leber, the West German Defence Minister, is said to have described such proposals as both 'wrong and unwise'.[40] What so alarmed and irritated the West Germans, tired of being lectured by Kissinger on the need to do more for their own defence, was the fact that the Americans also favoured trading in intermediate range nuclear systems in return for asymmetric cuts in Soviet conventional forces, and the fact that within NATO West Germany was alone in opposition to the idea. Only part of the story leaked into the press. The *Financial Times* reported from Brussels: 'The Dutch argument was given some support in an airport statement here by Dr. James Schlesinger, the U. S. Secretary of Defence, who said on his arrival for the NATO Defence Ministers' conference here that if forward-based systems were to come under discussion, the natural place would be Vienna'.[41] This was enough to strike fear and resentment into the heart of every defence-conscious West German. Schlesinger's willingness to discuss limits on forward-based systems found form in an offer made to the Russians at Vienna on 16 December 1975. It amounted to the proposal to withdraw 36 Pershing missile launchers, 54 F-4 Phantom nuclear-capable fighter-bombers, and 1000 nuclear warheads (unspecified), plus the previous offer—totally unrealistic in its original incarnation—to withdraw 29 000 American troops, in return for the withdrawal of 68 000 Soviet troops and 1700 Soviet tanks.[42] The Soviet Government responded in February 1976 by cutting out the demand for the withdrawal of its tank force and in its place proposing withdrawal of equal numbers of Pershing IA and Soviet Scud missiles, equal numbers of Sukhoi–17 (Western codename 'Fitter') and F-4 aircraft, equal numbers of air defence SAM-2 and Nike Hercules missiles, and equal numbers of nuclear warheads. The difference in the two offers reflected the different, indeed opposing, positions held by the two sides: the Russians mainly concerned to reduce Western nuclear power, the NATO powers primarily concerned to reduce Soviet conventional capability. Nothing came of the two offers. The West rejected the Soviet counter-proposal and later withdrew the initial proposal.[43]

NATO held an overwhelming preponderance in tactical nuclear weapons, so its new offer scarcely jeopardised the allied deterrent, particularly if the Russians reduced their tank army in East Germany. The West Germans were nonetheless extremely uneasy. Although keen to maintain *détente* with the East they were simultaneously zealous to maintain the existing balance of power in Europe; the West German Defence Ministry was unhappy about the Vienna talks and it watched Soviet moves to match Western theatre nuclear capabilities at each level of escalation with growing anxiety. In this respect the appearance of the Tu–22M ('Backfire') in 1974 and the testing of the SS-20 from 1975 fed pre-existing concerns.

The evolution of the US negotiating position of SALT II did not help. During the negotiations at SALT I the Russians had attempted to restrict the development of French and British forces by proposing a 'non-transfer' provision in the forthcoming treaty, which would have prevented the USA from transferring technology to its allies to further the development of their nuclear weapons systems. The Russians gave up this attempt when the US consistently refused to concede. However, they raised it again at SALT II. This time instead of merely blocking the proposal the USA offered in its place a 'non-circumvention' clause which was essentially designed to assure the Russians that 'the United States would not circumvent ceilings on central systems by augmenting forward systems' (FBS).[44] The West Germans and others in NATO were assured that this would not jeopardise existing defence co-operation. It nonetheless made them nervous.

What made matters worse was that, having conceded on FBS demands at Vladivostok, early in 1975 the Russians made proposals for 'not only a *non-circumvention* provision but also a *non-transfer* provision under which each party would undertake "not to transfer offensive arms to other states, and not to assist in their development, in particular, by transferring components, technical descriptions or blueprints for these arms" '.[45] This put the British (and the French) in a position similar to that of the West Germans. Both had at one time or another benefited from the transfer of US nuclear weapons technology and the British certainly hoped to continue to do so in the future. The Soviet 'non-transfer' proposals sensitised them all to any hint of weakness in the US negotiating position at SALT. It was the West Germans who felt the most strongly about US concessions to the Russians. Prohibited from possessing their own nuclear weapons by the West European Union Treaty of 1954 confirmed by signature of the Non-Proliferation Treaty in 1969, the West Germans were totally dependent on the US nuclear guarantee. They had the most to lose. US reassurances—deployment of the F-111; promulgation of the Schlesinger doctrine; allocation of more Poseidons to

NATO; further development of tactical air capability in Europe—
were never sufficient because the sense of insecurity and the feelings
of mistrust ran too deep. Once aroused, these insecurities were not
easily satiated. The failure of the United States to take them
sufficiently seriously only worsened the situation. It was not so much
that the Ford administration neglected the modernisation of theatre
nuclear weapons—such programmes were proceeding slowly but
surely—but that the United States appeared ready to bargain away
nuclear weapons already deployed (the Vienna proposals of
December 1975) or of potential value as a deterrent to a Soviet
attack (the Cruise missile). What made matters worse was the fact
that consultation between Washington and allied capitals in Europe
was seen as inadequate, and not merely during the early phase of
SALT II.[46]

It was because of growing insecurity that the West Germans joined
the Pentagon in opposition to restrictions on Cruise missiles. 'Some
German officials began to express anxiety about the imbalance of
"Eurostrategic forces", underscored by the existence of the SS-20,
and suggested that Cruise missiles might help redress this imbalance',
Thomson recalls. He adds that 'European concerns about American
SALT policy were magnified into suspicions when it was learned that
the United States had included a ban on long-range SLCMs and
GLCMs in its SALT proposal of February 1976'.[47]

4.3   THE LIMITS OF *DÉTENTE* IN EUROPE AND THE THIRD WORLD

The Pentagon and the West Germans would not now countenance
a compromise on Cruise; the Russians—under pressure from their
military—could not now accept anything less. Despite the decision
to proceed with the SS-20 the Soviet military leadership came to
blows with Brezhnev over his withdrawal of Soviet insistence on
compensation for FBS and relations further soured with the realis-
ation after Vladivostok that the Americans refused to accept the
inclusion of Cruise in the restrictions on warhead numbers. First
Deputy Minister of Foreign Affairs Georgii Kornienko later told a
senior American official that 'Brezhnev had to spill political blood
to get the Vladivostok accords',[48] and Arbatov used similar words
in conversation with Senator Bradley in August 1979.[49] The blood
was still all over the carpet when *Krasnaya Zvezda* hinted at dissent

within the Soviet armed forces. In an article published on 1 December 1974, very soon after the Vladivostok summit, Colonel Alexei Leont'ev raised the issue of FBS in Asia: 'the Vietnam war showed that foreign bases are a source of military danger', he asserted. Focusing on the threat to the oil-producing countries— these were the days of Pentagon planning to use force to safeguard Western oil supplies—Leont'ev added: 'It is enough to state that the war against the people of Vietnam, near whose shores, by the way, oil was also discovered, was waged from American bases in the Philippines, Thailand and Okinawa'.[50] This certainly suggested dissatisfaction within the military over Brezhnev's concession on the FBS at Vladivostok; and the results of the summit continued to disturb Brezhnev's relations with the military for some time to come.

The discontent showed itself in various ways, including a loud silence in *Krasnaya Zvezda* and in Marshal Grechko's speeches with respect to Brezhnev when the Party and the government were praised for the contribution to enhancing the country's defence. There was also an increasingly vociferous emphasis on the need for vigilance, in both speeches and press comment from the military. Not that Brezhnev was losing his grip. On the contrary, at the Central Committee plenum of 16 April 1975 he finally succeeded in removing rival Alexander Shelepin from the Politburo. But a resolution supporting the policy of *détente* was suitably buttressed with warnings about the forces of war, reaction and aggression.[51] Although it reported on the plenum in terms identical to those of *Pravda*, on 27 April a further editorial appeared on the subject of the plenum in *Krasnaya Zvezda*. The leader was more significant for what it omitted than for what it said. It stated that 'the troops of the Soviet Armed Forces express their warm approval of the foreign policy course of our party and of its Central Committee and Politburo', yet made no customary reference to General Secretary Brezhnev.[52]

By the autumn of 1975 the Soviet military had grown more restless. The debate on SALT in Moscow took on a new acuity because of the continued failure to resolve the Cruise missile issue. Pessimism was evident, and not only among the professionally pessimistic military. Referring to the talks on force reductions in Vienna, the Foreign Ministry journal *Mezhdunarodnaya Zhizn'* on 21 October 1975 acknowledged that 'there are still many difficulties in resolving the problems of European detente, particularly military *détente*; a complex and thorny path still has to be travelled'.[53] The NATO offer delivered on 16 December 1975 (see p. 68), incorporating the Dutch proposals, did not substantially alter this assessment. Because of the tensions aroused within NATO in the course of attaining West German acquiescence, the offer on force reductions was presented as a once-and-for-all proposal. It thereby took on the character of an ultimatum which the Russians were unlikely to accept. Although welcoming the fact that the West had at last thrown some nuclear weapons and some (but only truly tactical) air forces into the pot, the Russians objected that the NATO Powers were still aiming at asymmetrical reductions (which was true); they objected to the fact that the Western offer was made conditional upon acceptance of the West's overall scheme for arms reductions; and they began questioning how one could trade off nuclear against conventional weapons, which was disingenuous since it was they who had always insisted that all weapons be counted into the talks.[54]

The problems associated with military *détente* took on greater importance now that political *détente* in Europe had run its course. The high point of political *détente* had been the Conference on Security and Co-operation in Europe (CSCE). Thereafter only progress in military *détente* could lead to the solution of more intractable political problems in Europe. For the Russians the CSCE was a mixed blessing. It really left them only marginally more secure than before. They had failed to obtain Western recognition of the postwar frontiers of Europe as 'unalterable' even by peaceful change; 'inviolable' was as far as NATO would go. Second, in order to obtain this much the Russians had been obliged to concede on human rights—'basket three'—which received embarrassing prominence in the multilateral declaration, the so-called 'Final Act', which ended the conference on 1 August 1975.[55] Former Soviet diplomat Shevchenko recalls: 'In various meetings of senior Foreign Ministry officials during the years I served as Gromyko's adviser, I heard several colleagues as well as KGB and Central Committee participants in the discussions caution against the trend in East-West negotiations to expand beyond Soviet goals. Their warnings went unheeded'.[56] 'Although few Westerners recognized the success their diplomats scored in the relatively unpublicized talks, the Final Act emerged as a notable advance for their ideas and a setback of sorts for the Soviet Union', Shevchenko concludes.[57] Only some of the more cynical KGB officers wrily noted that 'basket three' might have the beneficial side-effect of enhancing their own role in the scheme of things.[58]

With the image of *détente* increasingly tarnished, the debate on SALT sharpened. On 13 November 1975, evidently relying on

Western official sources, the *Daily Telegraph* reported that the Soviet military was holding back progress on SALT. Grechko was 'reported to have been supported by other spokesmen for the eight ministries relating to the military-industrial sector which are uneasy about too quick an accommodation with Washington'. It was also reported that the Cruise missile was the centrepiece of their concern.[59] As though distantly echoing the *Daily Telegraph* on 19 December 1975 *Mezhdunarodnaya Zhizn'* published an article on 'The Soviet Union's Struggle for Military Detente', which indicated the existence of a struggle in Moscow over SALT:

> One must take into account the fact that the problems under discussion are unusual in being extremely complicated; they concern the vital interests of states and dictate the need for deeply thought-out and responsible decisions. Therefore there can be no justification for the demands of certain circles for the adoption of hasty, hurried decisions in this sphere, for attempts to interfere in the progress of the negotiations. Clearly, equally great significance is attached to the atmosphere in which the talks are held and an understanding of the importance of the steps already taken towards the resolution of these problems.[60]

A further article, which appeared in the military Party journal *Kommunist Vooruzhennykh Sil*, indicated that a debate was under way as to the value of further defence expenditure and the role of the armed forces in Soviet foreign policy. Colonel Tyushkevich wrote:

> Doctrine on war and the army shows that in the complex contemporary international situation an extraordinarily important role is played by the military power of the countries of socialism, the constant readiness of their armies to defeat any aggressor. There is no doubt that all other factors in the struggle for peace would not have played their role if the powerful armed forces of the socialist states and primarily of the Soviet Union did not exist.
>
> Consequently, the special political role of the socialist armies and in particular of the Soviet armed forces consists in the fact that they represent an effective factor promoting the development of progessive social processes. They exert their influence on the course of the historical process both by deterring the forces of the aggressor, reliably protecting the socialist community and limiting the activities of the imperialists in other regions of the globe, as

well as in the form of a force for direct action in the event of aggression against socialism.[61]

The Russians did indeed become more assertive in the Third World and elsewhere during the era of *détente*, though one should certainly not assume that US strategic superiority had ever effectively intimidated the Soviet regime into throwing aside revolutionary internationalism for fear of the consequences. It is also true that some, at least, in Moscow were aware that this assertiveness was jeopardising *détente*. But partly out of concern not to appear submissive to American dictates, the Brezhnev leadership continued to buttress national liberation movements in the Third World, highlighting the assertion that *détente* would facilitate the class struggle and raising to the point of dogma the assertion that the correlation of world forces was moving to Soviet advantage. Given the accusations levelled at the leadership in 1972 for tolerating 'selective co-existence' in signing the SALT accords while the Americans bombed allied North Vietnam and in negotiating SALT II while the Americans ejected Soviet influence from the Middle East, Brezhnev was in no position to draw back from opportunities to expand Soviet influence at the expense of the West elsewhere in the world, even had he wished to do so, which is doubtful. Moreover, Soviet commentators were totally frank in acknowledging that *détente* was not supposed to end the larger conflict between the two social systems, but was designed merely to prevent that conflict erupting into war:

Co-existence does not remove competition between the two systems, although it does shift the centre of gravity of this competition to non-military spheres of human activity; it removes neither the class nor the ideological struggle. It is precisely within these bounds determined by history that the process of detente is taking place, the process of transition from an era of confrontation to negotiations and from negotiations to the regulation of co-operation. This process cannot be other than a process of struggle, a process of competition between the two systems. Non-class politics does not exist—no such thing has yet been invented—and the class politics of the bourgeois states consists precisely in the fact that any turning-point in the international arena, any transitional—and, consequently, also largely unknown—period is utilised in their own interests to the advantage of capitalism, to the detriment of socialism. And the turn towards detente is no exception.[62]

The more perceptive of the *mezhdunarodniki* (the specialists in international affairs) were well aware of the way in which revolutionary internationalism was hindering the progress of *détente*, though it took time for the message to penetrate. One of the first to signal the change in public was *Novosti* political observer Vadim Nekrasov, appearing on Moscow television's 'International Observers' Roundtable' towards the end of September 1976. Nekrasov referred somewhat pessimistically to the importance of securing the 'preservation' of *détente*, in contrast to the usual platitude about the need for the 'extension' of *détente* into other fields. 'You did not make a mistake?', asked programme moderator Alexander Kaverznev. 'No,' Nekrasov replied, 'I used the phrase intentionally, although it may sound a little unusual . . . inactivity in this direction, taking into account that the opponents of detente have particularly intensified their activity recently and that the arms race is continuing, can indeed have a kind of eroding effect.'[63] Nikolai Shishlin, head of a consultants' group of a section of the Central Committee apparatus, was more explicit about the connexion between the downturn in *détente* and the resurgence of world revolution, though he necessarily avoided linking the process to Soviet aid for revolution: 'we all see that with detente, better conditions have been created for social progress and for the triumph of the cause of the peoples' liberation [*sic*] . . . As a result, this aspect of detente is frightening imperialism'; hence attempts on the part of the West 'to slow down detente'.[64] Another side to the Western response was, as already indicated, evident during the negotiations at the CSCE from 1973 to 1975: the presentation of 'basket three'—human rights, freer communication across frontiers, and so on. The Western powers were seeking to undermine Soviet power through the propagation of liberal democratic values. The foreign affairs editor of *Izvestiya* indignantly referred to this as an attempt by the West to assert 'the right to export its ideology to the socialist countries'[65]—indignation not without a trace of hypocrisy.

4.4   US COMMITMENT TO NATO IN DOUBT

The NATO countries moved to counter the Russians in the military field as well as in the arena of ideological combat. As we have seen, the impression that NATO was indifferent to the condition of its theatre nuclear forces is largely unjustified. Moreover, the Russians were inevitably prone to exaggerate the significance of NATO's early moves to modernise its theatre nuclear arsenal since they threatened to nullify Soviet attempts to match NATO nuclear forces at each level of escalation. 'Newspapers in the West have much to say about NATO's plans to develop new systems of weapons', an unattributed commentary on Moscow radio asserted in July 1976.[66] 'There is work underway on building an American-West German tank, on creating new spy planes and low-flying aircraft with a large range, on equipping their land forces with the "Lance" and "Pershing–2" rockets, with Cruise missiles and other systems.' Vadim Nekrosov noted:

> The so-called 'nuclear threshold' is being lowered, that is, it is deemed permissible to use tactical nuclear weapons under conditions in which this was previously not contemplated. The framework of the activity of the joint military system is being expanded. The adoption of the principle whereby its members plan general and financial commitments has introduced a substantially new element in the coordination of the NATO countries' actions and makes it possible to mobilise to a greater degree the financial and human resources of the West European states for military purposes.[67]

Similarly Professor Major-General Simonyan raised the issue of the Schlesinger doctrine once again: on this occasion in the context of NATO weapons modernisation. 'In accordance with the concept of "selective targeting", in the United States intensive work is being carried out to improve nuclear missile weapons, not only strategic weapons, but also operational-tactical and tactical weapons. The plans for their use are constantly discussed at sessions of the NATO nuclear planning committee', he wrote in *Krasnaya Zvezda* on 28 September 1976.[68]

NATO Europe's increasing sense of insecurity *vis-à-vis* the USSR was due to a combination of factors, among which growing uncertainty as to the unalterable nature of the US commitment to NATO during an era of strategic parity was no less important than the apparent shift in the balance of military power in Europe to Soviet advantage. As we have seen, in 1975 the British *Statement on the Defence Estimates* emphasised that in a period of strategic parity Western strategic nuclear forces did not necessarily constitute a credible deterrent against lower levels of aggression.[69] The West Germans were, of course, even more concerned than the British—'The Federal Republic of Germany will be affected first and hit hardest by any

attack in Central Europe',[70] their Defence *White Paper* reminded
one and all; and an unusually explicit passage bears witness to their
anxieties about the possible loss of US forward-based systems:

> In the talks of the two world powers on the limitation of nuclear
> strategic arms the Soviet Union has demanded that forward-based
> systems (FBS) be included in the negotiations. The Soviet Govern-
> ment understands forward-based systems to comprise all strategic
> systems of the United States other than land and sea-based inter-
> continental weapons, which are capable of reaching targets in
> the Soviet Union . . . The nuclear capability of NATO which is
> integrated in the conventional forces is above all the link between
> the conventional forces in Europe and the strategic nuclear
> weapons of the United States . . . In the Nuclear Planning Group,
> NATO develops the political guidelines governing the release and
> employment of nuclear weapons. Understanding and frankness
> between the allies on these critical issues has grown.[71]

The growth of what is here euphemistically referred to as 'frankness'
was hardly a welcome development. This 'frankness' was to develop
into something more acute by 1977.

The uncertainty in Western Europe as to US intentions highlighted
not simply the extent of the American commitment to the defence
of NATO Europe but also the need for greater unity within Western
Europe itself. The energy crisis following the October war (1973)
had shaken European unity. The British *Statement on Defence Estimates* in 1975 thus laid greater emphasis than before on the importance of 'political cohesion' in the face of the world economic crisis
as a factor in NATO's overall strength.[72] The *Statement* in 1976 was
even more explicit, arguing that 'the social and economic problems
now facing the West could, if not satisfactorily resolved, have consequences for the external security of Western countries'.[73]

Given the intractability of these economic and social problems, it
was easier for Western Europe to focus on the growth of Soviet
defence capabilities and on seeming American indifference rather
than concentrate on economic and social reform. In these conditions
the further accumulation of armaments in Western Europe drawn
from the United States came to acquire a symbolic significance only
loosely related to the true state of the theatre nuclear balance and
to the actual utility of the weapons deployed. We have noted the
US contribution to theatre nuclear modernisation from 1974 to 1975
following the introduction of the powerful F-111 (1971) and the

promulgation of the Schlesinger doctrine (1974): the decision to proceed with the development of the Pershing II (1974) and the allocation of more Poseidon re-entry vehicles to the alliance (1975). In 1976 Secretary of Defense Donald Rumsfeld listed improvements in NATO capabilities, current and planned, including the introduction of the Lance missile and the proposed eight-inch artillery shell (for battlefield use), as a result of which a number of nuclear-capable aircraft could be reallocated to conventional force roles which, together with 'the introduction of the Air Force's A-10, F-15, and F-16 aircraft, should improve significantly our conventional air power'.[74] Indeed, whereas Soviet tactical air procurement had risen markedly in 1970 and reached a peak in 1973, it had then dropped; after a dip following the Vietnam war, US tactical air procurement rose steeply from 1975.[75]

Among these aircraft newly introduced, the A-10 was a close-support attack aircraft for battlefield deployment. The F-15 'was designed primarily to provide an air-to-air combat capability superior to that of enemy aircraft projected for the early 1980s'.[76] The Chairman of the Joint Chiefs of Staff described it as 'the most advanced air superiority aircraft in the world'.[77] 'With its huge wings and mighty engines it can either out-climb, out-turn, or out-run any aircraft in the Soviet inventory'[78]; it became operational in 1977.[79] The F-16 is a multipurpose fighter with an enormous bombload and unprecedented accuracy of delivery.[80] It was reported that in an 'RAF-sponsored bombing competition, a team of F-16s finished first, with 98 per cent of the maximum points possible, a perfect bombing score on all four days of the exercise, fewer valid SAM . . . launches than any other team, and . . . F-16s "shot down" eighty-eight of the fighters that were sent to intercept them, without jettisoning their bomb loads and without ever resorting to fuel-guzzling after-burner power. The F-16s suffered only one kill during the entire competition. The other teams averaged almost three losses per mission'.[81] The first units were deployed in USAFE in 1981.[82] The F-15 had not originally been scheduled for deployment as early as 1977.[83] The decision to deploy earlier was a result of pressure from NATO Europe. Similarly, on the introduction of the F-15 the Department of Defense decided to increase the number of aircraft in the European theatre by retaining the F-4 as well. Furthermore, as a result of pressure from the US State Department, which wanted the way clear to bargain away the Cruise missile at SALT II, a second F-111 wing was despatched to Britain to replace a wing of F-4s and the decision was taken to equip the F-16 with nuclear weapons. 'These actions will substantially improve U.S. tactical air capability in Europe and reinforce the evidence of our commitment to a strong European defense', Secretary of Defense Rumsfeld stated in 1977.[84] Yet what the West Europeans noticed was less what the United States added to the burgeoning arsenal than the one weapon it was not so readily prepared to commit to their defence: the Cruise missile.

4.5 CARTER MAKES MATTERS WORSE

The advent of the Carter Presidency at the beginning of 1977 brought the problem of trust in US relations with Western Europe to crisis point. In his inaugural address in January, Jimmy Carter pledged to move towards the eventual elimination of all nuclear weapons.[85] This was enough to make all West European Governments, the West Germans in particular, extremely nervous, given their great dependence upon nuclear weapons as a deterrent against superior Soviet conventional land forces. While Carter's messianic vision of a nonnuclear future disturbed the West Europeans, his excessive and self-righteous emphasis on the importance of human rights—political freedoms rather than social or economic rights—provoked the Russians, who were far happier with the cynical *Realpolitik* of Nixon and Kissinger rather than the flamboyant and self-serving ideologising of Carter and Brzezinski, which set their teeth on edge. The West Europeans had long-standing doubts about America's aptitude for old-fashioned power politics. The activities of Nixon and Kissinger allayed those doubts, even if they awakened other anxieties; the activities of Carter and Brzezinski simply confirmed old fears without offering anything in return. By the time Carter reached the White House the strategic arms limitation talks were no closer to a successful conclusion. The dispute over the Vladivostok agreement remained unresolved. Worse still, relations between Moscow and Washington were drifting into choppy seas. The backlash against strategic arms control and *détente* had begun to affect administration policy. Carter's first moves to resume the negotiations with the Russians demonstrated a near-fatal combination of unrealistic expectations, tactless presentation, and lack of consultation with NATO Europe.

Paul Nitze, a senior figure in the US SALT delegation under

Nixon, had resigned in 1974, deeply disturbed by the apparent willingness of the Nixon-Kissinger administration to attain a SALT II
agreement at any cost. In January 1976 Nitze went public with a
fierce polemic in *Foreign Affairs* arguing 'there is every prospect that
under the terms of the SALT agreements the Soviet Union will
continue to pursue a nuclear superiority that is not merely quantitative but designed to produce a theoretical war-winning capability'.[86]
The validity of Nitze's melodramatic assessment of the US-Soviet
strategic balance is doubtful but his central purpose is in retrospect
only too obvious: to mobilise the will of the United States to regain
the higher ground *vis-à-vis* the Soviet Union which the Americans
so evidently possessed in the pre-Vietnam era. To this end he and
others set up the Committee on the Present Danger. Nitze's reaction
to the post-Vietnam and post-Watergate malaise and its deleterious
impact on US prestige and ultimately also on US power was certainly
not an isolated response. Senator Henry Jackson, aided by his
assistant, the diehard Richard Perle, was moving along similar lines.
Nitze was expressing sentiments which others already harboured,
though he articulated these ideas with greater authority, force and
eloquence than others could muster. The impact of this lobby soon
made itself felt.

   Following his defeat by Ronald Reagan in the Nebraska primary
in May 1976, President Ford nervously postponed signing an agreement with the USSR on limiting the size of peaceful nuclear
explosions. This was a straw in the wind. Even after the election of
Jimmy Carter as President on a disarmament ticket in November
1976, the impact of the new defence lobby continued to grow. Its
arguments were largely accepted by Professor Zbigniew Brzezinski,
a leading Polish-American sovietologist from Columbia University,
who was appointed Carter's special assistant for national security
affairs. No sooner was the appointment announced than Brzezinski
declared in public that he was not entirely pleased with the dimensions of the existing US-Soviet relationship, including the strategic
arms limitation agreements.[87] Carter, already wavering between
alternatives, told reporters that he would not necessarily accept
everything already negotiated by the Ford Administration.[88] Those
alternatives were personified by the anti-nuclear Paul Warnke, newly
appointed head of the Arms Control and Disarmament Agency who,
with Secretary of State Cyrus Vance, favoured continuing not merely
within the framework of the Vladivostok accords but also within
the framework of the Soviet interpretation of those accords, which

entailed sacrificing the Cruise missile (a position which would cause consternation in NATO Europe); and the anti-Soviet Brzezinski, who favoured reconstructing negotiations on an entirely new basis, aimed primarily at cutting the numbers of the newly deployed RS-20 (known in the West as the SS-18) and the RS-18 (SS-19) missiles on the Soviet side, combined with no concessions on Cruise and restrictions on the Tu–22M (Western designation 'Backfire').[89]

Contrary to popular belief, Carter did not suddenly present the Russians with an entirely novel set of SALT proposals when Secretary Vance arrived in Moscow on 28 March 1977 for negotiations. On 1 February Carter had asked Soviet Ambassador Anatoly Dobrynin for the reaction in Moscow to a series of hypothetical proposals including lowering ceilings on bombers and missiles of both sides.[90] Moreover, addressing the UN General Assembly on 17 March, even before he had met with the US National Security Council to finalise the new SALT negotiating position, Carter announced:

> My preference would be for strict controls or even a freeze on new types and new generations of weaponry and with a deep reduction in the strategic arms of both sides. Such a major step towards not only arms limitation but arms reduction would be welcomed by mankind as a giant step towards peace. Alternatively, and perhaps much more easily, we could conclude a limited agreement based on those elements of the Vladivostok accord on which we can find complete consensus, and set aside for prompt consideration and subsequent negotiations the more contentious issues and also the deeper reductions in nuclear weapons which I favor.[91]

Carter clarified this point at a news conference on 24 March. He stated that 'our first proposal' would be an 'actual substantial reduction that the Soviets will agree', and that 'the second fall-back position will be, in effect, to ratify Vladivostok and to wait until later to solve some of the most difficult and contentious issues'.[92]

By the time Vance arrived in Moscow Soviet opinion was visibly hardening against the United States. The refusal of the Americans to concede on Cruise prompted plain speaking in public, though not yet in the central organs of the Soviet press. A Novosti commentator, K. Georg'ev, published an article on SALT in, of all places, *Kazakhstanskaya Pravda* on 3 September 1976, arguing:

> The positions on these issues taken by the American side are not

only unrealistic but are generally notable for their lack of logic. While striving to exclude long-range Cruise missiles if not totally then partially from the limitations stipulated by the new agreement, at the same time the United States would like to extend these limitations to the 'Backfire' type of aircraft which is a medium-range bomber. In other words, on the one hand it is proposed not to limit that type of weapon which falls within the agreement in every respect and, on the other hand, they want to include a weapon which has nothing to do with the subject of the talks.[93]

This position was restated by Brezhnev in his letter to Carter of 25 February. Carter's letter was an unrealistic mélange of arms control proposals, including the futile suggestion that the SS-20 be prohibited, which the Russians were unlikely to accept, and other issues including human rights which were scarcely made more presentable by being put alongside unctuous expressions of goodwill.[94] The combination of Brzezinski's bullish *Machtpolitik* and Carter's moralistic naïveté was an inflammatory mixture which not only gave the Russians acute heartburn but also left both American domestic opinion and allied governmental opinion with the uneasy feeling of White House incompetence.

Boxed in by the compromises he had obtained from the military in order to reach the Vladivostok accords, Brezhnev made plain that a SALT II agreement would have to be based on the Vladivostok principles: 'in January of last year a concrete formula for the accounting of air-to-surface Cruise missiles within the aggregate of strategic arms was practically agreed upon', he argued. Brezhnev also insisted on the exclusion of the Tu–22M (Backfire) and protested at Carter's provocative exchange of letters with the 'renegade' Nobel Prize winner Dr Andrei Sakharov (which achieved nothing for Sakharov). Brezhnev's letter also contained the tactless and condescending warning: 'We would not like to have our patience tested in any matters of international policy, including the questions of Soviet-American relations'—the sort of tone that Queen Victoria adopted in scolding her wayward children who headed the various kingdoms of Europe in the 19th century.[95]

Secretary Vance thus arrived in Moscow on 27 March with no great reason for optimism and with the atmosphere already poisoned by flamboyant posturing on human rights and public statements incautiously unveiling the outlines of the US SALT proposals. Not surprisingly the visit was a disaster. Brezhnev dismissed the US proposals out of hand as 'unconstructive and one-sided' and as 'harmful to Soviet security'.[96] The reaction to this in Washington was to stand firm, while simultaneously pretending in public that all was well. Thus on 30 March Brzezinski wrote in his diary that 'if the American public stands fast and we do not get clobbered with the SALT issue, I think we can really put a lot of pressure on the Soviets. We have developed an approach which is very forthcoming; on the one hand, we are urging reductions, with the other hand we are urging a freeze, and at the same time we are urging more recognition for human rights. All of that gives us a very appealing position, and I can well imagine that the Soviets feel in many respects hemmed in'.[97]

The Russians did indeed feel 'hemmed in', but they were prepared to leave matters where they stood and wait for the next meeting with Vance in the late spring to resolve the issues in dispute. However, when Vance returned to the US Embassy residence at Spaso House on 30 March he gave a press conference in which he presented an outline of the American proposals on comprehensive reductions which made the Russians appear entirely unreasonable—a move which confirmed Soviet suspicions that the US was going public (as Carter had done at the UN) in order to win a propaganda coup and thereby hem them in still further.[98] That same day Carter not only insisted that he was still optimistic, and that he would 'hang tough', but also warned the Russians publicly that 'if we feel at the conclusion of the discussions that the Soviets are not acting in good faith, then I would be forced to consider a much more deep commitment to the development and deployment of additional weapons'.[99]

The Soviet reaction was an unprecedented outburst reflecting the accumulated frustrations of the previous two years prompted by several factors: the shift in the US position after Vladivostok; the retreat from the undertakings with Kissinger early in 1976; the raising of human rights issues; the presentation of a new negotiating basis for SALT loaded to the advantage of the USA; and the public statements as to the content of the Moscow talks immediately after their ignominious collapse. On 31 March Gromyko held an impromptu press conference where he delivered a fierce and damning condemnation of US behaviour. Gromyko recapitulated the story of the Vladivostok summit and the subsequent struggle over Cruise in such a way as to imply more consensus between the US and Soviet sides than had ever been the case. With more justification Gromyko assailed the Americans for raising the issue of the Tu–22M—'We say that this question is being raised artificially in order to complicate the situation on the road to the conclusion of an agreement'. He vented his exasperation at the appearance of a new US adminis-tration which sought to 'nullify' all that had been previously attained. He went on to attack the 'version' that the US had proposed a broad programme of disarmament which the Russians had refused. 'This version is false in its very essence', Gromyko asserted. The US had suggested cutting the number of strategic warheads to 2000 or even to 1800 units, and missiles with MIRVs to 1200–1100. 'In addition, they simultaneously proposed liquidating half of those of our missiles which someone in the United States simply does not like' (the RS-20 and RS-18). 'One has to ask: is such a one-sided presentation of the question the road to agreement?' Moreover, Vance had proposed a prohibition against either side modernising existing missiles (which would have prevented the USSR from MIRVing their missiles while the USA had already MIRVed most of theirs): 'to put forward such demands is a doubtful approach, not to say cheap', Gromyko asserted. The accusations continued. Gromyko turned Carter's refer-ence to the need for 'good faith' onto the President. Moving from the comprehensive proposals to the narrow proposals Gromyko objected to the fact that they excluded Cruise in return for exclusion of the Tu–22M: 'They called a non-strategic plane strategic, and then say: we are now ready to exclude this bomber from the agreement if the Soviet Union agrees to give the green light for the production and deployment of Cruise missiles'. Gromyko also raised two further questions, both of which touched a raw nerve within the Western alliance: the issue of a 'non-transfer' provision and the issue of forward-based systems. The Soviet Government had, said Gromyko, raised the issue of 'the non-transfer of strategic weapons to third countries . . . in order that no activity whatever is undertaken to circumvent the agreement whose signature is currently under discussion' (a reference to SALT II). This was, he insisted, considered a matter of 'no small importance'.

By publicising the issue in this way Gromyko was consciously throwing a spanner into NATO's works, as he was by raising the issue of forward-based systems, a fact which he all but admitted:

> At the conclusion of the first agreement on the limitation of stra-tegic armaments we issued an official declaration to the effect that we would have to return to this question. At Vladivostok in the

interests of reaching agreement we did not propose as a necessary precondition the inclusion in the agreement of a provision on the liquidation of American nuclear forward-based means [of delivery]. But now we are reconsidering this question in the light of the latest proposals from the USA. This is a question of our security and the security of our allies. We have every right to raise the question of the liquidation of American forward-based means [of delivery]. This covers atomic submarines, bombers, capable of carrying nuclear weapons, [and] aircraft-carriers in the appropriate region of Europe (you well know what region we are talking about). Call it what you will: a hardening of position, a change in positions. But; I repeat, this question is now raised by us in connexion with the latest American proposals.[100]

Two years later a Congressional delegation from the United States reported the remarks of First Deputy Chief of Staff Sergei Akhromeev on this issue: 'When Secretary Vance proposed major changes in the Vladivostok formula *without* also being willing to put FBS back on the bargaining table, the General concluded, the Soviets saw the United States asking for new concessions on top of those already given'.[101] Thus instead of caving in under pressure from the United States the Russians exerted more pressure, correctly calculating that Washington would sooner or later be forced back within the framework of the Vladivostok accords. It was also at about this time that Moscow decided to proceed with the deployment of the SS-20, a move which was to spark off exaggerated alarm among Europeans mistrustful of US intentions.

West European mistrust was deepened by the seeming inconstancy of American policy under President Carter. Carter had no firm sense of direction, and the pressures on his policy towards the Soviet Union came not only from different sources of power but also from forces in headlong collision. As a result the Carter Presidency had all the buoyancy of a cork upon water but without a deadweight to counteract and counterbalance conflicting forces acting upon it. Carter had set to sea with no experience in navigation, with only the vaguest notion of his destination, with a fractious and divided crew who, on taking turns at the wheel, were constantly altering course, and all of this at a time when, with squalls blowing and a major storm on the horizon, the surest sense of direction and the firmest hand were absolute essentials.

The Europeans were quick to take alarm and the West Germans

were naturally to the fore. From the outset Helmut Schmidt viewed Carter with some contempt. As an editorial in the *Frankfurter Allgemeine* noted on 21 March 1977: 'Bonn is concerned that Jimmy Carter is a man ruling the White House whose moral and religious convictions are incompatible with the demands of world politics'.[102] Not only were the West Germans anxious at Carter's anti-nuclear pronouncements, they were also infuriated because his sermons on the observance of human rights in Eastern Europe jeopardised the arrangements following from the CSCE for the emigration of Germans from Russian, Polish, Romanian and East German territory.[103] Allied confidence in the United States had been further undermined by the debacle at Moscow in March. 'After the March talks in Moscow', Vance notes, 'the allies were deeply concerned that the SALT negotiations and detente were in jeopardy. Repeatedly, they stressed a fervent desire that the talks get back on track'.[104] No prior consultation between Americans and West Europeans on the US negotiating position had taken place before Vance arrived in Moscow. The Europeans were briefed only on the eve of the presentation of US proposals to the Russians.[105] And lack of proper consultation continued to be a problem.

When Carter met allied leaders in London for an economic summit and a meeting of the North Atlantic Council from 7 to 9 May, differences soon emerged between him and Schmidt not merely on human rights but also on the lack of consultation between Washington and Bonn over defence planning. British Prime Minister James Callaghan recalls 'Helmut Schmidt coming to London in a smouldering mood, exacerbated by Carter's method of handling discussions'.[106] In February Carter had sanctioned a review of force posture in the European theatre (Presidential Review Memorandum 10). Well before the report was complete, one of its more controversial proposals had reached German ears: the suggestion that a temporary withdrawal from forward zones might be advisable in the event of a conflict with the East—a rather uncomfortable proposition for those whose population stood on and close to the front line.[107] This and other issues led to friction between the two leaders. Schmidt pointedly remarked to the North Atlantic Council 'that a consensus on military strategy is of decisive significance for European-American cohesion'; Carter was obliged to reaffirm US adherence to the principle of front-line defence.[108] However, as Brzezinski notes in his memoirs, 'differences on the nuclear issue were only papered over'.[109] And when Secretary Vance met Gromyko in Geneva on

18–20 May the proposals he tabled had not been cleared beforehand with the allies. Furthermore, although the West Europeans were concerned that Moscow and Washington should continue towards a SALT II agreement, they were alarmed when they heard what Vance proposed to Gromyko. This included a three-year ban on the deployment of long-range GLCMs and SLCMs—a proposal reminiscent of the offer Kissinger had made in February 1976. 'Up to then, we had not given our allies adequate information about the state of development of these new weapons, nor had we made clear to them our strategy in negotiating short-term limits on the deployment of Cruise missiles at the May talks in Geneva', Vance records.[110] James Thomson, then at the Office of the Secretary of Defense (OSD), recalls:

> When news of this suggestion reached Europe, it aroused a response which combined with suspicions about President Carter's anti-nuclear preferences to produce a strong and negative reaction. The United States appeared to be more concerned about limiting the nuclear threat to the United States than the nuclear threat to Europe, and to be willing to bargain away weapons important to Europe to obtain limits on Soviet strategic forces. The British and the Germans expressed European concern most vocally. Allied governments intensified earlier requests for technical and operational American analyses on the Cruise missile issue, which the Carter administration had refused to supply for fear that they would whet the European appetite for the missiles.[111]

After disputes between the Departments of Defense and State, the view that the allies should receive further information was finally accepted and Leslie Gelb, then director of the State Department's Bureau of Politico-Military Affairs, was instructed to prepare an 'evenhanded' paper on the subject of Cruise for distribution to the allies.[112] This paper was written under the direction of James Goodby. 'At that time', he recalls, 'I believed that deployment of INF [intermediate-range nuclear forces] would be divisive in the Alliance. The UK fed the German fears, unfortunately I suppose because the Cruise was a UK strategic modernization option.'[113] Thomson tells us:

> From the point of view of the administration, the effect of this 'policy evenhandedness' on the Europeans was disastrous, for those aspects of the US paper that described negative policy,

especially the arms control implications of potential Cruise missile deployments, exacerbated European anxiety about US intentions. The paper suggested that Cruise missiles might have negative arms control implications—for example, by posing verification problems—and raised the possibility of vigorous and negative Soviet reaction to any deployments. The paper went on even further in implying that Cruise missile deployments might be unwise because of a 'decoupling' effect—they would suggest a Eurostrategic balance independent of US strategic forces and thus reduce the credibility of the US strategic nuclear commitment. In addition, Europeans were again not satisfied with the repeated suggestion that because US strategic forces provided ample coverage of targets in the Soviet Union, NATO did not need long-range Cruise missiles. But the West Germans were already thinking in terms of a European balance independent of the total balance.

The Bureau's memorandum thus 'led the German government to suggest that the United States alter its SALT position to permit the deployment of long-range GLCMs and SLCMs'.[114] It was in this atmosphere of acute tension within NATO that the Soviet Union began to deploy the SS-20.

5 The Reaction in Western Europe, 1977–79

5.1 THE IMPACT OF SS-20 DEPLOYMENT

The threat that the SS-20 would pose to the security of Western Europe had been discussed by Defence Ministers as far back as January 1976 at a meeting of NATO's Nuclear Planning Group (NPG) in Hamburg.[1] But by the time the SS-20 was deployed no response had yet been orchestrated. Moreover, the Americans had failed to consult with their allies over the agenda of SALT II, and when the NPG reconvened in Bari on 11–12 October 1977 the Americans brusquely rejected the West German proposal that the United States alter its negotiating position in SALT to accommodate the deployment of Cruise missiles in the European theatre.[2] Thus although the Bari meeting resulted in the creation of a High Level Group of senior officials from member countries to examine options for forward planning on nuclear issues, it was not specifically set up to deal with the SS-20. Furthermore, it was a belated response to the need for a framework of consultation within the alliance, which in no way appeased the West Germans, who were incensed at American behaviour.[3]

On 28 October Chancellor Schmidt delivered his counterblast at the International Institute of Strategic Studies Alastair Buchan Memorial Lecture in London. As Schmidt recalls: 'Jimmy Carter, who became President, did not accept my opinion that the SS-20's posed a growing political and military threat to West Germany, and he decided not to tackle this problem within the framework of SALT II . . . Annoyed, I went public with my concerns in a speech in London in the autumn of 1977 . . .'.[4] The key passage was drafted by the Chancellor himself: 'strategic arms limitations confined to the United States and the Soviet Union will inevitably impair the security of the West European members of the Alliance *vis-à-vis* Soviet military superiority in Europe if we do not succeed in removing the

89

disparities of military power in Europe parallel to the SALT negotiations'.[5]

The United States was now under strong pressure to reverse its position on Cruise. But those concerned to appease Soviet anxieties in order to obtain an agreement in SALT II were reluctant to concede. Asked at a Senate hearing on 3 November whether there were 'any viable alternatives' to the deployment of the Cruise missile in Europe Secretary of State Vance replied:

> The question of Cruise missile deployment is related to theater nuclear force modernization and improvements in opposing Soviet forces. Possible alternatives to Cruise missile deployment include additional F-111 deployments, extended-range Pershings, commitment of additional SLBM RVs [submarine-launched ballistic missile re-entry vehicles] to SACEUR [Supreme Allied Commander Europe], etc. These, as well as the arms control alternatives for Cruise missiles, will be analyzed in detail within the Alliance.[6]

The Americans had already increased F-111 deployments in Britain to some 170 in 1977. But the British were still dissatisfied, not least because they had serious doubts whether the F-111, dependent as it was on long concrete runways, and even when dispersed on warning, could be relied upon to survive a pre-emptive strike by the more accurate SS-20.[7] This did not leave many options. The alternative of increasing the number of SLBM RVs allocated to SACEUR did not reassure the West Europeans either. 'The Germans had argued in Nato all through 1976 for a Europe-based counter to the SS-20'[8] and the British were, by the summer of 1977, aligned alongside the Germans. At a meeting of the NPG at Ottawa in June 1977 Secretary of Defense Harold Brown had asked Britain's Defence Minister Fred Mulley if NATO would accept an off-shore response to the SS-20. Early in August a letter drafted jointly by senior Foreign Office and Defence Ministry officials was sent by Mulley to Brown rejecting this as a solution.[9] The objections have since been outlined by Michael Legge, at that time handling the issue at the British Ministry of Defence:

> If missiles are to be deployed on existing ships or submarines, their TNF (theatre nuclear force) function will often conflict with the platform's primary role, which may well require it to operate out of range of European land targets. Dedicated platforms on

the other hand are very expensive, particularly the more survivable submarines. Moreover, the firing of a small number of missiles as part of a selective strike would greatly increase the vulnerability of the platform by revealing its location. Command and control arrangements for sea-based systems also present some problems that would restrict flexibility for limited strikes. Finally, sea-based systems lack political visibility: They neither provide a clear link between European theater forces and the U.S. strategic deterrent, nor do they permit the sort of direct European involvement that is possible with forces based on European soil.[10]

This may sound an odd critique from a senior official in the service of a Power so dependent upon submarine-launched ballistic missiles for its own security. But the British were thinking about Cruise missiles as an alternative to acquiring Trident missiles (SLBMs). London eventually dropped this option because of the uncertainty as to whether Cruise would maintain its penetration ability in 30 to 40 years' time compared with the more assured penetration ability of a ballistic missile system.[11] British consideration of Cruise in 1976–77 thus played a major part in causing Britain to side with West Germany in blocking US efforts to bargain away the system to secure a SALT II agreement.

Legge's emphasis on the importance of the political and symbolic elements in theatre nuclear forces was a point also made by others. 'The TNF [theatre nuclear forces] problem is mainly a political and psychological one', a veteran NATO diplomat pointed out.[12] 'At one level the problem is a military one for the NATO theologians, but the important level is the political one', an American journalist remarked. 'It's there that you have Europeans looking at U.S. policy in Korea and Taiwan, in Angola and Ethiopia, in Afghanistan and Iran, in the oil markets and the currency exchanges and, even if they might concede that each decision was right on its merits, they wonder what the hell the United States is up to. They see it sliding downhill, and they don't like what they see.'[13]

With the creation of the High Level Group the battle continued. Vance's replies to questions from the Senate indicated that there was still no consensus in Washington as to whether the West Europeans were right. Thomson, then at the NSC, recalls:

In these meetings, held in late 1977 and early 1978, British and German officials pushed hard for the adoption of a consensus that there should be an 'evolutionary upward adjustment' in the long-range portion of NATO's theatre nuclear forces. US Defense Department officials initially agreed to this formulation, which implied that GLCMs should be deployed. The State Department and the National Security Council (NSC) staff became angry that the Defense Department could have permitted the United States to become committed to such a position in the absence of a US policy on Cruise missile deployments. The NSC staff directed that the consensus be watered down and that formal interagency procedures be established within the US government to manage American participation within the HLG. However, US attempts to back away from the HLG consensus again deepened Europeans' concern about American policy and whetted even further their appetite for Cruise missiles.[4]

In retrospect the years 1977 to 1978 proved a turning-point in East-West relations. By deploying the SS-20 the Russians had inadvertently set in chain a process which ultimately only damaged Soviet interests. Moscow was not wrong to see the relationship with the United States as paramount. It was right to see NATO Europe as essentially a military and political dependant of the United States. But the Russians failed to see that, although the West Europeans were subordinates, they nonetheless exerted significant influence within the amorphous and unpredictable foreign policy process in the United States, particularly at a time when the incumbent administration was infirm of purpose, and elements within its ranks as well as outside were reacting increasingly assertively against the tide of revolution rising in the Third World and blatant Soviet involvement in the revolutionary advance.

Like all Powers the Soviet Union underestimated the extent to which others were responding to its own behaviour. Instead of seeing the moves to deploy the SS-20 as critical to the growth of hostility to Moscow in Western Europe, the Russians tended to believe everything was a 'propagandistic screen to conceal imperialist policy' directed towards rearmament.[15] Moreover, they saw all this as orchestrated from Washington. The Americocentrism in Soviet foreign policy which characterised the SALT years blinded the Russians to the role of others in the system.

The Russians found it easier to understand American objections to their attempts to offset the capability of US forward-based systems than to acknowledge West European anxiety to retain that capability at a level effectively superior to Soviet counter-measures. Inevitably

Moscow tended to view US hegemony over Western Europe as in some essential sense a mirror-image of Soviet hegemony over Eastern Europe. Slipping into such an assumption was somehow easier than finding a path through the complex, ambivalent and uneasy relationship of dependence which characterised the West European alliance with the United States. And when they did recognise that Western Europe could influence the direction of American policy, they saw it as a force moderating American behaviour. For example, the Soviet press never betrayed any awareness of the fact that West European objections were central to the US refusal to include the FBS on the SALT agenda from the outset in 1969. But there was never a shortage of Soviet references to West European attempts to attenuate American excesses: ironically as late as 1977–78.

Even with the press in Western Europe increasingly alarmist at the overkill represented by Soviet military power on the continent, the Russians chose to focus instead on the role of the West Europeans in drawing the United States away from the unrealistic SALT proposals carried to Moscow by Vance in the spring of 1977. Commentator Vadim Nekrasov acknowledged that the Vance proposals meant that the 'situation' had 'become aggravated' and went on to say that 'All the more important in our view is the European component in the whole complex of issues and affairs connected with the relaxation of international tension'.[16] Barely a week later, on 10 April, Nekrasov was reassured by the fact that 'To a certain extent the West European public and politicians are now attempting to put pressure on their transatlantic partners in order to bring them to their senses.'[17]

But the Russians took all this for granted. They took *détente* with Western Europe for granted. After all what choice had the West Europeans? Public opinion in the region had drifted to the Left since the early 1970s, high military expenditures were difficult to sustain and, as the 'neutron bomb' episode (see below) was to demonstrate, there was an evident aversion to further nuclear armaments among the receiving populations, particularly in West Germany. By taking Western Europe for granted and deploying the SS-20 to strengthen their hand in the expectation of negotiations with the Americans on theatre nuclear weapons in SALT III, the Russians effectively not merely liquidated Western Europe as a critical factor moderating the increasing assertiveness of the hawks in US foreign policy-making, they also unwittingly drove the West Europeans into the anti-Soviet camp at a crucial moment.

When the campaign to introduce Cruise missiles into Europe got under way in the summer of 1977, Soviet press coverage was almost obtuse in its inability to recognise where the pressure for Cruise in Europe originated; and there was nothing in the Soviet Government's behaviour which indicates that either the Foreign Ministry or the Central Committee apparatus was any more aware of the real dimensions of the problem than their mouthpieces in the Soviet press. One might have expected the Europeanists at the Foreign Ministry to have rectified such misconceptions. However, there is no indication that reports received from the appropriate Soviet embassies sufficiently relayed the true depth of the disturbance caused by the deployment of the SS-20.

There was no one of any stature serving as Soviet ambassador in Western Europe with the exception of Valentin Falin in Bonn. A self-made man, a hard worker of considerable intelligence, as head of the Ministry's Third European Department, Falin had framed the Soviet response to Brandt's *Ostpolitik*.[18] But he fell from favour and was passed over in the appointment of the Deputy Foreign Minister responsible for Western Europe in 1971.[19] Instead he was sent to Bonn. Given his poor relations with Gromyko thereafter, it is unlikely that Falin's reports carried much weight. In 1978 he was recalled, leaving the Foreign Ministry to serve under Zamyatin as Deputy Head of the newly formed Central Committee International Information Department. The man who succeeded Falin in the post of Deputy Foreign Minister covering Western Europe was Anatoly Kovalev, also a one-time Germanist, though very much as representative of an occupying Power. He had served as political counsellor to the Soviet Control Commission in Germany from 1949 to 1953, remaining in East Berlin and moving to the newly formed Soviet Embassy before being recalled to Moscow in 1955.[20] He thus became a protégé of Vladimir Semenov, High Commissioner and then ambassador to East Germany, who rose to become Deputy Foreign Minister. From 1965 to 1971 Kovalev headed the First European Department which encompassed France and the Mediterranean. Here he identified with the opening towards the French Government. In 1966 he was elevated to membership of the Collegium, the collective decision-making body at the top of the Foreign Ministry. His subsequent and further promotion in 1971 to the post of Deputy Foreign Minister testified to the fact that Gromyko had taken

Kovalev under his wing. However Kovalev's influence suffered a severe setback when he lost positions to the West in negotiating at the European Security Conference at Helsinki from 1974–75; acceptance of 'basket three' (see pp.72–5), although cleared at the top, ensured that he failed to obtain a seat on the Central Committee in 1976 at the 25th Party Congress and again at the 26th in 1981.[21] Thus at the very time when the West Europeans were seriously reconsidering the premises of *détente* as envisioned in Moscow their grievances found no effective echo in the Soviet Foreign Ministry.

Novosti political observer Dimitry Ardamatsky typically entitled an article on the subject of Cruise missiles: 'America is Now Trying to Involve Europe in the Strategic Arms Race'. Emphasising the role of the United States undoubtedly served a propaganda purpose, but such material does not convey the impression that the writer was conscious of what he was assuming. The Ardamatsky article appeared on 10 June.[22] On 3 July an article in *Krasnaya Zvezda* also pressed the argument that 'the Pentagon has decided to involve its North Atlantic block partners in its "Cruise" missile strategy. At a NATO nuclear planning group session last month in Ottawa, the USA's Secretary of Defense H. Brown proposed the armament of NATO forces in Europe with Cruise missiles'. He went on to say that the West Europeans were not enthusiastic.[23] Yet this was the meeting at which Brown sought to persuade the British to accept an alternative to Cruise!

As late as 1982, when the consequences of their policies were evident in Europe, the Russians still underestimated the extent to which the West Europeans played a leading role in initiating the confrontation over the state of the nuclear balance in Europe. A book printed by the Foreign Ministry publishing house and edited by Nikolai Lebedev, then head of the Moscow State Institute of International Relations (MGIMO), responsible for training, among others, diplomats and foreign correspondents, argued:

In circumstances in which the USA undertook dangerous steps aimed at disrupting the process of detente, trying to take the world back to the times of the 'Cold War', certain circles in the FRG [Federal Republic of Germany] did not demonstrate a sober and realistic approach in evaluating the . . . international situation that was unfolding and in fact associated themselves with the anti-Soviet position of the American administration.[24]

Once more the Russians attributed the initiative largely if not solely to the United States.

In 1977, with no sign of a forum in which to negotiate intermediate-range nuclear forces and with their eyes focused almost exclusively on the US Government, the Russians saw no incentive to halt deployment of the SS-20. Indeed they had every incentive to complete deployment before the opening of the SALT III negotiations. The West Europeans had no incentive to open negotiations before that time because, as they saw it, the deployment of the SS-20 was already tilting the nuclear balance in Europe to Soviet advantage. To accept negotiations in 1977–78 without a corresponding augmentation in US forward-based systems at a new technological level (and neither Cruise nor the extended range Pershing II was yet ready) would mean negotiating from a position of weakness. Apart from bargaining away the Cruise missile in order to secure a SALT II agreement, the Americans themselves had little enthusiasm for burdening the already difficult SALT process with further talks in related areas. And many in Washington also felt that the West Europeans were making much ado about nothing in respect of the SS-20.[25]

Soviet complacency towards Western Europe was reinforced not only by what they saw as West European pressure on Washington to accommodate the Russians over SALT II but also by the neutron bomb fiasco. The tragic irony was that the lessons the Russians drew from this episode were misleading in the extreme: it appeared to confirm that the United States would concede to pressure from NATO Europe against nuclear rearmament and that the governments of Western Europe were in turn compelled to reject the neutron bomb as a result of pressure from their own public, pressure pumped by skillful Soviet propaganda. In fact the entire episode became a negative reference point for both West Europeans and Americans alike, a lesson learned with a vengeance.

5.2   THE NEUTRON BOMB FIASCO

On 6 June 1977 word of the neutron bomb—an enhanced warhead designed for US tactical nuclear missiles in Europe—reached the public through the revelations of Walter Pincus of the *Washington Post*. This sparked an extraordinary controversy: the weapon was designed to kill people (Soviet soldiers) rather than destroy property (industrial infrastructure)—a concept of limited war with politically explosive implications since Germans inhabited the future battlefield. The Russians undoubtedly fuelled the fire. By the end of July the Soviet Committee in Defence of Peace had condemned the decisions to produce both the neutron bomb and the Cruise missile.[26] The World Peace Council—a Soviet front organisation—more aware of the propaganda potential of the neutron bomb than the Cruise missile, then announced an action week from 6 to 13 August to launch a mass campaign against the bomb.[27]

The World Peace Council had its distant origins in the Amsterdam-Pleyel movement: a non-party anti-war movement set up by the Soviet-dominated Communist International on 27 April 1932 at the suggestion of the unorthodox German Communist Willi Münzenberg.[28] Its purpose was to mobilise the forces of pacifism within the capitalist camp, as Lenin had advocated.[29] That same philosophy in similar conditions prompted the Russians to back, initially with some reluctance, the Wroclaw World Congress of Intellectuals for Peace convened at the initiative of Polish Communist journalist Jerzy Borejsza in August 1948.[30] The Russians soon took over the enterprise and the First World Conference of Peace Supporters was held in Paris (and Prague for those refused French visas) in April 1949.[31] The Conference set up a Standing Committee which on 19 March 1950 moved into action with the Stockholm Peace Appeal. The Appeal called for nuclear disarmament and in November 1950 a second world conference was convened in Warsaw because the British Government banned the conference scheduled in Sheffield. The assembly concluded its deliberations by establishing the World Peace Council.[32] The WPC was active into the 1970s under the nominal leadership of the Indian Communist Romesh Chandra. Its relationship with Moscow was symbiotic: 'The USSR invariably supports the movement of peace supporters. In its turn the WPC responds positively to the call of every Soviet initiative in the world arena', Chandra told *Novoe Vremya* in July 1975.[33] Financial support for the WPC comes from the Soviet Peace Fund and supervision of its activities is directed from the Soviet Communist Party Central Committee's International Department.[34] From 16 August 1970 overall direction came within the purview of Vitaly Shaposhnikov, one of six deputy heads of the Internatinal Department.[35] The Department also works in close co-operation with Section [*Sluzhba*] A of the KGB's First Directorate.[36] In 1976 Shaposhnikov emphasised the importance of Western public opinion in securing *détente:*

In recent years there has been a significant increase in the authority and influence of public opinion, supported by the actions of peace-loving forces . . . Peace-loving forces are now becoming not only the material basis of public opinion but also key factors actively influencing its formation, its moral stance [*printsipial'nye pozitsii*], in particular on problems of international relations . . . Public opinion . . . is increasingly becoming an essential factor related to the direction taken by states' foreign policies . . . in the formation of world public opinion, alongside the social forces within each state, an increasingly active role is played by the international democratic movement for the elimination of the threat of world war, for an end to the arms race and for disarmament. . . .

Significantly Shaposhnikov also made reference to building on the traditions of the anti-war congresses of the 1930s.[37]

Orchestrating opposition to the neutron bomb was thus not difficult: the international infrastructure was already in place. Operating from the Finnish capital, Helsinki, the Soviet-directed peace movements sprang into action: its monthly journal *Peace Courier* appeared with a special issue to meet the action week in August; the headline on the front page read 'WPC Calls for Worldwide Action Against Neutron Bomb. UNITE, SAY "NO" TO HORROR-BOMB!'[38] In January 1978, after many successful demonstrations which reflected a natural sense of alarm within West Germany, *Peace Courier* appeared with a headline which in retrospect appears remarkably prophetic: 'World Peace Council's Call for New Year: MAKE 1978 YEAR OF BANNING N-BOMB'.[39] Veteran Soviet journalist Yuri Zhukov, later chairman of the Soviet Committee in Defence of Peace, was to claim some success for this campaign: 'In the 1970s the third wave of mass activity by the supporters of peace, in the course of which about 700 million signatures were gathered for the second Stockholm appeal, forced the then President of the USA J. Carter to cool his bellicose ardour, which had some impact on [*skazalos' i na*] his decision not to deploy in Europe that truly diabolical weapon—the neutron bomb'.[40] It is undoubtedly true that without a receptive audience in Western Europe, particularly in West Germany, no amount of organisation could have got the campaign under way. The peace movement had indigenous roots. But it is also true that without WPC organisers and funds the campaign might well have just fizzled out without accomplishing anything.

The reaction to the furore over the neutron bomb revealed a

vacuum of leadership at the head of the NATO alliance as President Carter wrestled with his conscience in a vain and untimely attempt to square personal conviction with *Realpolitik*. As Thomson, then at the National Security Council, recalls:

> The lack of an internal U.S. government consensus during the early phases of the neutron bomb affair in the summer of 1977 had contributed substantially to administration dithering over whether it was for or against the neutron bomb. While Washington dithered, the public debate over the weapon careered out of control. Secondly, the importance of American leadership on nuclear issues within the alliance was highlighted. Partly as a consequence of internal divisions, in the fall of 1977 the administration had requested that its allies provide the United States with a decision for or against the neutron bomb. Used to following an American lead on such matters, the allies did not know how to respond and instead asked for U.S. views; these, of course, were not forthcoming. While this inconclusive double-act was under way, the public debate on the neutron bomb spread to Europe and got further out of control, now spurred by Soviet propaganda efforts.[41]

Carter told his subordinates that 'he did not wish the world to think of him as an ogre'.[42] And Schmidt did not want to inflame West German public opinion by sharing publicly in a decision on the neutron bomb. The Americans ultimately persuaded the Germans to share some of the responsibility along with their allies; the United States would bear the initial burden of deciding on production of the bomb. But at the last minute, after inter-allied agreement had finally been forged, Carter demanded more explicit public statements from Schmidt and British Prime Minister James Callaghan. Barely a week later, on 26 March, Carter 'said, in effect, that he did not wish to go through with it; that he had a queasy feeling about the whole thing; that his Administration would be stamped forever as the Administration which introduced bombs that kill people but leave buildings intact; and that he would like to find a graceful way out.'[43] On 8 April it was announced that production of the bomb would be deferred. The President had retreated.[44] To all intents and purposes the Russians had won. The allies were furious. As Secretary of State Vance subsequently noted: 'Militarily, little was lost by the postponement of the ERW [enhanced radiation weapon] decision'. But 'politically, the costs were extremely high. The president's standing in the alliance received a strong blow'. More importantly 'The incubus of the ERW haunted subsequent alliance consultations on the far more significant issue of modernization and enhancement of NATO's long-range theater nuclear capabilities'.[45]

The neutron bomb episode acted as a catalyst within the US administration. In Thomson's words: 'the neutron bomb affair changed the view of the NSC [National Security Council] officials about whether it would be wise to conduct a full-scale policy review of the LRTNF [long-range theatre nuclear forces] issue within the U.S. government. Up to that time, the NSC staff had agreed with the State Department that such a review was bound to generate leaks (suggesting impending decisions on Cruise missiles) that could harm U.S. efforts to negotiate a SALT II agreement. However, now NSC officials became convinced that the LRTNF issue could boil over, just as the neutron bomb question had, with far more disastrous consequences for America's strategic position, to say nothing of the prospective SALT II treaty'.[46]

Having succeeded in putting a stop to deployment of the neutron bomb, the WPC then launched its campaign against the rearmament of Western conventional forces decided upon at the NATO summit on 30–31 May 1978. By July the *Peace Courier* had appeared with the headline: 'NATO's Escalation of Arms Race Must be Stopped. UNITE, SAY "NO" TO NATO PLANS!'.[47] West European Governments could see that if this trend continued there would be little left of NATO. The response to the SS-20 thus came to hinge upon the need to reassert US leadership of the alliance. Those who had long favoured an enhancement of NATO theatre nuclear capability now found themselves in the majority, even among those sceptical of the need for deployment of more nuclear weapons and those most concerned to secure a SALT II agreement with the Russians. The decision to deploy extended-range Pershing II and Cruise missiles was thus reached through a series of meetings between agencies within the US administration and between the allies within NATO in response to this need as much as, if not more than, the need to increase theatre nuclear capabilities to offset the accretion to Soviet strike power represented by the SS-20.

By 5–6 January 1979 when the leading allies met in Guadeloupe, Carter announced that the USA not only favoured the deployment of further theatre nuclear forces but was also ready to lead the way in creating a NATO consensus on the issue.[48] This was no easy task. The reassertion of American resolve was regarded by some as sufficient, particularly when the prospect of deploying more nuclear weapons in Western Europe would excite the anti-nuclear movement into further growth, directly jeopardising the position of coalition governments. The frustration such backsliding induced in Washington is evident in a comment made by Brzezinski which was prompted by Schmidt's behaviour in Guadeloupe: 'throughout he was the one who was most concerned about the Soviet nuclear threat in Europe and the least inclined to agree to any firm response'.[49] Under attack from the Left, Schmidt insisted that if new theatre nuclear weapons were deployed they should be positioned not only in Germany but also in the rest of NATO Europe. This was known as the 'non-singularity' principle.[50] The United States responded by becoming increasingly assertive, to the point where the Americans grew into the role the Russians had already created for them. When, for instance, the West Germans and the Dutch began pressing for a theatre nuclear arms control policy parallel to the programme for modernisation, the Americans were reluctant to concede. Although the US Government accepted the need to develop an arms control policy, it nonetheless insisted on the principle that 'arms control should be viewed as a complement to not a substitute for force modernisation'.[51]

5.3   THE DUAL-TRACK DECISION

In acquiring the role already attributed to them by the Russians, the Americans inevitably reinforced the false Soviet assumption that the West Europeans were merely the objects of policy. With the United States taking the lead in introducing new weapons into Europe, the solution to the problem for the Russians appeared to lie in direct negotiations with the USA at SALT III: So why appease West European anxieties? In large part the inertia which characterised Soviet policy towards Western Europe during this crucial period can be attributed to such reasoning. Otherwise Soviet policy made little sense. Indeed as 1979 proceeded the Americans became baffled by the fact that even with the West Germans visibly backsliding on the need to deploy Cruise and Pershing II the Russians failed to make any significant gesture towards West European opinion. Thomson at the NSC recalls: the Americans kept expecting that 'the Soviet Union would execute some political or diplomatic manoeuvre that would precipitate negative political reaction in Europe and destroy the

official NATO consensus on the deployments. They kept waiting for
the Soviet dog to bark'.[52] But to the Russians the original strategic
and political rationales for the SS-20 were still the same. If theatre
nuclear weapons were to be put on the table at SALT III, further
bargaining chips were still needed. Moreover, the Russians still saw
the United States as the crucial actor. The securing of a SALT II
treaty at Vienna on 18 June 1979—once again omitting any restriction
on US forward-based and allied nuclear systems—reinforced this
impression. They therefore ridiculed the 'ballyhoo raised in the West'
about deployment of the SS-20:

> We may indeed ask those who are talking about the 'Soviet military
> threat', and linking it with the SS-20 missile, about the targets
> assigned to the numerous US forward-based facilities located near
> the Soviet Union, including several hundred nuclear-armed aircraft
> which are capable of carrying nuclear weapons and are based on
> aircraft carriers plying the seas day and night? There are several
> hundred of these planes, and their operational range makes it
> possible to reach very important objectives in the Soviet Union.[53]

This 'ballyhoo' was thus seen not as genuine alarm at the deployment of the SS-20 or at the tendency of the Super-Powers to find
common ground at the expense of others, but as an artificial
campaign to mobilise Western opinion in favour of further strengthening US forward-based systems in Western Europe, thereby bols-
tering the US bargaining position on theatre nuclear weapons at
SALT III. By focusing on this aspect of the issue, the Russians lost
a vital opportunity to halt progress towards a NATO decision to
deploy Cruise and Pershing II missiles in Western Europe. The
Americocentrism of Soviet foreign policy under Brezhnev and
Gromyko obscured the role of others in the international system and
for this the Russians were to pay a high price.

The other reason for Soviet inertia was the extraordinary success
made in halting deployment of the neutron bomb. This inevitably
encouraged Moscow to believe that Cruise and Pershing II deployment could similarly be forestalled. In February 1979, one month
after the Guadeloupe summit, a special session of the World Peace
Council was held in Berlin. The journal of the East German Peace
Council reported: 'The Berlin Special Session of the World Peace
Council considered the favourable experience gained in, and the
results produced by, the campaign against the neutron bomb and
drew conclusions for other important aspects of the struggle of the

masses against the arms race.' The journal went on to boast that 'Of all the social forces exercising a favourable influence on international developments, the organized world peace movement is particularly prominent'.[54]

That not everyone at the Soviet Foreign Ministry and in the Central Committee apparatus was blind to reality is evident from a belated move taken by the Soviet Government on 6 October, barely more than a month before a NATO decision was due. In a speech delivered in East Berlin Brezhnev announced his willingness 'to cut, compared with the existing level', the number of medium-range nuclear systems in the Soviet Union. Brezhnev also announced a unilateral withdrawal of 20 000 Soviet men and 1000 Soviet tanks from bases in East Germany. He also took the opportunity to reaffirm Soviet willingness to embark on SALT III as soon as the SALT II treaty was ratified and reasserted the Soviet intention 'to discuss the possibility of limiting not only intercontinental but also other types of armaments'.[55] The WPC duly came out in support of the Soviet proposals and gave notification of demonstrations in Bonn (3 November) and Brussels (8–9 November) under the slogan 'No New US Missiles in Europe!'[56] The Soviet leadership had finally been persuaded to make some gesture towards West European opinion. But the offer to reduce medium-range weapons missed the mark because the most salient point about the SS-20 was that it would replace *single* warhead missiles with *multiple* warhead missiles: a cut in the number of missiles would not necessarily reduce the number of warheads; indeed Soviet replacement of the SS-4 and SS-5s by SS-20 would actually increase the number of warheads. Brezhnev's offer testified to Soviet acceptance of the need for a gesture but it also indicated that he did not consider West European opinion worth more than that; no substantive offer was forthcoming.

Brezhnev had offered too little too late. In Moscow during the last years of the Brezhnev era there was a general reluctance to reassess existing policy positions even where they had evidently failed, and in this case the prospects for the peace movement still looked promising; there was a lack of tactical agility in any sphere except SALT II, where Gromyko was bent on securing an agreement; and, in order to forge a consensus with the military on SALT, it appears that deals were made whereby Soviet security was enhanced without attention to its impact on relations with Western Europe. Furthermore, the energy expended on SALT left other areas—relations with not only Western Europe but also China, Japan and the Third World—devoid of impetus and experiment. The Russians paid a high price for SALT.

The end result hurt Soviet interests. The NATO High Level Group proposed stationing 572 Pershing II and Cruise missiles in Western Europe. The plan was that all 108 Pershing II launchers would be deployed in West Germany, replacing the Pershing 1A. Of the Cruise missiles 160 would go to Britain, 112 to West Germany, 96 to Italy and 48 to both Belgium and the Netherlands. The HLG proposal was reviewed at a Nuclear Planning Group meeting on 13–14 November in The Hague. The Defence Ministers in attendance 'recognized that, as a consequence of the achievement of such parity [in strategic forces of the USA and USSR], disparities in theatre nuclear forces became especially significant to the overall balance of nuclear forces'. They 'considered that the introduction of the SS-20 missile and Backfire [Tu–22M] bomber was a cause of particular concern'. They agreed on 'the need for modernization of NATO's theatre nuclear forces' and 'reaffirmed the need for arms control to be pursued in parallel'. Modernisation would, 'by augmenting NATO long-range theatre nuclear forces, close a gap in the spectrum of escalation and provide increased options for restrained and controlled responses'.[57] This decision was then confirmed when Foreign and Defence Ministers met on 12 December. The resultant communiqué emphasised the future threat rather than the existing threat, 'trends' rather than an existing imbalance: 'These trends have prompted serious concern within the Alliance, because, if they were to continue, Soviet superiority in theatre nuclear systems could undermine the stability achieved in intercontinental systems and cast doubt on the credibility of the Alliance's strategy by highlighting the gap in the spectrum of NATO's available nuclear response to aggression'.[58]

Even had the Russians offered more in the form of concessions, it is doubtful at this stage whether NATO would have halted its progress towards a decision on deployment because the decision was as much a political as a military matter, as much a political gesture as an answer to military exigencies. The US *Fiscal Year 1981 Arms Control Impact Statements* issued in May 1980 made the point that 'Recent Soviet deployments of new and modernized long-range nuclear systems for theater uses—in addition to their direct military significance—have affected the NATO Alliance's perceptions with respect to the adequacy of NATO's present theater nuclear posture'.[59] Moreover, as the same document makes clear, even if the Russians agreed to cut their growing arsenal in an arms limitation agreement some Cruise and Pershing II missiles would still be deployed: 'It is the judgement of the Alliance', the *Statements* added, 'that any achievable arms control outcome involving TNF [theatre nuclear forces] would not, in the first step, eliminate entirely the Soviet LRTNF [long-range theatre nuclear forces] threat and would not obviate the need for some LRTNF modernization to meet the Alliance's own security requirements'.[60] In retrospect the problem the Russians faced by the end of 1979 was made all the worse by a lack of understanding on their part of the real processes at work. Under pressure from Western Europe and from Congress to demonstrate US resolve, the Carter administration now had its sights set firmly on Cruise and Pershing II deployment. The Russians, on the other hand, somehow supposed that the momentum of *détente* was irreversible, that with marginal adjustments on the propaganda front the Soviet Union could emerge from this situation unscathed. Under Moscow's direction WPC machinery thus moved into action. Its Bureau met in Helsinki to plan its campaign and on 18 December 1979 it invited sympathisers to send delegates to a World Parliament of Peoples for Peace which would meet in Sofia (Bulgaria) in September 1980.[61]

6 Negotiation from Weakness: The INF Talks, 1980–83

6.1 THE ROAD TO GENEVA

The shift in Western policy towards the Soviet Union represented by the dual-track decision found the Russians completely unprepared. They failed to see the significance of what was happening. Under the ageing Brezhnev, backed by the equally ageing Gromyko, the Soviet Government lost all diplomatic initiative. It was easier to assume that the correlation of forces was still to Soviet advantage, that *détente* was irreversible because the economic crisis in the West had undermined NATO's resolve to confront the Russians in Europe, and that the resurgence in Western determination to bolster NATO's defences was ultimately unsustainable, than to reconsider long-held assumptions and re-orchestrate policy along entirely new lines. For this reason it took a considerable period of time for the Russians to adjust to the new reality.

The issue could not entirely be avoided, however. During June 1980 and prior to a Soviet-West German summit towards the end of the month, Moscow undertook a policy review of the INF problem. Was negotiation really necessary? If so, what was the Soviet Government ready to concede? The idea that the Soviet Government might negotiate under duress displeased more than merely the military. The result of this review was agreement to negotiate but on terms which essentially left the Soviet position where it stood in the autumn of 1979. Thus when Brezhnev and Gromyko met Chancellor Schmidt and Foreign Minister Hans-Dietrich Genscher in Moscow on 30 June—1 July 1980 'the Soviet side offered to enter into discussions on the question of medium-range nuclear missiles simultaneously and in direct connexion with the question of American forward-based systems'.[1] They also made agreement on these issues conditional upon ratification of SALT II which, after the Soviet invasion of Afghanistan in December 1979, remained in limbo. Even this limited departure from the previous position was apparently achieved only after considerable disagreement. This is evident from the unusual way in which the results of the Soviet-West German summit were announced: a statement was issued as late as four days after the Germans had gone. It was published under the joint auspices of the Politburo, the Presidium of the Supreme Soviet and the Council of Ministers—a cumbersome and atypical procedure indicative of deep differences at the top.

The Russians had tentatively moved forward. But the offer had little hope of a favourable reception given the atmosphere in Washington during the approach to the Presidential elections, with Carter in humiliating retreat under a hail of Reaganite rhetoric. By the time Gromyko delivered a more elaborate version of his customary and ever implausible plea for world disarmament at the UN General Assembly on 24 September 1980 the Soviet Government had yet to receive a positive answer. The only consolation was that by making the offer on INF the Russians could at the very least play upon West German anxieties that lack of negotiation would harden public opposition to the deployment of Pershing II missiles. The gathering of the World Parliament of the Peoples for Peace in Sofia on 23 September—timed to coincide with and echo Gromyko's disarmament proposals delivered to the UN—was celebrated by the WPC as a great success, with the arrival of some 2260 instead of the 1500 delegates originally projected.[2] Brezhnev duly sent a message calling on the Parliament to give 'new stimulus to the development of the struggle and of mass action against the military danger'.[3] Chandra duly parroted the Soviet INF proposals for a trade-off between US FBS and Soviet MRBMs.[4] Head of the Central Committee International Department Boris Ponomarev was impatient for action: 'The entire international situation requires raising the struggle for peace to a new level . . . what is needed are not anonymous and abstract condemnations of war and of the arms race but urgent and energetic demands . . . It is necessary to turn the growing alarm of hundreds of millions of people into practical deeds, into mass, purposeful, agreed action'.[5] Once again the experience of 1977–78 was pointed up as the model, this time by Yuri Zhukov and his colleague Krushinskii reporting the proceedings for *Pravda* and recalling how 'mass action enabled [us] to avert the deployment of the American neutron weapon in Western Europe'.[6]

The WPC had called for demonstrations against Cruise and

Pershing II during UN Disarmament Week from 24–30 October. The demonstrations which resulted had yet to reach their peak. Nonetheless *Peace Courier* claimed that 'The response to the World Parliament's call for common action to safeguard peace was enthusiastically manifested in many countries during the U. N. Disarmament Week'.[7] If Washington failed to respond, Soviet proposals would surely drive a wedge into the uncertain and still divided Western alliance. It was evidently these considerations which impelled the Carter administration into eventual acceptance of the Soviet offer to negotiate.

Talks opened in Geneva in mid-October 1980, scheduled at American insistence to last no more than a month. The US team was led by Spurgeon Keeny, deputy director of the Arms Control and Disarmament Agency; the Soviet side was led by Viktor Karpov, who headed the SALT II delegation during the Carter era. Clearly the talks were no great priority on the American side. The US negotiating position was inequitable by the standards of the time: insisting that there be equal limits on longer-range land-based missile warheads (SS-4s, SS-5s and SS-20s matched by Cruise and Pershing IIs), yet omitting all US lighter delivery aircraft (still a focus of Soviet concern), F-111 and FB-111 bombers and, of course, all British and French nuclear systems.[8] As former deputy assistant director of the US Arms Control and Disarmament Agency, David Linebaugh, noted: 'the only conceivable result of an agreement confined to land-based missiles would be a substantial shift in the nuclear balance in Europe in favor of the West'.[9] Given Moscow's intransigence such proposals suggested that the USA had no interest in any deal which would jeopardise the installation of Cruise and Pershing II at the end of 1983. Indeed, this was to remain the essence of the US position for the next three years. The position was only partly qualified by the fact that in order to placate the West Europeans—above all the Germans—the United States had little alternative but to engage in negotiations, however futile they might be. The irony was that whereas prior to 1979 the United States was less than fully committed to the utility of the new missiles and the Europeans were almost uniformly in favour of them, after the Americans had done their duty by demonstrating their continued commitment to NATO Europe the positions were temporarily reversed. The minority in Washington which had early on seen a military advantage to be gained from implanting Cruise and Pershing II in European soil were now a majority within the US administration, seeking every possible accretion of military power *vis-à-vis* the Soviet union to compensate for the decline in US prestige associated with the era of *détente*. And even those in the new administration—like Assistant Secretary of Defense for International Security Richard Perle—who were sceptical of the value of the new weapons and were equally scornful of the allies in Europe, nevertheless hated the Russians to such a degree that in their view anything so heartily disliked in Moscow surely had something to commend it.

In turn, although now prepared to negotiate under duress, the Soviet Government as a whole was not about to legitimate the deployment of any Cruise or Pershing II missiles. Apart from the fact that in any negotiations these weapons would more than offset the advantages gained from deploying the SS-20, the Soviet military were particularly concerned about Cruise, given the weaknesses in the USSR's air defences. They were also concerned about the Pershing II. Although under Secretary of Defense Harold Brown the Americans agreed to ensure that the range of the Pershing would not be extended sufficiently to reach targets in Moscow—this was done to placate the West Germans who did not want to alarm the Russians excessively—the Reagan administration did not feel bound by such niceties. The Pershing II thus acquired a particularly alarming aspect to the Russians. It had a hard-target capability and from West German bases it could blast Soviet command and control centres in the Soviet capital within ten minutes of launching. Despite public denials from the administration, the Pershing II could hit Moscow. *Defense Electronics* leaked the news in August 1983:

> Pentagon planners have found new targets for the Pershing II missiles to be based in West Germany. Soviet command and control centers present opportune targets to NATO forces trying to stem a Soviet westward surge, considering few missiles are set for staging in Europe and the importance Soviet military doctrine places on centralized command of relatively minute details of warfighting tactics. With a range allowing strikes on Moscow from Germany, the removal of C^2 [command and control] capability by a comparatively small number of Pershings would render much of the Soviet ICBM first strike and retaliatory forces impotent. One high-up Reagan Administration official attested to the efficiency of using Pershing IIs to knock out Soviet C^2 installations saying, 'the number of minutes required to do the job is very small'.[10]

The furthest the Russians would go was to limit the deployment of the SS-20 (standing at 81 aimed at Europe in December 1979 and rising to 171 by November 1981) to match the existing long-range nuclear weapons arrayed against them from Western Europe and offshore. In this there were two considerations. First, the Soviet military argued that Cruise and Pershing II deployment would shift the balance of power in Europe to Western advantage. Second, deployment might be forestalled through a skilful combination of negotiation and propaganda: West German opinion in particular was so divided by the prospect of deployment that Moscow might be able to mobilise support for its position in Bonn and thereby scuttle the dual-track decision by merely negotiating without in any way sanctioning Cruise or Pershing II deployments. The Russians thus banked on being able to exploit 'inter-imperialist contradictions'. Their calculations were not entirely incorrect, though they invariably appeared more plausible than was justified.

Ronald Reagan, elected President in November 1980 on a Republican Party platform calling for military superiority over the Soviet Union, pressed for the reinforcement of Western military power as an essential precondition to any negotiation; in West Germany the argument was for immediate negotiation to obviate any need for further deployments. These differences surfaced very quickly. While Social Democratic Party (SPD) spokesman Karsten Voigt warned that the dual-track decision would have to be reconsidered if the US Senate voted against the SALT II treaty,[11] Secretary of Defense designate Caspar Weinberger told the Senate Armed Services Committee that the new administration would need at least six months before resuming talks with the Russians in order to close the 'gap' in the strategic balance.[12] In contrast the West German Government, under pressure from the peace movement, and the Russians, priming the peace pump, were by early 1981 converging in opposition to deployment. It was evidently the prospect of their convergence, combined with a complacent underestimation of Reagan's determination and ability to reverse the decline in US military power, which caused the Soviet Government to overplay its hand and to open in 1981 with proposals on INF that were difficult for any government in Western Europe let alone the United States to accept as a basis for negotiation.

The offer was outlined by Brezhnev at the 26th Party Congress on 23 February 1981:

Now, about nuclear missile weapons in Europe. Their accumulation is getting more and more dangerous. A vicious circle of its own has come into being: the actions of one side prompt counter-measures by the other. How can this chain be severed?

We propose that a moratorium on the deployment in Europe of new nuclear missile systems of medium range by the NATO countries and the USSR be agreed upon right away, i.e., to freeze in quantitative and qualitative terms the existing level of such systems, including, of course, the USA's forward-based systems in this region. This moratorium could enter into force as soon as negotiations on this question begin, and could take effect until the conclusion of a permanent agreement on limitations or even better—on the reduction of such nuclear systems in Europe. In this we assume that both sides will end all preparations towards the deployment of corresponding supplementary systems, including the American missiles, 'Pershing–2', and strategic ground-launched Cruise missiles.[13]

Although this was what Schmidt had suggested during an SPD campaign rally in Essen on 9 June 1980,[14] the Chancellor no longer faced imminent elections and not only had less need to appease the Left within his Party, he also had to maintain some measure of consonance with US policy. Thus on 25 February 1981 Bonn announced that the offer was unacceptable but nevertheless supported the proposal to commence talks.[15] The Russians now turned up the pressure. That spring they instructed the WPC to focus all its efforts—usually dispersed among a multitude of Third World issues—on the anti-missile campaign.[16]

If a major Soviet aim was to sow discord within the Western alliance—and it surely was—they succeeded. Despite the outward display of unity differences between Bonn and Washington became marked, indeed no less so than in the worst days of the Carter era. At the end of March 1981 Reagan administration officials met with alliance counterparts in Brussels. The West Germans, in particular, expressed concern that the United States was unprepared to commit itself to a date for the resumption of talks with the Russians; and early in April Schmidt declared that his government would face problems at home should the USA fail to open talks on arms reductions with Moscow.[17]

Such pressure began to yield results. At the end of April and on the eve of a NATO Foreign Ministers' meeting in Rome Reagan finally sanctioned arms control negotiations with the Russians. There

Secretary of State Alexander Haig pledged that INF talks would begin by the end of the year.[18] The US Government also announced that although it was not legally bound by the SALT I or SALT II treaties nothing would be done to undermine the two sets of agreements; however, the Americans also included the important caveat that this would apply only as long as the Russians adhered to the treaties, which left open the possibility of abrogation at some future date.[19] The Reagan administration was clearly adjusting under pressure, but the concessions squeezed out of Washington were limited: Schmidt's attempts in his talks with Reagan from 20–22 May to elicit a firm date for the opening of the INF negotiations proved unavailing.[20]

In August the WPC instructed its affiliated organisations to accelerate the peace offensive by recruiting more widely.[21] As summer gave way to autumn, pressure on the Americans from Western Europe increased. At a news conference held in Rome on 12 September, Chancellor Schmidt and Italian Minister Giovanni Spadolini called on the two Super-Powers to begin arms control negotiations. Schmidt announced that 'Italy and Germany believe negotiations are very important. But just as important are continued consultations with our countries. We intend to take the initiative and speak out on the progress of the negotiations'. 'Without parity, there cannot be negotiations, but without negotiations there cannot be peace', Spadolini declared. 'Italy and West Germany are well aware of their rights with regard to the nuclear powers, founded on their adherence to the nuclear nonproliferation treaty', Schmidt stated, adding: 'We have the right to expect that they will reduce their arsenals of nuclear weapons'.[22]

6.2 THE INF TALKS BEGIN

This pressure finally brought results. On 23 September Haig and Gromyko agreed that negotiations on theatre nuclear weapons would open in Geneva on 30 November.[23] The European allies had finally succeeded in reaffirming the second track of the dual-track decision as a reality of US policy. The WPC duly took credit: 'The will of the peoples for peace was a decisive factor to overcome [*sic*] obstacles to the opening of the negotiations between the USSR and the USA in Geneva'.[24] Apart from Reagan's *faux pas* during a press briefing on 16 October when he acknowledged that a nuclear war confined to Europe was conceivable—re-awakening the worst fears of 'decoupling' of the US deterrent from West European security—the differences between the United States and allied governments were in fact narrowing.[25] At a meeting of the NATO Nuclear Planning Group in Gleneagles, Scotland, on 21 October the Allies reiterated their joint position with the United States that 'the deployment of the modern SS-20 missile has upset the overall military situation in Europe and has created a potential source of instability and political pressure'.[26] They also reached a consensus in private on the forthcoming US negotiating position, later unveiled by the President on 18 November as the zero-option: 'The United States is prepared to cancel its deployment of Pershing 2 and ground-launched [Cruise] missiles if the Soviets will dismantle their SS-20, SS-4, SS-5 missiles'.[27]

The American offer, which was made at the suggestion of Schmidt,[28] was a proposal the Russians were at this stage unlikely to accept. They still had every expectation of being able to forestall Cruise and Pershing II deployments without having to liquidate their own medium-range missiles. The communiqué issued at the end of the NATO planning group meeting certainly indicated doubts about the negotiability of the zero-option. 'On the basis of reciprocity, the zero-level remains a possible option under ideal circumstances', the key sentence ran.[29] But who can recollect ever having negotiated 'under ideal circumstances'? In fact, as West German officials have subsequently admitted, 'the so-called zero-option . . . was crafted mainly to appease the anti-missile movement and not as a real negotiating goal'.[30] The fact that it eventually became the basis of agreement between the Soviet Union and the United States is surely one of the unintended ironies of history.

When the offer was originally made, the Russians announced it was unacceptable. On 23 November Brezhnev suggested a complete reduction of all medium-range nuclear weapons in Europe and the Far East: 'that would be a real "zero-solution" . . .'[31] But the West was not interested in agreeing to a withdrawal of existing US forward-based systems and the liquidation of French and British nuclear systems. The Russians evidently saw this offer as a useful piece of public relations designed to offset the propaganda value of Reagan's equally implausible proposal. The Soviet Government then made an announcement—again authorised collectively by the Politburo, the Presidium of the Supreme Soviet and the Council of Ministers—published on 1 December. It outlined four new proposals including a moratorium on the deployment of medium-range nuclear weapons in Europe including the FBS and allied nuclear forces, now buttressed by the offer of a unilateral Soviet reduction in medium-range systems; Soviet readiness to agree to mutual rejection of all types of medium-range weapons aimed at European targets; and, lastly, ultimately the removal of all nuclear weapons, both medium-range and tactical, from Europe.[32] This was the USSR's opening bid when the Soviet and American representatives met at Geneva on 30 November 1981.

At Geneva the Soviet side was led by Yuli Alexandrovich Kvitsinsky. Born on 28 September 1936, at 45 he was a rising star in Moscow's foreign policy firmament. Of Polish descent, his grandfather is said to have fought with Piłsudski against the Bolsheviks in his campaign to annexe the Ukraine in 1920 and then to have defected to the Reds. An aunt is said to have been a secretary to the famous Marshal Tukhachevsky who had perished along with most of his commanders in the terror of 1937. Graduating from the Moscow State Institute of International Relations (*MGIMO*) in 1959, he entered the diplomatic service and was posted to the embassy in East Berlin until 1965. Returning to Moscow as deputy head of the Third European Department, he went on to play an important role in the negotiation of the Berlin settlement (1970–71). He then served on the negotiating team at the Vienna talks in 1973–74 and was then moved to the embassy in Bonn to take up the post of Minister-Counsellor in 1978. From there he was despatched to take charge of the INF negotiating team in 1981.[33] He spoke not only Polish and German but also English and the Scandinavian languages. His appearance at the head of the Soviet INF team was a tribute not merely to his diplomatic and linguistic skills but also to the fact that he had a powerful patron in the Party: this was Valentin Falin, once Kvitsinsksy's superior as head of the Third European Department of the Foreign Ministry from 1968 to 1970 and now deputy head of the newly created International Information Department of the Central Committee set up in March 1978 and led by Leonid Zamyatin, another ex-diplomat.[34] Kvitsinsky's counterpart was Paul Nitze, whose involvement with the foundation and activities of the Committee on the Present Danger (see p.80) had propelled him once more into the upper reaches of government. An extremist of the 1970s, circumstances had so altered that he became the moderate of the 1980s. US diplomats nicknamed him the 'silver fox'; the Russians,

on the other hand, knew him more ominously though no less respect-
fully as the 'grey hawk' (*sedoi yastreb*).

Despite the fact that both Nitze and Kvitsinsky took seriously the
idea of reaching a compromise somewhere midway between the
opening positions of both sides, the negotiations were destined to
fail. The very idea of negotiating had been a point of contention
with the diehards in both camps. In Washington they were led by
Perle and ultimately and instinctively backed by the President; they
were not prepared to accept a deal which prevented a substantial
number of Pershing II and Cruise missiles from being deployed in
Europe.[35] In Moscow some elements understood 'that compromises
must be reached'.[36] However, it appears that diehards aligned with
the military were not willing to countenance any agreement which
sanctioned the arrival of even one Pershing II or Cruise missile in
Europe.

The talks which opened on 30 November were little more than
exploratory during the first round. Both sides enlarged upon the
declarations of their respective leaders but neither side had much
room for manoeuvre, and it was too early to present drafts for
detailed discussion. The round thus closed in late December with no
sign of progress but with an agreement to reconvene in the New
Year. By then the Polish crisis had risen to new heights and the talks
resumed on 12 January 1982 with the Russians nervous lest the
United States walk out as a consequence of the imposition of martial
law and the suppression of the independent trade union movement
in Poland.[37]

6.3   THE RUSSIANS AND THE PEACE MOVEMENT

The suppression of the independent Polish trade union movement
and the suppression of all spontaneous manifestations of pacifism in
Eastern Europe—where the official East German peace movement
talked only of stopping 'the imperalist arms race',[38] not the East-West
arms race—weakened Soviet influence among pacifists in Western
Europe. The resulting complications presented the World Peace
Council with an unaccustomed dilemma: it would lose influence if it
continued to be so closely aligned to every step of Soviet policy; on
the other hand the WPC could scarcely bite the hand which fed it.
All this was ultimately the responsibility of Vitaly Shaposhnikov at
the International Department, and it was Shaposhnikov who now

aired the dilemma in the Institute of World Economy and International Relations journal in December 1981.

'In its dimensions, social structure and methods', Shaposhnikov wrote, 'the anti-war movement has gone so far beyond its former limits that this raises an entire complex of new problems.' Before outlining the problems, he first outlined the results. Extending the evaluation he had made in the mid–1970s, Shaposhnikov now emphasised that 'The anti-war movement is becoming an increasingly important factor of international life'.[39] 'Now this movement is so white-hot [*dostiglo takogo nakala*] that it is increasingly becoming a real obstacle to the attainment of the plans of the North Atlantic bloc.' Quoting SACEUR General Bernard Rogers and West German Defence Minister Hans Apel to illustrate the level of anxiety within NATO, Shaposhnikov went on to state that a special directive had been issued by the alliance demanding that the member countries 'take steps against the anti-war movement'.[40] Particularly important was the movement in West Germany, where the scale of the movement was especially broad. In Bonn on 10 October 1981 the anti-missile demonstrations reached unprecedented heights—more than 300 000 people participating.

This then led Shaposhnikov to the problems which stemmed from the very size of the movement and its extraordinary heterogeneity. The current movement was often compared to that of the 1950s—the Stockholm Peace Appeal, and so on. This was in his opinion both true and untrue:

> Above all one must bear in mind that those campaigns were carried out at the initiative of the World Peace Council, which to a certain extent coordinated mass activities of the peace-loving forces of society in that period. The WPC today, too, takes the initiative in such campaigns. However the situation in the anti-war movement as a whole is now fundamentally different. First, it is developing in circumstances [which are] completely different* from that period in the international arena, second, it is on a significantly greater scale compared with the fifties and has a heterogeneous composition . . . [41]

The ideal model was the neutron-bomb campaign. 'As we know', Shaposhnikov wrote, 'several years ago "the movement against neutron death" became such an effective form of public protest that

---

* wrongly written as 'excellent' [*otlichnoi*] instead of 'different' [*razlichnoi*].

it forced J. Carter to retreat. This was made possible thanks to the high degree of solidarity of social forces attained.'[42] Other writers, however, complained of the challenge thrown up by the heterogeneity of the movement. 'The numerous anti-war movements . . . face Marxists with a range of problems connected with the formulation of the theory of the struggle for peace', two writers in *Kommunist* commented months later.[43] But none of these commentators, least of all Shaposhnikov, could afford to be too overt. The issue was too important to be discussed entirely frankly in public. And many in the peace movement were either ex-Communists who knew Moscow's methods only too well or were sensitive to accusations that they were stooges of the Russians. Leading nuclear disarmer and former member of the British Communist Party E. P. Thompson warned in February 1981: 'To allow the Western peace movement to drift into collusion with the strategy of the World Peace Council—that is, in effect, to become a movement opposing NATO militarism *only*—is a recipe for our own containment and ultimate defeat'.[44] Such problems were new to the WPC. It was accustomed to a degree of control more typical of the Stalin era. Unease was voiced at the Bureau meeting of 8 January 1982 in a statement lamenting 'attempts to disorganise, disorient, and weaken the peace movement'.[45] Clearly Thompson was not far from their minds. And when the International Liaison for Disarmament and Peace—yet another front organisation presided over by Chandra—met in Vienna on 29 January–2 February, it failed to draw significant attendance, and some who did attend attempted to use the forum to attack Soviet policies, particularly in Poland.[46]

These difficulties should not be exaggerated. Despite such setbacks the impact of the peace movement as a whole could still be felt in the INF negotiations where Nitze, in particular, became increasingly fearful lest the bottom suddenly and irrevocably drop out of his entire negotiating position as a result of a loss of nerve in the capitals of Western Europe. 'Many of these movements have no clear conception of where they are going', Soviet commentators noted, but they also consoled themselves with the thought that 'it is perfectly obvious that they are not on the same road as capitalism'.[47]

6.4 BACK TO THE TALKS

The Americans were the first to table a draft for detailed discussion on 2 February 1982. It consisted of the zero-option. This represented what Richard Burt, then director of the State Department Bureau of Politico-Military Affairs, disarmingly called 'the simple, straight-forward US approach'.[48] 'I believe that we will succeed in Geneva if we are firm and deliberate, if we stand by the substance of our proposal', Perle insisted. 'That substance is fair and equitable; it must not be sacrificed to the negotiation.'[49] This meant that the negotiations were for the Americans in reality merely an exercise in public relations; unless, of course, one assumed the Russians were likely to capitulate, and at this stage there was no evidence that they would. Frustrated by US intransigence and no longer nervous lest the US team walk out, Brezhnev responded by questioning American good faith and by breaking the strict secrecy hitherto adhered to by both sides in the negotiations. At a reception for representatives of the Second International in Moscow on 3 February and referring to the Geneva talks, 'Brezhnev remarked that their initial stage prompts a degree of vigilance in view of the evident unwillingness of the American side to seek a basis for a mutually acceptable under-standing'.[50] He also unveiled part of the Soviet negotiating position.[51] It was self-evidently in Soviet interests that the public in the West should know the true position of each side, and the Russians—finding the USA uninterested in compromise and only too aware of the way allied pressure had brought the Americans to the negotiating table in the first place—were not likely to let an opportunity pass without placing any blame for lack of progress squarely on American shoulders. Referring to these disclosures and further revelations by TASS on 9 February (see below), Richard Burt later vented his irritation that 'The Soviets have . . . put details of their negotiating position at Geneva into the public domain, in a transparent attempt to gain public support for their position and to undermine alliance support for the US position.'[52]

Based upon Brezhnev's Bonn proposals the Soviet draft tabled on 4 February and published by TASS five days later clung to familiar positions: compensation for US forward-based systems as well as British and French forces, and no deployment of Cruise or Pershing II. In detail what Kvitsinsky proposed was the following: first, the agreement should encompass all medium-range nuclear weapons launchers with a combat radius of 1000 kilometres (621.37 miles) or more, 'deployed in the territory of Europe and in the adjacent waters or intended for use in Europe'. This definition thus covered both US carrier-based aviation in the Second and Sixth Fleets and the FB-111's stationed on the US northeastern seaboard and allocated to the European theatre—refuelling over such bases as Fairford, Gloucestershire, in England—as well as US land-based aircraft in Western Europe. All were designed to buttress the American commitment to the defence of Western Europe. None was limited by the SALT agreements. Second, the treaty should reduce the number of these weapons to 300 units each by the end of 1990, with an intermediate level of 600 each by the end of 1985; by later agreement the terms could then be extended beyond 1990. Third, the Russians were clearly concerned to allow for further replacement of SS-4s and SS-5s by SS-20s and future substitution of the SS-20s by later generations of weaponry: 'The sides will have the right to determine themselves the composition of the armament being reduced and within the limits of the agreed reduced levels to carry out, at their own discretion, replacement and modernisation of armaments, whose framework is to be determined additionally'. Fourth, the Russians sought to avoid having to liquidate the SS-20s withdrawn under the agreement: 'The main means for the reduction of medium-range armaments will be their destruction, which does not exclude the possibility of withdrawing a part of the armaments behind some agreed lines'. Fifth, the Russians left the form of verification open. Sixth, both sides would freeze their weapons at existing levels; the sweetener here was that if the USA agreed to a freeze, the Soviets would unilaterally reduce their armaments in anticipation of future mutual cuts.[53]

The Soviet plan was categorically rejected by the United States on 10 February; it was based on 'familiar themes which we and our NATO allies have long made clear cannot provide an acceptable basis for an arms control agreement', the State Department announced, joining in the new spirit of open diplomacy initiated by the Russians. The objections cited were essentially two-fold: first, the Americans claimed that by including French and British systems the Russians were not accepting the principle of equality between the Super-powers. In fact they were unequal because the USA had nuclear-armed allies and the USSR had not and was not to be allowed compensation for that fact; the USA also had forward-based systems in Asia, against which a part of the Soviet missiles were aimed—as well as against the Chinese who had no intention of discussing arms control at all. And second, but more convincingly, the Soviet proposal would allow the Russians to continue to replace SS-4s and SS-5s by SS-20s; and they were counting launchers rather than warheads, so the actual threat to Western Europe would scarcely diminish were these replacements allowed.[54]

This was not the last word, however. Addressing the 19th Komsomol Congress in Moscow on 18 May, Brezhnev stated that the unilateral moratorium observed by the USSR in ceasing to deploy intermediate-range missiles in the European zone of the country applied also to Soviet missiles that could reach the German Federal Republic and other countries of Western Europe from positions immediately East of the Ural mountains. He also made clear that the moratorium envisaged cessation of not merely deployment but also the construction of bases for the missiles. Yet Brezhnev made no movement towards the counting of warheads, whose number increased with the substitution of SS-20s for SS-4s and SS-5s, instead of missile launchers. The Russians were certainly not alone in seeking a margin of advantage. The Americans, for example, still insisted on the need for restrictions on Soviet missiles targeted on Asia. Brezhnev ridiculed this as 'absurd' and called the American bluff: 'A resolution of the question of these missiles—their limitation and reduction—is possible', he said. 'But only through negotiations with those who possess nuclear systems which our missiles confront'.[55]

6.5   PROBLEMS WITH THE SOVIET MILITARY

Further movement in the Soviet negotiating position was circumscribed by the difficulties Brezhnev was encountering from the Soviet military. These difficulties stemmed from the diminishing rate of economic growth which heightened competition between the defence and the civilian sectors of the economy for priority in the allocation of investment. The problem had first made its impact in 1975–76 when growth rates fell, and it had been worsening ever since. With the drop in the growth of national income the military found the rate of increase in their resources reduced[56]; with the severe deterioration in the economic situation in 1981–82 after yet another disastrous harvest, the problem demanded urgent attention. The Soviet public was clamouring for more consumer goods, including regular supplies of meat, dairy produce, vegetables and fruit. Clearly if the economy was to be put back on its feet, agriculture would have to become more productive. Only then would there be an incentive for labour to raise industrial productivity, only then could greater discipline be enforced without causing social unrest (the example of Poland was never far from their minds), and additional capital be raised to re-equip Soviet industry at levels comparable to those in the West.

The issue of investment allocation came to a head when Brezhnev addressed a plenum of the Central Committee on 24 May 1982. After one of its committees had explored solutions to the problem, the Politburo agreed upon a programme 'to guarantee food products to the population of the country in the shortest possible time'. Brezhnev sought approval from the plenum. He knew he could count on the Central Committee's support best by putting the issue in terms of the need to break Soviet dependence on hostile Powers for supplies of grain—memories of Carter's grain embargo of 1980 were still fresh. Yet given the massive increases in the US defence budget the Soviet military were bound to be unsettled by Brezhnev's reordering of the country's economic priorities: the Soviet Union would maintain its defence capability 'at the necessary level' and would 'continue to struggle for international detente—both political and military detente'. 'But', Brezhnev emphasised, 'we are well aware of something else: the successful fulfillment of our plans [for agriculture] is an important precondition to the strengthening of peace'— butter before guns.[57] It is worth noting at this point that the Politburo member responsible for agriculture—with a vested interest in the reallocation of resources from the military sector—was Mikhail Gorbachev, Central Committee secretary since 27 November 1978 and member of the Politburo since 21 October 1980. And Brezhnev's shift of emphasis from military to agricultural priorities must have resulted not only from the urgent need to solve the problem of food supplies but also from growing pressure from those such as Gorbachev, arguing for a far-reaching reform of the economy as a whole.

Disagreements between Politburo members were not usually aired in public but signs of discontent with the new line soon surfaced from the military. On 12 July, two weeks after the opening of the Strategic Arms Reduction Talks (START) at Geneva and with the INF negotiations still staggering on, member of the Politburo and Minister of Defence Marshal Dimitrii Ustinov published an article in *Pravda*. For the first time he made public the military's discontent with the government's unilateral commitment to 'no first use' of nuclear weapons, the first of several indications of deep misgivings shared by the officer corps about Politburo priorities as a whole:

> In the light of the increasingly aggressive policy of the United States and the NATO bloc, it was not easy for the Soviet Union to take upon itself a unilateral obligation to no first use of nuclear weapons. And it is perfectly natural that the Soviet people, our friends, [and] progressive people of the world should raise the question: was this the right moment chosen for such a move, and do we not subject our people, our Motherland, the cause of socialism and progress throughout the entire world to excessive dangers with unilateral obligations? Did we not have a difficult historical experience when an aggressor stopped at nothing [and] put his machine of destruction into full gear? Can we ignore all this?

Referring specifically to the INF negotiations, Ustinov warned that 'The impression is being given that . . . the USA is not determined to make constructive steps in response to our initiatives. they are not going further than their notorious "zero-option" '. He asserted that the Americans were seeking either the 'unilateral disarmament of the Soviet Union' or to stalemate the talks in order to keep them going indefinitely, accusing the Russians of lack of good faith and implementing their preconceived plan for rearming NATO. Then came the warning:

> In this respect I would like to make one thing clear: the USSR will not embark upon unilateral disarmament. If the Americans continue to insist that their nuclear forward-based systems and the nuclear systems of Britain and France are not taken into account within the scope of the negotiations, then this will hinder any advance.[58]

6.6   THE 'WALK IN THE WOODS'

These were scarcely auspicious conditions in which to release a *ballon d'essai*. It was Nitze who made this move. Nitze's nightmare was that the West Europeans, the Germans in particular, would cave in to pressure from the peace movement and from the East. It was this motive which impelled him to break through the established US negotiating position. But Kvitsinsky was also interested in breaking through the barrier represented by the zero-option, though he had good reason to be uneasy about engaging in off-the-record discussions. The subsequent breach of confidence in Washington certainly bore out these fears. What gave the two men hope was that in the summer of 1980 and again in 1981 the Soviet leadership had undertaken a major review of its INF position. A further review was now due. Both Nitze and Kvitsinsky embarked upon exploratory and informal talks in the hope of influencing the policy-making process before the review was complete. On 16 July and after preliminary soundings, the two took their legendary 'walk in the woods' outside Geneva unencumbered by interpreters. Although Nitze knew no Russian, Kvitsinsky's English was more than adequate for their purpose. Sitting on a log in the woods, Nitze handed Kvitsinsky a typescript—a 'package' of proposals according to which the USSR could retain 75 IRBM launchers, the United States 75 GLCM launchers; the Russians would end up with 225 warheads, the USA with 300 (since the GLCM launchers would each have four missiles). The rationale behind this imbalance was that since Cruise was slower than the SS-20, the United States had to be compensated elsewhere. Furthermore, an important US concession would be that no Pershing II missiles would be deployed. But neither British nor French forces would be included, and the number of SS-20s aimed at Asian targets would be limited to 75 (Kvitsinsky obtained Nitze's agreement to raise this to 90). Nitze also proposed a ceiling of 150 fighter-bombers, but excluding US carrier-based aircraft which, as Kvitsinsky noted, would have meant only symbolic cuts in US forces but major cuts in Soviet forces.[59]

The two men returned home to obtain a response to the package. But Kvitsinsky arrived in Moscow only to find that the INF policy review was already over and, what is more, that tension between the military and the political leadership was at new heights; certainly not propitious conditions for acceptance of the Nitze package. Moreover, Nitze himself arrived back in Washington to find that there was no more interest in compromise than there had been when Reagan inaugurated the zero-option.

Pressure on Brezhnev to retreat from the position outlined at the Central Committee plenum in May increased throughout the summer and into the autumn. 'Perhaps, never since the Second World War has the situation been so grave and so dangerous', intoned Marshal Kulikov, Soviet Commander-in-Chief of the Warsaw Pact, towards the end of September, in a statement typical of the hyperbole then current among the Soviet military.[60] When Gromyko met the new US Secretary of State George Shultz in New York at the opening of the UN on 28 September Shultz told him nothing of the American response to the Nitze package and nothing of the supposed summit Nitze had invented to lure Kvitsinsky into accepting the package for consideration. But there was no real likelihood of Moscow accepting the offer anyway. When Kvitsinsky arrived for the re-opening of the Geneva talks and spoke to Nitze on 29 September, he made this clear and referred to Nitze's failure to include the British and French forces as the main reason for the rejection of the proposals.[61] Nitze thus came away with the impression that the Russians would not accept any US INF deployments.

What made matters worse was that, after the European allies were briefed on the Nitze-Kvitsinsky exchanges, the French leaked the news to the press—an article appeared in the *Chicago Tribune* on 22 October giving only a brief outline of the moves made. But any such leak was bound to irritate Moscow, adding to discontent among the military at the direction taken by the political leadership. Matters soon came to a head. On 27 October Brezhnev was obliged to address a meeting of armed forces commanders in the Kremlin in an attempt to reassure them that he was indeed very much concerned with the state of the country's defence capability.

At the meeting Brezhnev highlighted problems in various sectors of the economy. He defended the decisions taken by the May plenum as of 'exceptional significance'. But he also took great care to reassure officers present that 'Dmitrii Fedorovich Ustinov is continually informing me about the state of our armed forces. Yes, I too . . . continually deal with the question of the strengthening of the army and navy and I know how things are with you'. He added: 'The Central Committee of the Party is taking measures so that you will need for nothing'. It was a necessary gesture. 'The personal participation of Comrade L. I. Brezhnev in the recent conference of Soviet army and navy commanders in the Kremlin was a vivid new manifestation of the Party's concern for the army and navy', readers were assured.[62] How far this went to appease discontent among the military is a matter of debate. But it gives one a real sense of the difficulty faced by Soviet leaders in devising policies which clashed with the priorities of the military, and this applied to negotiations at Geneva no less than to other vital matters. Here the Russians had made no decisive shift in their position despite the fact that only a year remained before Cruise and Pershing II missiles were due to be deployed in Western Europe.

The Soviet leadership were constrained by concern not to alienate the military by making concessions at Geneva but only too aware of the deadline approaching. One indication of increased concern came two days before Brezhnev's speech, when Shaposhnikov took direct operational control over supervision of World Peace Council activities in Western Europe by formally becoming head of the Central Committee International Department's West European section on 25 October, just prior to the meeting of the WPC Presidential Committee on 30 October—2 November.[63] 'Time is running out. The year 1983 is crucial . . . The power and success of the struggle for peace depend upon the unity of peace forces, notwithstanding the differences of viewpoint and respecting the independence of each', the Committee pleaded.[64]

The speech to the military had been Brezhnev's last public performance. Since early 1977 he had been increasingly debilitated. On the morning of 10 November 1982 his heart finally gave out. Two days later a Central Committee plenum approved Yuri Andropov's appointment as General Secretary. Andropov's top priority was the reform of the economy: 'the Party is guided by Lenin's far-sighted injunction that we exercise our main influence on the world revolutionary process through our economic policy', he told a Central Committee plenum on 22 November.[65] 'It is easy to see that the greater our successes, the stronger our economy, the better the state of affairs in our national economy, the stronger will be our international positions', he told workers of the Sergo Ordzhonikidze machine-tool plant at the end of January 1983.[66]

6.7 ANDROPOV TAKES POWER

Andropov's statements indicated that domestic economic reform was his first priority. But he had long been involved in foreign policy matters. From the Central Committee secretariat in 1953 he had been transferred to the Foreign Ministry as head of the Fourth European Department. In 1954 he was appointed Soviet ambassador to Hungary, where he proved his worth during the uprising in 1956. In 1957 he was appointed head of the Central Committee's International Liaison Department (dealing with foreign Communist Parties). From 1962 to 1967 he served as a secretary of the Central

Committee and then became head of the KGB, where he served until May 1982. It is interesting to note that his transfer back to the Central Committee apparatus at that time coincided with Brezhnev's shift of priorities away from the military and towards the consumer.[67] As former head of the KGB he may well have had excessive expectations for the progress of the peace movement in Western Europe. For although there was a shift under his direction towards an accommodation over theatre nuclear forces, Andropov proved unable or unwilling to make sufficient concessions to secure a settlement which alone could have prevented the arrival of US deployments in Europe.

By the time Andropov came to power, the INF talks were at impasse. Neither the military in Moscow nor the US Defense Department were prepared to countenance a 'walk-in-the-woods' solution. Moreover, the Soviet military not only sounded increasingly pessimistic, they also came close to stating openly their opinion that the negotiations themselves were useful only to the Americans, as a screen behind which the US Government was making long-planned preparations for the deployment of Cruise and Pershing in Europe. 'If the United States does not develop in a constructive direction, then the Soviet Union will naturally have no reason to develop its own position further, and the talks will become deadlocked. I would say they are already approaching this condition,' warned Colonel-General Nikolai Chervov, spokesman for the Soviet General Staff, on 3 November, a week before Brezhnev's demise.[68] Then no sooner had Andropov come to power than Marshal Ustinov went one step further in an interview with TASS published on 7 December. Having accused the Reagan administration of seeking military superiority over the USSR, the Defence Minister said: 'And we are more and more coming to doubt the sincerity of the USA's intention to reach a mutually acceptable agreement at the talks in Geneva on medium-range weapons. Willy-nilly, one reaches the conclusion that the American side, using the "zero-option" as a cloak in the negotiations, is in actual fact building a case for the full-scale deployment of its new missiles in Europe'.[69]

These were not propitious conditions for Andropov to launch a new initiative. But to forestall the arrival of the US missiles, the only means open to the Russians were either to entice or cajole the Europeans into rejecting or at the very least postponing deployment on their territory. Andropov's policy combined both elements. On 21 December, in a speech at the Kremlin marking the 60th anniversary of the formation of the USSR, Andropov announced that 'We are prepared . . . to accept that the Soviet Union would keep in Europe only as many missiles as England and France possess and not one more. This means that the Soviet Union would cut hundreds of missiles, including more than one dozen of the most up-to-date missiles, which the West calls the SS-20.'[70] In an interview with an American journalist, which appeared in *Pravda* ten days later, Andropov added that 'as to aircraft, we are for complete equality at a significantly lower level than now'.[71] This would have meant an end to Cruise and Pershing II in Europe. It certainly gave the British pause for thought. On the day following Andropov's original announcement, 22 December, the Soviet chargé d'affaires in London, Dolgov, called in at the Foreign Office in order to clarify the offer. The Foreign Office, then under the Prime Minister's rival, the pliant Francis Pym, was sympathetic: Andropov's proposal was described as a 'step in the right direction'.[72] Yet on 23 December the tough-minded Margaret Thatcher ended any such optimism by making clear that she still stood behind the United States which, like France, spurned Moscow's latest gesture.[73]

The scuttling of the offer by the NATO Powers was a blow, but some compensation could be found in its impact on West European public opinion. Pressure on the Americans to offer something more than the unconvincing zero-option had been mounting within West Germany, in particular since the autumn. The Andropov proposal accelerated a process already in motion. The opposition Social Democrats suggested that the inclusion of British and French nuclear forces in the INF account was not an unreasonable demand. The Free Democrats, in uneasy coalition with the Christian Democrats under Chancellor Helmut Kohl, were anxious about the elections forthcoming on 6 March 1983. They now broke ranks.

In a press conference on 5 January 1983 Foreign Minister and leader of the Free Democrats Hans-Dietrich Genscher openly pressed for an 'interim' agreement in place of the zero option.[74] Barely a week later in a speech to the European Parliament at Strasbourg he emphasised that all proposals from the USSR and the Warsaw Pact should be given 'serious and careful scrutiny'; every negotiating opportunity should be exploited. Genscher was insistent on the need to meet the demands of the growing anti-nuclear movement in Europe.[75] The existence of the movement, the initial hesitancy of the British and the dissonant voices in West Germany's coalition gave Andropov some cause for hope. He needed it. The

United States was immovable. Moreover, the East European allies were unenthusiastic when the Russians raised the issue of counter-measures—such as the forward deployment of operational-tactical nuclear missiles—in retaliation for the deployment of Cruise and Pershing II missiles. The matter was tabled at the Prague meeting of the Warsaw Pact on 4–5 January.[76] Once again, as in Brezhnev's latter days, it took a joint communiqué from the Politburo, the Presidium of the Supreme Soviet and the Council of Ministers, to underline the unity of opinion in the Kremlin on these delicate issues.[77] Moreover, some indication of sharp exchanges between the Russians and their subordinates at the Prague meeting was evident in Andropov's acknowledgment of the 'candid character of the discussion'.[78] Here lay further incentive for the USSR to reach a deal on INF: NATO was not the only alliance system disrupted by the SS-20 problem.

Moscow was making a special effort to appear reasonable. On 11 January Karpov (leading the Soviet delegation to START) and Kvitsinsky told members of a 13-man Congressional delegation in Moscow that the Soviets would 'consider destruction of the missiles' withdrawn under the Andropov scheme.[79] On the following day Andropov confirmed as much in conversation with Hans-Jochen Vogel, SPD candidate for Chancellor in the forthcoming election.[80] This was intended to meet certain Western misgivings about the 21 December offer. Certainly Andropov was having some impact.

From Moscow Vogel went on to Paris but was given short shrift by fellow socialist, President François Mitterand. The French, whose equivocal position within the Western alliance was now more than compensated for by their unexpected eagerness to maintain NATO's firm stand, now began exerting pressure on Bonn not to break ranks. Gromyko had been in Bonn from 16–19 January 1983 in an indelicate attempt to dissuade the West Germans from deployment, empha-sising the need for the Federal Republic to follow its 'own interests' and maintain 'good relations with the USSR', and threatening that the USSR would increase its theatre nuclear capability should the INF talks fail. No sooner had Gromyko left than Mitterand called on his neighbours across the Rhine to hold firm. 'The common resolution of members of the Alliance and their solidarity must accordingly be strengthened with all clarity in order for the Geneva negotiations to lead to success', the French President told a special session of the Bundestag.[81]

Despite Mitterand's warning both the West Germans and the

British continued to dissent from the declared US position. A further blow came on 23 January when leading conservative Franz-Josef Strauss, former Defence Minister and head of the Christian Social Union(CSU), publicly ridiculed the zero-option as 'unattainable' and 'absurd'.[82] Kohl now found it difficult if not impossible to continue as before. On the following day and after a meeting with Nitze—en route to Geneva for the re-opening of the talks on 27 January— Defence Minister and Christian Democrat Manfred Wörner qualified his government's enthusiasm for the zero-option by adding that the Western position was not one of 'all or nothing', that the West was prepared to be flexible.[83] Then on 25 January Britain's Foreign Secretary Pym announced on television that he was considering an 'intermediate' agreement which would settle for a reduction of missiles on both sides.[84]

The Americans were becoming increasingly isolated from their allies, who were under pressure from their own public opinion, and Nitze was increasingly alarmed at the consequences for the cohesion of the alliance. On 30 March Reagan announced his hope that the Russians 'will at least join us in an interim agreement that would substantially reduce these forces [INF] to equal levels on both sides . . . we are prepared to negotiate an interim agreement in which the United States would substantially reduce its planned deployment of Pershing II and ground-launched Cruise missiles, provided the Soviet Union reduce the number of its warheads on longer-range INF missiles to an equal level on a global basis'.[85] The US administration had come around to endorsing the spirit of the walk in the woods proposals, though Reagan remained adamant that the Pershing II should not be sacrificed in its entirety.

But the Russians had rejected that package and, still immobilised by opposition from the military and other hardliners, they were just as likely to reject the latest offer for three main reasons: first, there was to be no compensation for British and French forces; second, dual-capable aircraft were to be excluded (which meant those forward-based systems still of some concern to the military); and third, the Americans were still insistent on reducing the SS-20s targeted on Asia without also limiting existing US nuclear-capable forces in the Pacific as well as Chinese forces, all of which played a role in determining the balance of power in the region. These objections were initially pointed out by Kvitsinsky to Nitze the day before Reagan's speech;[86] they were reiterated by Gromyko at a press conference on 2 April. The interim option was 'unacceptable',

Gromyko insisted.[87] And Gromyko's was the more moderate position. Within the Soviet apparatus itself opposition to the continuation of these negotiations had been welling up for months. The belated and disappointing Reagan offer did nothing to stem the tide. Opinion dissenting from the declared position of the Soviet leadership had been expressed in the form of a question from Soviet citizens published in *Argumenty i Fakty* on 22 February, an indirect but nevertheless significant airing of discontent with the official line:

> From newspaper reports it is known that, in the negotiations on the questions of limiting and reducing nuclear arms, the USA's delegations have been taking an unconstructive position, trying to thrust upon the USSR agreements which would bring about a change in the correlation of forces to the advantage of imperialism. Furthermore, they are 'stalling for time' and openly trying to use the very fact of the negotiations to cool down the anti-war demonstrations in Europe and the USA, to mollify public opinion.
>
> In such a situation would it not be better for the Soviet Union to break off negotiations and wait until an administration with a realistic cast of mind comes to power in the USA, and then continue the negotiations?[88]

Marshal Ustinov would have concurred. On a visit to East Germany at the head of a military delegation from the USSR, he not only restated Gromyko's remarks, but he also warned all West Europeans that a Soviet retaliatory strike against countries accepting the new US missiles would very likely be fatal for those concerned. This took place on 6 April.[89] That same day the Committee of Foreign Ministers of the Warsaw Pact met in Prague to review INF and other issues. With this we see the extent of disagreement in the East. The tone of the subsequent communiqué issued on 7 April had little or nothing in common with Gromyko's statements, let alone Ustinov's bluster. The Warsaw Pact Foreign Ministers all concurred that 'the forces of peace' were still 'more powerful than the forces of war' despite the 'far-reaching escalation of imperialist policy'. And in place of Ustinov's menaces there was repeated emphasis on the importance of developing 'bilateral contacts with states belonging to the North Atlantic Treaty Alliance'.[90] Nothing could have been further from the views of dissentient hawks in the Soviet Union. If, as seems likely, the Russians were still attempting to squeeze a commitment to retaliatory measures from their clients and subordinates in the Warsaw Pact, they were greatly disappointed.

These efforts by the Russians came to the attention of the Western press only later, in the summer of 1983, a difficult summer for the Soviet leadership and for Andropov personally: his hospitalisation in March for treatment of heart and kidneys indicated that his spell in power might prove all too brief. Nonetheless on the foreign front he had continued to stagger on with further refinements of the existing Soviet negotiating position: hammering home Soviet opposition to the interim solution, ridiculing the Western stance on British and French weapons, damning the one-sided proposals on the Asian SS-20s, and threatening the West Germans with 'the most severe consequences', all addressed in an interview with *Der Spiegel* on 19 April.[91]

6.8   RESISTANCE FROM EASTERN EUROPE

As the *Spiegel* interview indicates, Andropov's policy contained both 'carrots' and 'sticks'. On the one hand he had increased the flexibility of the Soviet position, though not to the extent that Kvitsinsky and more *détente*-minded elements would have liked; on the other hand, he was attempting to raise the costs of non-compliance for the West. The balance was important. The trouble was that his Warsaw Pact subordinates stubbornly refused to subscribe to the threatened counter-measures. They did not see it as in their interests to raise the temperature further in Europe. It was implicit in their position that the Russians had gone too far in attempting to safeguard their own security at the expense of others. Even the normally compliant East Germans proved obstructive. On 3 March *Neues Deutschland* had published extracts from PCI leader Enrico Berlinguer's speech, in which he 'said that in medium-range weapons in Europe there is possibly an imbalance to the advantage of the USSR'.[92] Erich Hönecker, general secretary of the SED (Communist Party equivalent) and chairman of the East German state council, then arrived in Moscow on 3 May for a four-day visit. Despite the fact that the atmosphere of the visit was described as one of 'fraternal friendship and complete mutual understanding', this was a rather luke-warm attribute in the Soviet lexicon. Although Andropov used the opportunity to announce further flexibility on INF, he did not succeed in winning the East Germans around to his position in respect of counter-measures against NATO in the event of Cruise and Pershing II deployment. 'The Soviet Union', he announced, 'stated its readiness to have in Europe not one missile more, not one aircraft more than the countries of NATO have today. We are told that in this case the Soviet Union would have more nuclear warheads on the missiles. Fine, we are prepared to agree upon an equality of nuclear capabilities in Europe, both in respect of launchers and in respect of warheads, taking into account, however, the relevant armaments of England and France . . . In so far as the number of warheads on English and French missiles is reduced, so too will the number of warheads on our medium-range missiles be reduced.' But Andropov also spoke for his visitors in asserting that should deployment of Cruise and Pershing II occur, 'a chain reaction' would be 'inevitable': 'The USSR, the GDR, [and] other countries belonging to the Warsaw Pact would have to take counter-measures', he warned.[93]

But the GDR, among others, had not agreed to such counter-measures. Instead of referring to East German support for these actions, Hönecker took the opportunity to stress his country's support for the Soviet negotiating position at Geneva (the proposals on the table) and laid heavy emphasis, indeed unusual emphasis, upon the Warsaw Pact position enunciated at the Prague meeting in April. He also went out of his way to mention the growth of 'resistance' to Cruise and Pershing II deployment within Western Europe, and played up the importance of establishing a nuclear-free zone in Europe.[94] By the time Hönecker was due to depart on 7 May, he had still not surrendered to Andropov's position. The joint communiqué published on 8 May thus reflected East German priorities in referring to 'the massive significance' of the Warsaw Pact declaration of the previous month, and made mention of only 'the Soviet Union', not the USSR *and* the Warsaw Pact, taking counter-measures in the event of deployment of Cruise and Pershing II.[95] Despite the fact that only a few days later a commentator in *Pravda* referred to counter-measures by both the Soviet Union and the Warsaw Pact, the East Germans and the East Europeans had yet to be brought into line on this delicate issue.[96]

On 28 May, as statesmen from Britain, Canada, France, West Germany, Italy, Japan and the USA gathered at Williamsburg for their annual summit, the Soviet Government thus adopted an ambiguous turn of phrase in warning that should Cruise and Pershing II be deployed, the USSR would not only end its moratorium but that 'The need would also arise . . . to deploy additional weapons with the aim of establishing a necessary counter-balance to the increase in the USA's forward-based nuclear systems in Europe and in the nuclear weapons of other NATO countries, by agreement with other states belonging to the Warsaw Pact'.[97] That agreement had yet to be obtained.

By the time the Party Central Committee gathered in Moscow for a plenary session on 14 June preparations were already under way for the deployment of Cruise and Pershing II in Western Europe. But the Russians had still to obtain the consent of their allies for the forward basing of operational-tactical missiles on their territory. Moreover, Andropov reportedly faced the plenum with a divided Politburo behind him,[98] a situation reflected in contradictory statements released on the eve of the plenum concerning prospects for a resolution of the INF issue: on 11 June the Russians were quoted as saying an agreement 'still can and must be found'; on 12 June they were quoted as ruling out any chance of agreement.[99] Then in his address to the plenum on 15 June Andropov omitted any mention of the INF problem. He did, however, expatiate at length on the importance of unity within the diversity of the Warsaw Pact camp, and went out of his way to assure the military that defence capabilities would be enhanced.[100]

The failure to mobilise the Warsaw Pact left a hole gaping in the Soviet negotiating position which was not compensated for by the peace movement in the West. Moreover, the Western peace movement had begun to extend its influence unofficially into Eastern Europe. Pressure on the allies to conform to Soviet wishes mounted. They were asked to attend a one-day meeting in Moscow on 28 June—the eve of a visit to the Soviet capital by the recently re-elected West German Chancellor Kohl, due on 4 July. The aim was clearly to have the Pact in agreement on retaliatory measures in order to exert maximum pressure on West Germany. Four days before the Pact assembled, an editorial appeared in *Pravda* ominously entitled 'Unity and Solidarity'. Elaborating on appropriate sections of Andropov's speech to the plenum, the editorial not only dealt with the importance of CMEA economic integration but also, and rather enigmatically, stressed that it was important for ruling Communist Parties to react deftly to changes 'at home and abroad': 'There is nothing that the enemies of socialism would like better than to undermine the trust, sow discord, between our peoples and parties'. Clearly this was more than an oblique reference to the Polish Crisis; it applied also to inter-Party and inter-state relations.[101]

The Soviet military were less tactful. Referring to the threat of Cruise and Pershing II deployment in an address to graduates of the military academies on 27 June—the day before the Warsaw Pact summit—Marshal Ustinov attempted to pre-empt the decisions of the forth-coming meeting by wilfully re-interpreting the ambiguously phrased Soviet Government statement of 28 May to mean Pact acquiescence in Soviet counter-measures: 'In the announcement', he said, '. . . it is clearly stated that it [the Soviet Government] will take counter-measures together with its friends'.[102]

But when 'its friends' assembled on 28 June the Soviet Govern-ment suffered a major setback once again. In a phrase at odds with the thrust of Soviet strategy towards Western Europe, Warsaw Pact leaders condemned 'the false thesis that the expansion of military power can serve the interests of peace and the security of nations [*narodov*]'. The allies could agree that they should not permit the establishment of Western military superiority. What they would not agree upon was how to prevent such an eventuality. Moreover, the resultant communiqué made no mention of the 'atmosphere' at the meeting; such an omission is extremely unusual and supports the conclusion drawn by foreign diplomats in Moscow at the time that the discussion had deteriorated to a point where no euphemisms could hide the blatant differences of view.[103] Indeed the Novosti press agency went out of its way to deny any discord on the subject of counter-measures. On 30 June it lamely argued that 'There is no need to talk now about possible reprisals because the socialist coun-tries are prepared to fight for the very rapid success of the Geneva negotiations. They have not lost hope for an accord acceptable to all'.[104]

By the end of the summer differences between the Russians and their allies were no nearer resolution. They were still evident at a dinner given on 20 July in Moscow for Hungary's Party Secretary Janos Kadar, the most enlightened among the leaders of Eastern Europe. Whereas Andropov sounded a pessimistic note—'the conse-quences of a military and political character which would substan-tially complicate the entire situation in the world' should Cruise and Pershing II be deployed—Kadar played up the prospects for agreement with the West. To him this was 'a real, achievable goal'. And, interestingly, like the hardliners in Moscow, though to different purpose, Kadar rested his case on the growth of the peace movement in Western Europe: 'In the most advanced capitalist countries increasingly broad sections of the public are joining the ranks of anti-

war and anti-nuclear movements', he asserted.[105] To the hardliners in
Moscow this was an argument against the need to negotiate; to the
Hungarians it gave hope for the progress of the negotiations.

Kadar's optimism was scarcely justified. The peace movement's
bark was louder than its bite. Moreover, the Soviet military, among
others, were still obdurate. They insisted that 'the Soviet Union in
any event must and will have an equivalent' to British and French
systems.[106] But particularly after Thatcher's successful re-election in
June 1983 it was most unlikely that London would concede. The
British were still turning somersaults in order to make some sense
of their position. The updating of their Polaris submarines with the
Chevaline refit was complete by 1982—raising the number of
warheads targeting the USSR—and in July 1980 the British had
announced their decision to purchase the advanced Trident
submarine from the United States.[107] The fiction of an independent
nuclear deterrent was now even more difficult to sustain. With barely
a leg to stand on Britain's Defence Minister Michael Heseltine told
the House of Commons on 12 July 1983 that he had indeed 'included
the British Polaris system in the balance between the Soviet forces
and the NATO alliance'. But, he was at pains to point out: 'The
important point is that we have included it under the heading of
strategic systems, not under intermediate range systems, to which
the Geneva talks are directed'.[108] Ironically, while covering one set
of tracks with no great conviction the British simultaneously exposed
another. All of a sudden it appeared that Cruise and Pershing II
were not merely a riposte to the SS-20. Heseltine's deputy at the
Ministry of Defence, Peter Blaker, inadvertently acknowledged to
the House that 'Cruise and Pershing II missiles were intended partly
to replace out-of-date weapons systems such as the Vulcan bomber,
and partly to match the very big build up of SS-20s'.[109] The British
felt a need to justify their anomalous position. The French never
found anything illogical in simultaneously enlarging their nuclear
capabilities and pressing for Cruise and Pershing II in Europe while
claiming France was entirely independent of NATO defence
planning.

In an interview with *Pravda* on 27 August Andropov vented his
frustration at the Reagan administration's position. He also tried to
answer Western complaints that the Russians were counting nuclear
launchers instead of warheads in calculating the INF balance in
Europe. Once again he offered to retain only as many weapons as
France and Britain. He also publicly reaffirmed what had already

been said in private: 'the basic method of reducing medium-range nuclear weapons in Europe would be their dismantling, [their] destruction': this would include 'a significant number of up-to-date missiles, known in the West by the name SS-20'. These assurances were, he acknowledged, at least in part designed to appease the Soviet Union's Far Eastern neighbours: 'It will remove any basis for the anxiety now expressed by China and Japan' concerning the possibility of transferring such SS-20s to Soviet bases in Asia.[110]

These were moves preparatory to the resumption of the INF talks on 6 September, after a summer recess. While Nitze and Kvitsinsky manoeuvred to secure a last-minute compromise the Reagan administration pressed òn with preparations for deployment. The Russians had not yet entirely despaired of making progress but the failure to mobilise their clients into a common front firmly committed to retaliatory measures made their threats unconvincing. Without a clear price to be paid by the West Europeans in the event of deployment, and in the absence of timely concessions to West European anxieties, no progress was likely. The Russians lacked leverage. A meeting of Central Committee secretaries from the Warsaw Pact took place in Moscow on 20 September to discuss international and ideological questions. But once again the Russians failed to secure a collective statement threatening retaliatory measures.[111] The contrast between East European attitudes and those of the Soviet military, in particular, is striking. On 22 September Chief of Staff Marshal Nikolai Ogarkov issued a bellicose statement via TASS entitled 'Peace Needs Reliable Protection': 'Is it really that the lessons of the Second World War have been forgotten in West Germany?', he intoned. He went on to attack 'the sharply increased aggressiveness of international imperialism, Zionism and reaction led by the USA in recent years'; he suggested that 'their actions have been to a large extent reminiscent of the actions of fascism in the thirties'—the sort of militaristic hyperbole indulged in by the Reagan camp.[112]

The Politburo—which met as usual on Thursday 22 September— did not go as far as Ogarkov. But the delay in publishing a summary of the proceedings indicated disagreement at the top, and it is most unlikely that East European resistance to retaliatory measures could have been sustained in the face of a united Soviet leadership. Reference in the summary to the fact that 'the Soviet Union will henceforth take decisive counter-measures to the aggressive plans of imperialism . . . in close co-operation with other countries of the socialist commonwealth' appeared to indicate Moscow had finally closed ranks in its determination to override allied resistance.[113] But this had little immediate effect. Even Marshal Jaruzelski refused to accept deployment of Soviet operational-tactical missiles on Polish territory, and when Warsaw Pact commander Marshal Kulikov visited Romania to draw Ceausescu into line, he was greeted with mass demonstrations calling for a reduction in nuclear missiles in the East as well as the West.[114]

The only country thus far willing to support the Russians was Czechoslovakia. On 26–27 September the Czech Foreign Minister visited Moscow. The communiqué stated that in the event of US deployments 'the USSR, the CSR [Czechoslovakia], [and] other states belonging to the Warsaw Pact will face the need to take counter-measures to guarantee their security . . . Their declarations on this count are known and remain in force', the statement added disingenuously.[115] A meeting of Warsaw Pact Foreign Ministers in Sofia, Bulgaria, on 13–14 October not only failed (once more) to agree upon sanctions against the West in the event of Cruise and Pershing II deployment but also sounded the most conciliatory note so far, emphasising the dangers lying ahead and the importance of forestalling them through negotiation.[116]

The day of reckoning came less than a week later on 20 October when Pact Defence Ministers met in East Berlin. Arguments were apparently fierce: the meeting was euphemistically characterised as 'business-like'. Pointing to Pact declarations of 5 January and 28 June the communiqué argued that 'in spite of the constructive proposals' made by the East, the NATO countries had not only failed to respond positively, they had also continued to facilitate deployment of the American missiles on their territory. The crucial sentence was nevertheless still less than illuminating: 'the Committee of Defence Ministers took the appropriate decision'.[117] The precise nature of that decision was not made public until 25 October. An announcement from the Soviet Ministry of Defence stated that in response to Western preparations for Cruise and Pershing II deployment 'the Soviet Union is obliged to take additional measures to guarantee its own security and the security of its allies in the Warsaw Pact'. The governments of East Germany and Czechoslovakia had agreed to preparatory work 'for the deployment of missile complexes of an operational-tactical type on the territory of the GDR and CSR'.[118]

Having tried and failed to obtain the assent of others for the forward deployment of their missiles elsewhere in Eastern Europe, the Russians settled for a partial solution which nonetheless sat uneasily with both the Czechs and East Germans; rather as in Western Europe, an unequal distribution of the burden of these deployments was a far from satisfactory state of affairs. The East German leadership were clearly unhappy at the prospect of such deployments. Only two days after the Berlin meeting, *Neues Deutschland* published a letter from the congregation of the evangelical church in Dresden-Loschwitz, addressed to Hönecker. The letter expressed 'horror' at the idea not only of American nuclear missiles deployed in Western Europe but also at the initiation of 'analogous nuclear counter-measures on our territory and [that] we and our children will have to live side-by-side [*unmittelbar*] with nuclear missiles'. 'You yourself have repeatedly expressed the opinion that more armaments do not bring more security', the letter accused.[119] Discontent was also apparent in Czechoslovakia. On the day *Rudé Právo* announced the deployment of operational-tactical missiles in Czechoslovakia in the event of Cruise and Pershing II deployment by the United States, a commentator on Prague domestic radio acknowledged that 'As has been shown at numerous recent peace rallies, our general public does not want this dangerous competition because it leads to constant growth of tension and to the possibility of confrontation'.[120] Clearly these protests met with some sympathy within the Czech Party apparatus. Little more than a week later, on 5 November, an article in *Rudé Právo* referred to the 'pile of letters' from the public which included awkward questions such as 'who in fact started this[?]', 'What will the West European peace defenders say?', and as the author of the article acknowledged: 'In some [letters] one can sense the doubt whether the recently announced measures for the strengthening of defense "are necessary already today"; "whether one should not have waited for the deployment of Pershings to take place" . . .' 'If we have missiles, we ourselves will become the target', one reader had written, echoing concerns expressed in Western Europe.[121]

6.9   THE DEADLINE APPROACHES

At Geneva Nitze and Kvitsinsky were still attempting to square the circle. We have the accounts of both as to what precisely occurred. However, there are major differences in interpretation. Both concur that the USSR was in fact willing to cut the number of missile launchers below the figure of 140 (420 warheads) publicly proposed by Andropov in an interview with *Pravda* on 27 October.[122] But there is open disagreement over whether the Russians would be compensated for British and French forces. The two also disagree as to who initiated the new sounding, and whether Nitze also sought to allow for some Cruise and Pershing II missiles in the final balance.[123] But a report from Washington in *The Times* of 19 November stated: 'The Reagan Administration yesterday rejected the new informal Soviet offer to reduce to 120 the number of Soviet missiles aimed at Western Europe, saying that it would still leave Moscow with a sizeable monopoly of intermediate-range nuclear force missiles'. With this the talks broke down irreparably. By now the first Cruise missiles were already arriving at Greenham Common in England. The Russians sounded increasingly shrill. The WPC Bureau met in Athens on 18–20 November. *Peace Courier* duly appeared with the headline '*WPC Bureau Demands:* STOP THE MISSILES—HALT REAGAN'S DRIVE TO WAR'. But its message was also awkwardly defensive. Unity was vital: 'This unity is particularly important not least because the peace movement is operating under conditions of extreme difficulty. The slanderous defamations levelled at it by its enemies, presenting the movement as being manipulated by one side, need to be met forcefully'.[124]

West Germany's Foreign Minister Genscher had stated that if no agreement had been reached by 21 November his government would proceed with deployment. As water-cannon kept demonstrators back from the building, the Bundestag held its final debate on the issue and decided on deployment. On 23 November the meeting of the two delegations at Geneva lasted only 20 minutes. 'During the meeting the delegation of the USSR announced the discontinuation of the present round of talks without setting any date for their resumption', TASS announced.[125] Two days later Andropov issued a statement to the effect that talks could resume only if the Cruise and Pershing II missiles were withdrawn.[126]

Throughout the negotiations the Russians worked under the illusion that although they were negotiating under duress—the threatened deployment of US missiles by December 1983—they were not in fact negotiating from a position of weakness. Hopes of growing 'inter-imperialist contradictions' on the one level and illusions about the real strength and impact of the West European peace movements on another level all proved misleading as a guide to tactics at Geneva. Similarly, throughout the talks the Americans—Nitze in particular—

increasingly felt that, with West European support for deployment slipping, with conflicts of interest growing between the British and the French on the one hand and the West Germans on the other, plus the mobilisation of West European public opinion by the anti-nuclear cause, the United States was not negotiating from a position of strength. It was in fact the Russians who were negotiating from weakness. For all its scope and power, the peace movement in Western Europe never lived up to expectations; NATO held together; and the East Europeans gave the Russians more trouble than they were accustomed to.

7 Reversing from the Cul-de-Sac, 1984–87

7.1 THE DECISION TO NEGOTIATE

One of the main problems during these years was the fact that due to the advanced age of the Soviet leadership there was both too much and too little continuity in the direction of policy: too much in the sense that the core of the leadership had remained the same since the high-point of the Brezhnev era when a firm consensus had been formed; too little in the sense that the post of General Secretary changed hands all too frequently from 1982 to 1985, and that the reigning General Secretary was often too infirm to rule, far less impose innovations in foreign or domestic policy. The changes that did occur were more apparent than real, more a matter of words than deeds. This was perhaps most evident with respect to the problem of nuclear weapons in Europe.

By walking out of the INF and START negotiations at the end of 1983 in retaliation against the decision by NATO to deploy Cruise and Pershing II missiles in Western Europe, the Russians had not slammed all the doors behind them as they left. Less than a week before the talks broke up, but at a time when their collapse seemed inevitable, Chief Editor of *Pravda* Viktor Afanas'ev gave his 'personal opinion' that 'if these negotiations are ended, and this will probably be the case, then there will certainly be negotiations again, but at another level and taking into consideration the fact that new missiles have been deployed. When such negotiations will take place, and at what level, that I cannot tell you. But there will be negotiations . . . because controversies cannot be solved by force but only through negotiations and compromise, and we are ready for that'.[1]

But how ready were they? The Powers were due to meet in Stockholm at the initiative of the French in order to discuss 'confidence-building measures' in Europe. But, still licking their wounds, the Russians denied any interest in discussing more than the limited

141

issue of confidence-building measures when Gromyko met Shultz on 18 January 1984.[2] Not only did the Soviet Government move to deploy SS-12 (model 2) and SS-23 operational-tactical missiles in Czechoslovakia and East Germany, they also constructed more SS-20 bases in 1984 than in any other year.[3] The Russians were in fact still operating under the old assumptions. And the death of Andropov from kidney failure in the afternoon of 9 February further complicated matters. What is remarkable is less that he died than that he had remained politically active at all through most of the previous year while on hemodialysis.[4] His death left no easy succession.

The rising star was the relatively young Mikhail Gorbachev. Born on 2 March 1931 into the household of a Party member who worked on a collective farm in Stravropol province in the rich but famine-smitten Caucasus region, Gorbachev was a beneficiary of the Stalin era and its rapid social mobility, though he has since been critical of the arbitrary abuse of power which accompanied collectivisation of agriculture and high-speed industrialisation. He rose from being a mere farm-worker through an outstanding labour record to a much sought-after place at Moscow University's Law Faculty. Zdenek Mlynař, the Czech émigré, who was 'good friends' with Gorbachev at the university from 1950 to 1955, and in touch with him until 1968 when the Russians invaded Czechoslovakia, describes Gorbachev as a pragmatist yet a man of principle, very intelligent, open and self-confident without being arrogant, 'a man who attributes much more importance to his own experience, lived and felt, than to what is offered him on paper.'[5] It was clearly these qualities which led to rapid advancement. After spending just over a decade rising up the Party apparatus in Stavropol, he became a voting member of the Central Committee in Moscow in 1971. In 1978 he was appointed Central Committee secretary responsible for agriculture. In the following year he was also made a candidate (non-voting) member of the ruling Politburo and in 1980 a full, voting member. Unencumbered by the practices of the past, open to new ideas and critical of the stagnation which had settled in during the Brezhnev years, Gorbachev held the greatest promise. But it was evidently this very attribute which hardened the determination of others to block his path to supreme power. Instead the Politburo agreed on a compromise candidate, Konstantin Chernenko, who was unfortunately only marginally healthier than his predecessor and certainly no innovator;

a man more likely to work within the consensus than strike out in new and risky directions.

Under Chernenko many of the reforms initiated by Andropov were allowed to lie fallow. At Geneva the Russians had painted themselves into a corner. And the ageing Gromyko—increasingly bewildered by the extent and complexity of the demands placed upon him—was not the man to unthread the policies of the past and ease his country out of its accumulated international difficulties. His Americocentric vision meant any changes made were more likely to be directed at the United States than Western Europe. And with respect to the United States Gromyko certainly favoured negotiations but not if that also meant conceding positions built up during the era of *détente*. It would therefore take a bolder hand from above to force through the reversal of Soviet policy as a means of appeasing the West.

The catalyst was Moscow's increasing alarm at the prospect of a US-Soviet arms race in outer space when resources were badly needed for the renovation of the Soviet economy. At a time when the Soviet economy was staggering ahead and the US economy was bounding forward, in March 1983 President Reagan had announced the Strategic Defense Initiative (SDI). The SDI was promulgated in somewhat unreal terms as a system that would defend populations as well as forces from nuclear attack. But Reagan acknowledged that such a system might appear menacing to the Soviet Union if the shield were built while the United States retained its sword.[6] Even so, the Reagan vision seemed so hopelessly impracticable that the Russians appeared in no hurry to seek counter-measures. By the spring of 1984, however, there could be no doubt that he meant what he said. Worse still, the US Government was also upgrading its strategic counterforce capabilities. Clearly a new round of the arms race was in prospect at an even higher level of technology. We have no knowledge of what took place in Moscow during these momentous months. But it appears that those who believed the Soviet Union's disastrous economic performance required fundamental reforms and that fundamental reforms required *détente* with the United States argued that, since there was no way the Russians could compete in the nuclear arms race with the Americans, some form of negotiation was required, and these negotiations should be opened before the SDI became a reality.

Impressed by Reagan's resolve and uneasy at lack of contact with the United States, on 29 June 1984 the Soviet Government took the crucial step of proposing negotiations on the prohibition of the militarisation of outer space and observance of a moratorium on the testing and deployment of such weapons once the talks opened. It suggested Vienna as the meeting place and September as the date— the eve of the US presidential election. By now Soviet impatience was hard to hide. 'Considering the urgency and importance of the question, the Soviet Government expects a speedy and positive response from the government of the USA', the Russians declared.[7]

The Americans were prompt to respond. But the price for talks was a resumption of the INF negotiations. The US draft was a cunning exercise in studied ambiguity. It suggested the two sides 'discuss and determine mutually acceptable approaches to talks on arms limitations in the areas that cause concern to each side.'[8] 'Since we were eager to have negotiations on space weapons, the Americans figured that they should set a high price', one Soviet official said later.[9] For several weeks the Russians worked to draw the Americans over to their position: to get a commitment from them to ban space weapons. But the Pentagon vehemently opposed negotiating such systems in any forum. The State Department, on the other hand, envisaged the SDI as a bargaining chip which could force asymmetrical reductions on Soviet strategic forces. In Moscow counsels were equally badly divided. The problem was exacerbated by Chernenko's failing health. It left him incapacitated and absent from public life for the better part of July and August.[10] In an effort to smoke out the true US position, on 23 July the Russians put forward a draft joint statement reiterating what they proposed on 29 June. They then publicised these proposals in a Foreign Ministry press briefing.[11] The US Government refused to accept such terms. This left the INF issue unresolved and with little prospect of resolution.

The divisions in Moscow continued even after Chernenko's re-emergence in the public eye. Interviewed by *Pravda* (published on 2 September) he announced that an 'agreement' banning space weapons 'would not only prevent an arms race in outer space but, no less importantly, would facilitate the resolution of the questions of limiting and reducing other strategic weapons. I would particularly underline this.' Yet when questioned on this point First Deputy Head of the Foreign Ministry Press Department, Gromyko's son-in-law Vladimir Lomeiko was evasive.[12] A *Pravda* editorial then appeared on 4 September which failed to make any mention of Chernenko at all despite references to the previous Central Committee plenum.[13] In these uncertain times Reagan's invitation to Gromyko to meet when the Soviet Foreign Minister paid his annual visit to New York to address the UN General Assembly triggered further debate in Moscow. The Russians did not want to appear reluctant to advance the cause of peace but was it in their interests to help in Reagan's re-election by enhancing his doubtful image as a peace-maker? On the other hand, might it not be possible to pin him down as he desperately sought re-election?

The struggle in Moscow took a dramatic turn when on the evening of 6 September it was announced that Marshal Nikolai Ogarkov had been removed from his post as Chief of Staff and Deputy Minister of Defence, reportedly for 'unparty-like behaviour'. This proved extremely significant because when Ustinov died on 20 December Ogarkov was no longer in a position to replace him. Arms control was still the burning issue. Ogarkov had served as the Defence Ministry representative on the SALT delegations. This had given him a pro-*détente* image. However, in 1981 he had begun using Grechko's language in talking about the possibility of fighting and winning a nuclear war. He had since recanted. But his outspokenness did not endear him to Party leaders already at odds with one another, and therefore especially alert to the slightest sign of Bonapartism on the part of the military.[14] Leningrad Party secretary and Politburo member Grigorii Romanov, an outspoken supporter and hardliner, was then in Ethiopia. On his return the battle resumed. Attacks on the Moldavian Party leadership for bureaucratic conservatism began to re-appear in the Soviet press.[15] Under Andropov such attacks were interpreted as an oblique assault on Chernenko because of his close links to the Moldavian Party apparatus.

To those looking for a ray of light from Washington Reagan's speech to the UN General Assembly on 24 September provided it. The President spoke vaguely of the need 'to extend the arms control process to build a bigger umbrella under which it can operate . . . if progess is temporarily halted at one set of talks, this newly established framework for arms control could help us take up the slack at other negotiations.[16] Yet Gromyko's speech to the UN three days later, on 27 September, was unyielding. He did not go as far as Chernenko. The United States had to remove 'the obstacles which they created' before talks on strategic and theatre nuclear weapons could begin.[17] He did, however, visit Reagan in Washington at the end of the month; but the President made no headway trying to persuade Gromyko to drop Soviet preconditions. A perceptive diplomat in Moscow noted: 'it looks as if pro-detente forces in the

Kremlin were powerful enough to force the White House encounter but not strong enough to change entrenched Soviet policies'.[18]

Change was in the wind, however, and these changes were very much associated with Gorbachev's rise to power. By the beginning of October 1984 Western correspondents were reporting that Gorbachev also favoured 'urgent measures to get back to the negotiating table.'[19] And with talk of him as 'the second General Secretary' his influence was very soon evident in Soviet foreign policy. On 18 October the *Washington Post* published an interview with Chernenko in which the General Secretary avoided any mention of Soviet preconditions for talks and referred to the fact that, apart from space weapons, a moratorium on deployments, a test-ban and 'no first use', there were 'other important questions which . . . require resolution, the application of concrete effort'.[20] And when Lomeiko was asked about this on the following day, there was no mention of preconditions for talks; merely the remark that withdrawal of Cruise and Pershing II missiles would be 'common sense'.[21]

Gorbachev's rise to power was now certain. On 23 October a Central Committee plenum effectively relieved him of his cumbersome agricultural portfolio.[22] His new functions were not made explicit but this was evidently because they were all-embracing. There could be no doubt that he was the heir apparent when on 6 November his picture was placed next to that of Chernenko, out of alphabetical order, on the Gorky Street main post-office. Progress to talks with the United States paralleled Gorbachev's own elevation to power. On 26 October—three days after the plenum— Ambassador Anatoly Dobrynin, who, it is now apparent, had long chafed under Gromyko's cautious and restraining hand, approached Secretary of State Shultz with reference to Reagan's UN address. Dobrynin wanted to know precisely how the 'umbrella' talks would proceed. Five days later, on 31 October, this sounding was complemented by Gromyko's own conversation with US Ambassador to Moscow, Arthur Hartman.[23]

On 6 November Reagan won a landslide victory in the US Presidential election. This underscored the importance to the Russians of pressing ahead while the impetus to negotiate still existed. And the terminal illness of Defence Minister Ustinov made any further resistance from the Soviet military less effective. These soundings culminated in a Soviet response on 17 November agreeing to talks on both nuclear and space weapons.[24] The two Powers then announced the news five days later. Shultz and Gromyko would meet on 7–8 January 1985 to set the negotiating agenda.[25] By then Ustinov had died (20 December). His replacement Marshal Sergei Sokolov was denied full membership of the Politburo. Henceforth and throughout the subsequent and dramatic changes in foreign and defence policy the absence of a means of veto by the military made progress all the easier. The Soviet Government had now backed out of the cul-de-sac it had driven into in December 1983, though it had yet to fix on an alternative route.

7.2 RENEWED NEGOTIATIONS AT GENEVA

The Russians approached the Geneva talks warily, and with good reason. Reagan instructed Shultz to spurn any attempt to negotiate constraints on space weapons. Instead the Secretary of State was to urge the Russians to resume the negotiations on limiting intermediate-range and strategic nuclear forces. Should Gromyko insist on discussing the SDI, the US delegation was to seek to persuade them that research into space-based defence could increase nuclear stability.[26] But there was also a bottom-line to the instructions: if the Russians insisted on discussing space weapons, the talks on these would have to be conducted separately from the other subjects. Clearly the Americans were aiming to reduce Soviet intermediate-range and intercontinental missile forces without paying the price of sacrificing the SDI. Soviet interests pointed in precisely the opposite direction. On 3 January 1985 the Politburo agreed on the Soviet position, and in retrospect we can see that they insisted on linkage between progress on offensive missile force reductions and constraints on the SDI programme.[27] Given the conflict of interests between the two sides it is scarcely surprising that when they met in Geneva on 7 January the discussions were, in Gromyko's words, 'very difficult, at times very complex, not to say tense . . . frank in the sense in which this term is used when one speaks of conversations in the course of which the parties do not refrain from saying what they think, completely clearly, not always worrying about being polite'.[28]

Tough though the discussions were, the parties soon agreed on an agenda: the subject of the talks would be 'a complex of questions concerning space and nuclear weapons—strategic and medium-range'. Moreover, 'all these questions' would be 'examined and resolved in their inter-relationship'. The agreed aim included an understanding on the need to prevent 'an arms race in outer space' as well as an end to the one on earth.[29] The meeting was therefore a qualified success from the Soviet viewpoint. The Russians had surrendered their position of 1983 in order to obtain the chance of forestalling implementation of the SDI; the Americans were now obliged to put the SDI on the table in order to renew talks on the limitation of strategic and medium-range weapons. But reactions in Washington left no doubt that the advocates of the SDI—Perle and Secretary of Defense Caspar Weinberger in particular—were unlikely to accept seeing their hopes traded in. Politburo concern was evidently expressed at its meeting on 10 January. Reviewing the Shultz-Gromyko meeting, a summary of the Politburo proceedings stated:

> Opinion was unanimously expressed concerning the importance of the understanding attained at the meeting on the subject and aims of the Soviet-American negotiations on the questions of space and nuclear weapons, which will be examined and resolved in their inter-relationship.
>
> In this respect it was particularly emphasised that only strict observance of the understanding attained, in all its parts, in the course of the forthcoming negotiations, can guarantee real movement forward along the path of ending the arms race, of eliminating the threat of nuclear war and ultimately liquidating nuclear weapons.[30]

Concern about the SDI had not completely eclipsed Soviet concern about Cruise and Pershing II deployment. Although Gromyko had reached agreement with Shultz that space weapons, strategic and medium/intermediate range weapons should be discussed as a whole at the Geneva negotiations, indications that the Americans would turn the talks into 'a seminar' on the value of the SDI reinforced doubts about the wisdom of negotiating away the SS-20 while the Americans continued to deploy the new missiles in Europe. On 13 January Gromyko told Soviet television viewers:

> If the United States continues to deploy its medium-range weapons in Europe, then I must say bluntly that the situation will be made more complicated, and greatly more complicated. The fact that we proposed a freeze on these weapons is well known. Indeed in Geneva we warned the United States quite clearly that, if it did so—if it continued with the deployment; and it was at great pains

to emphasise that it had plans, and that it intended to carry out those plans—then it would put in question the talks that were due to begin in accordance with the understanding reached in Geneva. I repeat—we warned the United States about this.

Gromyko also insisted that in the forthcoming talks 'British and French armaments must be taken into account'. 'It would', he said, 'be most unjustified if the North Atlantic alliance obtained a kind of addition, or a bonus if you like, in the form of the British and French armaments. This is the crux of the disagreement in connexion with the discussion of the medium-range weapons problem.' He also raised the issue of US forward-based aircraft:

> Up to now, during the talks we have held, we have taken six American aircraft carriers into account—aircraft carriers which, by and large, either frequent European waters, for instance the Mediterranean, or which are found near European waters . . . Altogether, and this, at the end of the day, is a well-known fact, the United States has 14 aircraft carriers . . . Each of these aircraft carriers has 40 aircraft which carry nuclear weapons. Each aircraft has two or three nuclear warheads.

Gromyko's motivation for raising the issue was evidently to remind the Americans that if they proved obstructive over SDI, the Russians could be equally obstructive in other areas. 'We intend to keep this [the issue of US aircraft] in reserve', Gromyko warned, ' . . . If the talks go in such a way that the use of this factor is justified, we shall do that; we have the right to do so.'[31] Although he appeared to be concerned primarily with Cruise and Pershing deployments, Gromyko always considered the issue of armaments in Europe secondary. The state of the US-Soviet balance was what counted. Gromyko was concerned about the Eurostrategic balance only when the Americans appeared to be seeking a unilateral advantage in the European theatre in order to circumvent SALT I and II, thereby undermining the principle of equality between the Super-Powers. The West Europeans were, as ever, the mere objects of policy.

On 24 January the Politburo agreed upon the composition of the three-part negotiating team for Geneva: the section on space weapons headed by delegation leader Viktor Karpov, who had participated in SALT I and headed the SALT II team from 1978 and the START team in 1982–83; Yuli Kvitsinsky—promoted to strategic weapons; and Alexei Obukhov—a couple of years junior to Kvitsinsky and with an M.A. from Chicago University but still a veteran of SALT I, II and START—to handle INF.[32] These appointments highlighted the continuity between this and the previous set of talks, despite a stoic attempt to pretend that this set of talks was completely new (in order to camouflage the retreat from the intransigence of November 1983). The Americans were led by Max Kampelman—with no experience of the subject—dealing with SDI; former Senator John Tower, previously chairman of the Armed Services Committee overseeing strategic weapons; and Maynard Glitman, a veteran of the previous talks from the State Department, managing INF.

7.3   GORBACHEV TAKES POWER

The two delegations arrived in Geneva on 10 March. At 7.20 that evening Chernenko died after pulmonary emphysema, chronic hepatitis and cirrhosis finally precipitated heart failure.[33] This made no immediate difference to the negotiating position, which had been settled at a Politburo meeting on 6 March chaired by Gorbachev,[34] but it was to have a momentous impact in the long-run. The communiqué issued at the time of Chernenko's death had stressed 'the collective character' of his leadership.[35] This had resulted in some movement in foreign policy, but not without a good deal of resistance from Chernenko's colleagues, particularly Grigorii Romanov, a hardliner in foreign affairs and a spokesman for the military. In these circumstances Gorbachev's elevation to the post of General Secretary was a controversial move, even if he possessed qualities which men like Molotov could admire. It was Molotov's one-time protegé Gromyko who formally proposed Gorbachev for the post.

The qualities Gromyko cited—plain speaking, strong convictions, a sharp mind, decisiveness—when combined with Gorbachev's interest in world affairs promised fundamental changes in foreign policy. 'He is very good and quick at grasping the essence of the process taking place outside our country, in the international arena. I myself have often been taken aback by the speed and accuracy with which he grasps the essence of things, drawing conclusions, correct Party conclusions', Gromyko rhapsodied.[36] The intelligence was there, the interest was there, and the resolve was there. The experience was not. For two and a half years before becoming

General Secretary, Gorbachev 'had no less than a hundred and fifty meetings and conversations' with a variety of leading figures from all parts of the world. He has since described this as 'major school' for both himself and his colleagues.[37] Yet all of this plus a visit to Cittá del Mare, Italy, in 1971, a brief tour of Canada in 1983 and an even briefer visit to London in 1984 did not add up to much.[38] Even so, without a word of English he made a very favourable impression in Britain on the demanding Mrs Thatcher as firm of ideological conviction but a pragmatist on international questions. He evinced a particular interest in West European issues which reflected and extended a trend growing in Moscow's analysis of the international situation. This amounted to reordering Soviet foreign policy priorities so that issues secondary to the US-Soviet relationship but of primary importance to other Powers, such as Western Europe, would be dealt with by timely concessions. The hallmark of foreign policy under Gorbachev would be a new flexibility, a new realism, dispensing with the legalistic rigidity of the Gromyko school of diplomacy, itself a relic of the Stalin era.

Such innovations in Soviet foreign policy were vital. The Soviet Union needed peace in order to focus on reconstruction at home. The Soviet economy had run aground. Negative rates of growth were problem enough. But the problem was compounded by the fact that at a time when the technological lead held by the West, and indeed by the rising economies of the Far East, was increasing at an alarming pace, the Russians faced the prospect of an arms race with the United States in outer space at yet a higher level of technology. This would place intolerable additional strains on the Soviet economy, already floundering under the enormous weight of existing military expenditure. Indeed the situation was so bad that the Central Committee plenum which met in April 1985 concluded that 'the country finds itself on the verge of a crisis'.[39]

The first faint sign of new thinking in Soviet foreign policy and policy towards Western Europe in particular came when Gorbachev spoke to constituents on 20 February 1985, just before Chernenko's death:

Attributing great significance to the normalisation of relations with the USA, holding honourable negotiations with them on all the current problems of international life, we nonetheless do not for one moment forget that the world is not limited to that country; it amounts to more than that . . . Speaking of the problems of

European detente, the speaker emphasised that the Soviet people believe in the commonsense of the West Europeans, in their own interest in not allowing the transformation of Europe—our common home—into a theatre of military activity, into a testing ground for trying out Pentagon doctrines of 'limited' nuclear war. We note with satisfaction the striving of many West European states towards political dialogue. For its part the USSR was and remains dedicated to a policy of good-neighbourly relations between all European states.[40]

What was new and significant here was the deliberate emphasis on the importance of relations with Western Europe. The trouble was that the Russians had been far too active during 1979–84 trying only too clumsily to wrench apart the West Europeans from their American allies without offering any serious compensation in return. Brezhnev, Andropov and Chernenko had talked the language of accommodation towards Western Europe, but with the Soviet military always determining the bottom line of concessions for military *détente* in Europe and with the Foreign Ministry under Gromyko holding firm for fear of giving the Americans an advantage without anything concrete in return, the West Europeans had little reason to take Gorbachev seriously.

At first—with Gorbachev intent on consolidating control over the Party and state and with the programme for economic reform the highest priority—no real movement occurred. The INF talks began in Geneva on 28 March 1985. The substance initially remained secret. As a gesture, on 7 April the Russians announced a unilateral moratorium on the deployment of nuclear weapons in Europe.[41] But no progress was made. The Russians had already built more SS-20 bases in 1984 than in any other year. Moreover, the Soviet Government maintained its position of 1983: insistence on compensation for British and French warheads and removal of Cruise and Pershing II. Gorbachev made this much clear at a Kremlin dinner in honour of Italian President Bettino Craxi on 29 May.[42] The Americans, too, had not moved from their 1983 position: removal of the SS-20 or the maintenance of a balance between Cruise, Pershing II and the SS-20, with neither British nor French weapons counted in. 'Obviously, this is no basis for agreement', *Pravda* insisted, three days before talks resumed on 30 May.[43] This round—ending 16 July—also resulted in nothing. The lack of American willingness to discuss restrictions on the SDI gave the Russians no incentive to move on INF, at least within their customary framework of thought. The futility of continuing within this framework was becoming increasingly apparent. A necessary precondition to any major change in both the substance and form of Soviet diplomacy was not merely the suppression of opposition from the military—and the removal of Romanov from the Politburo on 1 July followed by the enforced resignation of chief of the main political administration of the armed forces General Yepishev saw to that[44]—but also the removal of the ageing Gromyko. Gromyko epitomised the rigidity of the last Brezhnev years. 'It is difficult, of course, to speak about flexibility or the absence of it when one is talking about Great Powers, about disagreements between them on the core questions of war and peace', Gromyko writes unrepentantly in his memoirs.[45] He was thus tactfully promoted to the largely decorative position of Chairman of the Presidium of the Supreme Soviet on 2 July. In his place Gorbachev put Eduard Shevardnadze, a Georgian, a fellow reformer with as little experience of the outside world as the General Secretary.[46] This ensured that control of foreign policy would be in Gorbachev's own hands, a move reminiscent of Stalin's substitution of Molotov for Litvinov in May 1939.

7.4 NEW APPROACH TO WESTERN EUROPE

Signs of a new policy immediately began to appear, particularly with respect to Western Europe. On 9 July talks were held in the Kremlin between select members of the two committees on foreign affairs of the Supreme Soviet and members of Britain's House of Commons Foreign Affairs Committee. Chairman of the Council of Nationalities Foreign Affairs Committee, Candidate Politburo member and head of the Central Committee International Department Boris Ponomarev suggested: 'To the extent that the countries of the EEC act as "a political whole", we are ready to seek a common language with it . . . on concrete international questions'.[47] This was a novelty. Never before had a senior Soviet official suggested treating the EEC as 'a political whole' and it is doubtful whether it was Ponomarev's own idea. Such ideas emanated principally from the Institute of World Economy and International Relations (IMEMO), then under the direction of Alexander Yakovlev (1983–85), former Ambassador to Canada (1973–83), and a man known to be the advocate of a less

Americocentric foreign policy. At IMEMO the intellectual inspiration behind this more serious approach to the EEC was none other than the former head of the Foreign Office's American Department and spy for the Soviet Union, Donald Maclean. Reviewing a collective work on the political aspects of West European integration produced at the Institute where Maclean directed research, M. Maksimova concluded with an epitaph for the man 'who was at the source of this work, who was its main initiator, organiser and soul of the collective of authors . . . doctor of history D. D. Maclean. . . .'[48]

The Russians were thus taking the EEC more seriously as a political actor in the international system. A more troubling issue was whether this was a positive or a negative development. Viewed purely from the Marxist-Leninist viewpoint, the EEC was clearly a bad thing. It represented the integration of monopoly capital and strengthened the power of capital collectively against the power of labour. But Soviet foreign policy did not rest exclusively on a class analysis. The issue for foreign policy-makers was whether the trend towards an all-West European foreign and defence policy would represent a threat to Soviet state interests by strengthening the foundations of NATO or represent a gain to Soviet interests by creating a barrier to US power in Europe. Although almost all Soviet commentators concluded that it was a bad thing from the vantage-point of Soviet interests, it did at least promise to complicate the American ability to have its way in Europe, as it had in the earlier years of the Cold War. The first sign of this more open-minded approach appeared on 'Studio 9', a television programme, on 31 March 1984. The panel were reviewing attempts in Western Europe to revive the West European Union as the basis for collaboration on defence matters exclusive of the Americans. Vitaly Zhurkin, deputy director of the Institute of the USA and Canada (ISKAN), argued that this meant more rearmament; he could see only the negative side to these initiatives. The perceptive Nikolai Shishlin, deputy head of the Central Committee International Information Department, also an Americanist, saw something intriguing about these developments. 'This fact is very, very curious. It would seem that, on the one hand, it is not a good thing that this West European alliance—generally a military and political organization—is reviving, whereas, on the other hand, there is something in this fact that prevents a simple assessment of this manifestation'. Shishlin was encouraged by the negative American reaction to the revival of the WEU: 'it seems to me that U.S. reticence at this West European idea is, to some measure, symptomatic, because the United States, it seems to me, to some extent lawfully sees another challenge in this to the North Atlantic bloc'.[49] Clearly change was in the wind, and, with Gorbachev's visit to France imminent, the new, more realistic and open-minded attitude towards Western Europe emerged with greater force in a column by Alexander Bovin, a good weather vane in both the best and worst of times, in *Izvestiya* on 26 September 1985.

Entitled 'The European Orientation' (*Evropeiskoe napravlenie*) it opened with the words: 'The European orientation is one of the basic, traditional orientations of our country's foreign policy'. Bovin had long been familiar with Western debates about Soviet intentions. In the past there had been warnings that the USSR would invade Western Europe. Now the 'Soviet threat' was being interpreted with more subtlety, 'more intelligently':

the Soviet Union,—as they represent our intentions—relying on its military-strategic superiority, wants, without any war, to place Western Europe under its political control, to turn it into a sphere of its overwhelming political influence. This is the aim. And the means—to embroil Western Europe with the United States of America and by this means break the American security guarantee, leaving Western Europe alone with the Soviet Union . . .

The Russians had repeatedly denied any such intentions. 'However, arguments about intentions do not always seem convincing: who knows what they or we have in mind. Therefore', he continued, 'we are raising the discussion to another plane'. Bovin emphasised the realism underlying Soviet foreign policy. He argued:

The social, class interests which tie Western Europe to its transatlantic ally are so strong and constant that to frame a policy based on breaking such ties would be unrealistic.

But this did not mean there were 'no contradictions' in relations between Western Europe and the United States. On the contrary, Bovin insisted that these antagonisms were both serious and permanent and the Soviet Union would take advantage of them, but in a different way:

I am not revealing any secret if I say that in its policy the Soviet Union does take into account the divergence of views between

Western Europe and the USA. But certainly not to dislodge the USA from Europe and find the so much sought after—in the opinion of 'penetrating' analysts in the West—political control over the continent. We have a modest aim. We would like to make use of Western Europe's potential via the transatlantic channel to meet the evident deficit in common sense on the part of the current administration in the USA.[50]

One does not have to take Bovin at face value to accept that Moscow was seriously beginning to reconsider the framework of the very policy towards Western Europe which had given rise to the development of the SS-20. But these ideas were still in genesis. The concept of using Western Europe as a channel to the United States was, and is, an enlightened one. But it assumed that a price need not be paid for that facility, that the West Europeans were willing to be used for that purpose, and it overestimated the degree to which Western Europe could influence a diehard administration in Washington possessed of a degree of resolve totally unlike the character of the Carter Presidency. The rise of the SS-20 and the subsequent deployment of Cruise and Pershing II in Europe had left the West Europeans more dependent upon the Americans than they had been for years. They were left with little or no leverage over US policy except at the extremes, and such leverage as there was had been used up to the hilt by the autumn of 1985. The collapse of West European resistance to the SDI was indication enough. Without offering the West Europeans greater security the Russians were and still are in no position to reduce West European dependence upon the US security guarantee; and the leverage of the Europeans over the Americans is inversely related to their degree of reliance upon the United States for their collective defence. In other words, a new West European policy would amount to no more than empty rhetoric on the part of the Russians unless it were also backed by deeds. Those deeds would have to begin by removing conditions laid down in the INF talks, above all insistence upon compensation for British and French nuclear forces. Such compensation might be justifiable in terms of the usual military rationale and accounting procedure. But it had clearly undermined Soviet diplomatic objectives in Western Europe.

Gorbachev arrived in Paris on 2 October. There he stressed the Soviet Union's wish to resolve 'accumulated European and world problems'.[51] He also made no secret of what lay behind the new sense of urgency to resolve these problems. In a speech to Deputies of the National Assembly on 3 October Gorbachev stated: 'Our chief task is to make the economy more effective and dynamic . . . it is not difficult to understand that the most important conditions for the attainment of these goals is not only a peace we can count on but also a quiet, normal international situation. These priorities also determine our foreign policy'. He pointed to the Soviet moratorium on the further deployment of theatre nuclear weapons. He went on to say that the USSR would be prepared to resolve the INF problem apart from the issue of strategic and space weapons. He also said that the Soviet Government was willing to hold direct discussions—*pryamoi razgovor*—with France and Britain since these Powers, France in particular, objected to the Russians discussing the matter with the Americans. However, the Soviet Union could not turn the other way and ignore French and British arsenals: 'This capability is growing rapidly and we can no longer close our eyes to it'. As a gesture Gorbachev announced that the number of SS-20s capable of targeting Western Europe would be reduced to 243: the number deployed in June 1984. The rest of the SS-20s were now removed from operational readiness and the revetements would be dismantled over the next two months. The SS-5s had all been removed. The remaining SS-4s were still being moved out. Gorbachev went on to repeat Ponomarev's remark to British MPs about the EEC as a potential negotiating partner in international relations, politically as well as economically. He reiterated the gist of Bovin's article on Europe, though not going so far in attributing to Western Europe the role of channel to the United States.[52]

This was progress indeed. However, the brief Gorbachev took to Paris was once more too little, too late. Moreover, the brusque manner in which he dismissed requests for further details on SS-20 deployments raised by a Dutch correspondent at a press conference on 5 October—'I think that this is enough for the Netherlands'[53]—betrayed overtones of the kind of Super-Power arrogance which sat uneasily with attempts to appease the West Europeans.

As the spirit of Gorbachev's reply to the Dutch correspondent suggests, the Soviet Government was still only tentatively and as yet only marginally reorienting the course of its West European policy. Moscow had called a moratorium on SS-20 deployments (in April). It had announced a cut-back of SS-20s deployed to the number operational in June 1984. It had dropped its insistence on linking an INF settlement to a ban on US space weapons and had agreed to talk separately to France and Britain (in October). But the assumptions underlying the policies of the 1970s had yet to be supplanted, despite the much-vaunted concern about Europe 'the common home'. Clear evidence of this can be found in a *Pravda* editorial on 13 November hopefully entitled 'Europe—Our Common Home'. The leader repeated the suggestion made by Ponomarev and reiterated by Gorbachev that the EEC could play a role as an independent entity in international politics. *Pravda* once more denied that it was the Soviet Government's purpose to split NATO (they could hardly say that it was). But all this was somewhat implausible when set against the reprise of an age-old theme which must have passed unnoticed under the gaze of those habituated to the old line:

> If one examines the postwar period, then it is undeniable that to a significant extent it is the extra-continental forces, mainly the imperialist circles of the USA, that have provided the impulse behind the resurrection of militaristic tendencies in Western Europe.[54]

Meant as a means of reassuring everyone that the Europeans were more reasonable than the Americans, it seems harmless enough. But the assumption that the Soviet Union had nothing serious to contend with from Western Europe was the very mistake which led to the crisis over the SS-20.

The most important event of 1985 and undeniably the most disappointing event for Gorbachev personally was the Geneva summit of 19–21 November. Discussions with Reagan were subsequently described by Gorbachev as 'frank . . . blunt, at certain moments extremely blunt'[55] with, as *lzvestiya* noted, 'deep disagreement on the principal questions'.[56] Nothing was resolved with respect to space weapons—still the chief focus of Soviet concerns—and in this respect the summit was a failure. But both sides did agree to accelerate progress towards an agreement on a mutual 50 per cent reduction in the nuclear forces of both sides. They also agreed to accelerate progress towards 'an interim agreement on medium-range missiles in Europe'.[57]

However, the Russians still insisted on counting existing British and French missiles into the total. Both London and Paris refused to concede to this. What we do not know is the extent to which Gorbachev carried with him the remainder of the Politburo in separating resolution of the INF issue from resolution of the crucial issue of the SDI. In editorials on 'The Horizons of Geneva'[58] and in the summary of Politburo minutes following the summit[59]—oddly appearing on a Wednesday (the Politburo normally meets on Thursdays)—the agreement to accelerate progress on the INF question was conspicuous by its absence.

Yet on 15 January 1986 Gorbachev went still further; and the absence of a published summary of Politburo minutes that week suggests that he did so with less than a full consensus behind him. He issued a statement that within the next five to eight years the USSR and USA should 'reduce by one half the nuclear weapons that can reach one another's territory'. As to the remaining systems, each side would retain no more than 6000 warheads. This would be dependent upon mutual renunciation of 'the development, testing and development of space strike weapons'. The first stage would include 'the adoption and implementation of a decision on the complete elimination of medium-range missiles of the USSR and the USA in the European zone'. The Russians also included the non-transfer provision that they had consistently attempted and failed to get the Americans to accept during SALT I and SALT II: 'the United States should undertake not to transfer its strategic and medium-range missiles to other countries'. The most innovative element, however, was the disappearance of the insistence upon compensation for existing British and French systems by suggesting that 'Great Britain and France should pledge not to build up their respective nuclear arsenals'.[60]

By removing insistence upon compensation for existing British and French nuclear forces, Gorbachev had broken through an important barrier which had hitherto blocked the path to an INF settlement. It meant that for the first time the Soviet Union had separated British and French nuclear forces from the American total in Europe—a vital precondition to any policy based on the assumption that the EEC might eventually become an independent entity in international politics. This innovation therefore should not be underestimated. But it should be seen as a precedent, an augur for the future, rather than as the sum total of Soviet proposals. For the impact of this crucial innovation was seriously blunted by Soviet insistence on preventing the modernisation and expansion of British and French systems. This made good sense in strategic terms because the completion of British and French plans would result in the tripling or more of their nuclear warheads as well as in significant gains in accuracy and therefore lethality in the next decade. In the event of a major reduction in US and Soviet arsenals to 6000 warheads each—

somewhat unlikely without a prohibition on space weapons—the projected British and French systems would amount to 50 per cent of the Soviet systems (should the Russians trade off their theatre nuclear potential as well). But in political terms this was something neither London nor Paris could accept. The decisions had already been taken. Moreover, in Britain the Liberal, Social Democratic and Labour Parties all rejected modernisation; the proposal thus represented a troublesome intrusion into British domestic politics likely only to alienate the Thatcher government.

These were not the only elements unlikely to find acceptance in Europe. As mentioned, the proposals included the suggestion that 'Within the next 5—8 years the USSR and the USA will reduce by one half the nuclear weapons that can reach one another's territory'. This meant reducing 50 per cent of US forward-based systems without reducing 50 per cent of all Soviet theatre nuclear weapons, namely SS-20s and SS-4s. Although the proposal also referred to 'the adoption and implementation of a decision on the complete elimination of medium-range missiles of the USSR and the USA in the European Zone', this left existing Soviet systems in place—as it left existing British and French nuclear forces in place—until an agreement was reached and implementation of such an agreement took effect (from 1990–97). In other words, in the short-term the USSR would attain a goal which was not dissimilar to the Nitze-Kvitsinsky proposals: existing SS-20s would remain, but counterbalanced by a reduced level of US forward-based systems (the precise nature of the cuts was left to be negotiated) plus existing British and French systems. Moreover, it was not envisaged that tactical nuclear systems in Europe—such as the operational-tactical missiles deployed forward in Central Europe—would be eliminated on all sides until the second stage; yet those missiles were deployed in retaliation for Pershing II and Cruise which would be cut in the first stage. The package thus promised greater concessions in the medium than in the short term. Yet progress in the medium term could become hostage to progress in the state of Soviet-American relations and, from the Soviet viewpoint, progress in suppressing the SDI.

A further element needs more scrutiny: whereas the proposal to forestall the expansion of British and French systems threatened to accentuate divisions within Britain and France ('intra-imperialist contradictions'), the proposal that 'the United States should undertake not to transfer its strategic and medium-range missiles to other countries' threatened to accentuate friction within the North Atlantic alliance ('inter-imperialist contradictions'): amounting to what those in Whitehall usually refer to as 'a NATO-buster'. Whenever brought up, this issue has instantly provoked cries of alarm from NATO Europe. The SALT II treaty had been framed fastidiously by the Americans to avoid any allusion to a non-transfer provision; a non-circumvention provision was the most the Russians attained, and, as the deployment of Cruise and Pershing II indicated, this proved worthless. If the United States were committed not to transfer its weapons technology to NATO Europe, how would the British, in particular, modernise their existing systems? Even a discussion of the issue between Moscow and Washington would reawaken all the old insecurities within the alliance so evident during the Carter era. The non-transfer clause would cut the umbilical cord between London and Washington, thereby seriously undermining the unity of the North Atlantic alliance while leaving the Warsaw Pact intact. Another element—linking of this package of proposals with an end to the SDI—was later dropped as the Russians met with growing difficulty in the United States. The Soviet offer of 15 January thus reawakened fears in Western Europe that the Russians were once again trying to decouple US and Western European security interests. The view in Whitehall was that 'the Soviet Union is once again trying to divide NATO and to stir up anti-nuclear sentiment in West Europe as it did during the months preceding the deployment of Pershing 2 and cruise missiles in Europe during 1983'.[61] In Paris the reaction was even more negative. 'All Europeans fear that the United States will abandon the right to use the territory of its allies for the deployment of nuclear weapons that can reach the Soviet Union', a French arms control official said.[62] The fact that the French had not allowed US weapons on their territory for 20 years, let alone Cruise and Pershing II missiles, made such protestations somewhat unconvincing. But the fact of French opposition was something the Russians would have to face, and not only the Russians. An American diplomat later complained that in their response to the Soviet proposals 'The Europeans were all to the right of us. We wanted the zero outcome, but even the Dutch were uncomfortable with that. They pulled the rug from under us'.[63] Paul Nitze, Shultz's senior adviser on arms control, was sent to persuade the allies that the deal should be accepted. He failed.

Somewhat thrown off balance by the rebuff from Western Europe, the Americans finally rejected Gorbachev's offer on 23 February, just two days before he opened the 27th Party Congress.[64] Thatcher's reply to Gorbachev's letter of 14 January outlining the proposals did not reach the Russians until 10 March, but it reinforced the message the West Europeans had already given the Americans. She particularly objected to the freezing of British nuclear forces at current levels and the non-transfer provision the Russians were trying to get from the United States.[65] Nitze could be charming but not that charming. Even when Gorbachev told visiting US senator Edward Kennedy that an INF agreement could be concluded independently of an SDI agreement, NATO Europe remained unmoved.[66] Thatcher's objections were echoed by NATO secretary-general Lord Carrington on 10 March: Britain and France, he said, could not be expected to accept 'perpetual nuclear obsolescence'.[67] Clearly the Russians had underestimated the very forces which gave rise to the crisis over the SS-20 in the first place. They had yet to take the crucial decision to accommodate West European security concerns. But Gorbachev was moving in this direction, for he made a major advance at the 27th Party Congress in redefining the Soviet approach to security—a necessary precondition for making concessions to the British and French in Europe. It also raised major implications for Soviet military planning and Soviet military doctrine in general.

'The basic tasks of economic and social development of the country also determine the international strategy of the CPSU', Gorbachev announced. In essence the Soviet Union needed peace to implement its domestic reforms. For this reason Gorbachev sought a return to *détente*. And in a resolute attempt to reduce tension through the reduction of military power, he redefined the maintenance of Soviet security as 'a political task' which could be resolved 'only through political means'. Security, he declared, 'can only be mutual'. Soviet military doctrine was 'purely defensive'. 'Our country', he argued, 'is in favour of keeping military capability within the limits of reasonable sufficiency'.[68]

Yet Gorbachev never defined exactly what he meant by 'reasonable sufficiency' and there is by definition no objective standard by which to judge when enough is enough; enough relative to what or relative to whom? For over a year thereafter the term was bandied about with no clear definition, as a label applied equally and indiscriminately to existing Soviet force levels, to the maintenance of a balance with US forces and to future limits on Soviet force levels. This lack of definition was not accidental. The Soviet leadership had yet to bring the structure and operations of its armed forces into line with the officially proclaimed defensive character of its military doctrine. Thus far there was more 'new talking' than 'new thinking' and more 'new thinking' than 'new action'. This is not surprising. It was not easy to engineer such a fundamental restructuring of attitudes among the military. As TASS military observer Vladimir Chernyshev pointed out nearly a year later, with the battle only partly won: 'the new thinking came at the end of a long road and painful reflection, as a result of repudiation of some postulates that proved to be unshakeable . . . that road was especially difficult in the military field'.[69]

The redefinition of Soviet security as a political rather than a military problem placed the greatest responsibility upon the conduct of Soviet foreign policy where 'tactical flexibility' was the order of the day. To ensure its implementation Gorbachev moved to renovate the upper levels of the diplomatic apparatus.[70] Two new First Deputy Foreign Ministers were appointed, the one closely associated with European policy: Anatoly Kovalev, whom we have already encountered as a falling star in the twilight of the Brezhnev era—a man too closely associated with the appeasement of Western Europe. He was to oversee Western Europe, the Conference on Security and Co-operation in Europe, and the Overseas Evaluation and Planning Administration. The other, Yuli Vorontsov, was not a Europeanist proper but he had direct European experience. He had served under Dobrynin in the Washington embassy from 1966 to 1977, latterly as his deputy, before appointment as Ambassador to India and then Ambassador to France under Andropov in 1983.[71] Vorontsov soon became a general trouble-shooter for the Ministry covering the Middle East and Arms Control. The Europeanists were further reinforced by the promotion to Deputy Minister of Anatoly Adamishin, formerly head of the First European Department whose brief covered relations with Western Europe (excluding West Germany until the reordering of departmental structures in 1986) since 1978, and member of the Foreign Ministry collegium (its top decision-making body) since 1979;[72] he was now to supervise those dealing with Africa as well as Overseas Humanitarian and Cultural Ties. Europeanists were certainly in the ascendant though, as Vorontsov's new appointment indicated, so too were the more flexible and open-minded among the Americanists. This was undoubtedly due to the patronage of Dobrynin, who took charge of the International Department of the Central Committee and as such became the most influential figure in Gorbachev's entourage in foreign policy matters. All in all this meant further impetus to a more supple approach to international relations. But how far this would affect relations with Western Europe was still uncertain.

The trouble with all this flexibility was that the rest of the world had yet to overcome suspicions of the Russians reawakened after 1945 and exacerbated by the experience of *détente* in the 1970s. In Europe as elsewhere there was inevitably the suspicion that Soviet moves represented a change in tactics but no change in Soviet goals. The Russians had not renounced though they had played down their commitment to the world revolutionary movement which was reiterated at the 27th Party Congress. In Europe they seemed as committed as ever to splitting the Western alliance. Lenin's directives on the 'exploitation of inter-imperialist contradictions' were, as the Soviet diplomatic handbook advises, 'the theoretical basis for all the tactics of socialist diplomacy'; 'This kind of tactic in foreign policy has entirely proved its worth', the handbook notes.[73] At the Party Congress Gorbachev was not so direct. He was not likely to be so. But he did predict 'a future increase in the accumulated mass [*massiv*] of contradictions' between the three centres of power in the international system: the United States, Japan and Western Europe. He also went out of his way to play on West European irritation at the continuation of US hegemony over Western Europe evident in American insistence upon support for the SDI: 'does existing American policy coincide with Western Europe's notions about its own security; doesn't the USA go too far in its claims to leadership?'[74] Alexander Yakovlev, Central Committee Secretary, Politburo member and confidant of Gorbachev, also noted that 'The flexibility and dynamism of the USSR's foreign policy after the April plenum of the CC CPSU . . . has highlighted [*vysvetili*] among other things the depth and severity of existing inter-imperialist contradictions'.[75] In the light of such comments it was unlikely that the Soviet Union would make rapid progress in its West European policy.

7.5   THE REYKJAVIK SUMMIT

In October 1985 Gorbachev had dissociated any agreement on intermediate-range nuclear forces from any agreement on space weapons. At first sight this would appear to signify that the Russians were eager to settle the INF issue for its own sake. The Soviet military were indeed anxious about the presence of the Pershing II missile in West Germany with its hard-target capability and short firing time. Soviet air defence was unquestionably nervous about the potential of the Cruise missile. But for all the military's concern about the capability of the Pershing II and Cruise missiles it had never been so overwhelming that they were prepared to accept the Nitze 'walk-in-the-woods' proposals or push for an INF agreement in 1983–84. Similarly at the Soviet Foreign Ministry the Europeanists were undoubtedly concerned to draw the West Europeans away from the United States. But since Brezhnev this had never taken top priority in Soviet foreign policy. It took US adoption of the SDI to force the Russians back to the negotiating table on nuclear weapons in Europe and it was in the expectation of subverting the SDI programme that the Russians made concessions on intermediate-range forces. An INF agreement was seen mainly in the larger context, as the means by which Moscow could accelerate the process of disarmament, a process which would hopefully culminate in a ban on weapons in outer space. As Gorbachev told the 27th Party Congress: 'We must not let the "star wars" programme be used as a stimulus to further arms race and as an obstacle on the road to radical disarmament. It would seriously help to overcome this obstacle if we could make tangible progress concerning a decisive reduction in nuclear capabilities. Therefore the Soviet Union is prepared to make a real step in this direction by resolving the question of medium-range missiles in the European zone separately—unconnected with the problems of strategic and space-based armaments'.[76]

Concern over the SDI thus overshadowed everything else; the means towards its destruction might vary, but the end was always kept in sight. President Reagan wrote to Gorbachev on 25 July 1986 extending an invitation to visit the United States. But Gorbachev was reluctant to go without any assurance that a deal on the SDI was at hand; it was not. Not until 19 September did Shevardnadze hand Shultz Gorbachev's reply.[77] Side-stepping the invitation, Gorbachev instead suggested the two leaders 'personally involve' themselves in preparations for the summit. This amounted to a pre-summit summit.[78] To sweeten the pill Shevardnadze simultaneously— on 20 September—announced that the Soviet Government had dropped its demand that British and French nuclear systems remain frozen at existing levels.[79] At the very least the pre-summit summit might bring about an INF agreement, thereby giving further impetus to the disarmament process as a whole. But the Russians also had something else in mind. Under the illusion that

the West Europeans favoured an INF agreement and in the knowledge that they were unhappy about the SDI, Gorbachev was
persuaded that an INF agreement could be held hostage to a deal
banning the SDI.
Gorbachev and Reagan met at Reykjavik on 11–12 October. The
US delegation was not expecting too much to come out from the
meeting. But the Soviet team arrived in Iceland determined to get
results, throwing the Americans off balance with a bold new package
of proposals put together by 'the Politburo and the Central
Committee secretariat . . . the Ministries of Foreign Affairs and
Defence, other departments, representatives from academia, military
experts, specialists in various branches of industry'.[80] 'What is needed
are bold, unorthodox [*nestandartnye*] decisions!', Gorbachev kept
repeating.[81] What he suggested was that the two sides work on three
draft agreements 'which we together with the President could later
sign during my visit to the United States of America'. First, the two
sides should cut strategic weapons by no less than 50 per cent during
the first five years and the remaining 50 per cent in the following
five. After haggling, the Americans agreed to apply this to all intercontinental weaponry. Here the Russians conceded the position
adopted at the Geneva summit where they had insisted on the
inclusion of US forward-based aircraft. Second, the Russians
proposed the complete liquidation of US and Soviet
medium/intermediate-range missiles in Europe. British and French
forces would be totally excluded. This was Gorbachev emphasised,
'a very big concession' since both the British and French were
expanding and modernising their forces. The Russians also agreed
to freeze the numbers of operational-tactical missiles forward-based
in Europe—the SS-23 (Soviet designation OTR-23) with a 500 kilometre range and the SS-12 model 2 (OTR-22) with a 900 kilometre
range—as the prelude to negotiations on their removal. The Americans had initially proposed an 'interim solution' which would leave
a certain number of medium/intermediate-range missiles, including
some Pershing II missiles, in place. When Gorbachev deftly repro-
ached Reagan for deserting his own offspring—the zero-option of
1982—the President relented. Gorbachev in turn conceded a
reduction of medium/intermediate-range missiles in Asia to 100, to
be matched by 100 on US territory. Everything appeared to be
running smoothly until the Russians pulled the third part out of the
package: a draft treaty on anti-ballistic missile defence which would
effectively put an end to the SDI, and a prohibition of nuclear testing.

This was, Gorbachev argued, 'organically' part of the package. With the appearance of the third element the whole structure collapsed since the SDI was the one item Reagan would not bargain away, even to the extent of a Soviet proposed ten-year ban on testing in the field and deployment.

The surprise for Moscow was less that Reagan stood firm than that the collapse of the talks came as welcome news to Western Europe. There the news that the Americans were interested in abolishing nuclear weapons induced the same kind of trauma that Carter's statements on the subject had produced. The West Germans—with most to lose—complained the most vociferously in private. The French were the most vociferous in public. Deputy Supreme Commander of Allied Forces in Europe, General Hans-Joachim von Mack, expressed his discomfort at US acceptance of the Soviet position: the exclusion of operational-tactical missiles from the projected INF agreement. NATO Secretary-General Lord Carrington joined what was increasingly a chorus of alarm and the French Foreign Minister bluntly stated that the withdrawal of all US missiles 'would weaken the security of Europe, especially in view of other imbalances, such as those in conventional and chemical weapons'.[82] NATO Defence Ministers, in conclave at Gleneagles in Scotland following the summit on 21–22 October, agreed to meet West German concerns by providing for 'constraints' on operational-tactical missiles along with the reduction of medium-range missiles, but left both the British and French still uneasy about US willingness to trade away weaponry peripheral to US security (medium-range missiles) but reluctance even to negotiate on weaponry central to US security (the SDI).[83]

The Russians appear to have calculated that not only the West Europeans but also the Americans would be willing to press for concessions on the SDI in order to obtain a favourable INF agreement. They were therefore most reluctant to revert to the previous position dissociating the two issues after having made further concessions on intermediate-range nuclear forces. When Victor Karpov, despatched as part of the diplomatic diaspora to brief Western Governments on the summit, told counterparts in London and Bonn that a separate INF agreement was still on the cards, he was publicly corrected by Gennadi Gerasimov, Lomeiko's replacement at the Foreign Ministry Press Department.[84] Gorbachev pressed this point in a television address on 23 October: 'They say that the difficulties in Reykjavik supposedly arose as a result of the fact that we, the Soviet side, put forward our cardinal proposals in a package. But the package is a balance of interests, concessions, a balance of collective concerns [*snyatiya ozabochennosti*] a mutual interdependence of security interests . . . Our concessions are also a part of the package. No package, no concessions'.[85] Journalist Alexander Bovin pointed out that the aim was to direct world attention to the SDI as an obstacle to arms control. 'When the "package" has done this job it will be dissolved', he is reported to have said.[86]

The assumption that the West Europeans favoured an INF agreement soon proved false. Professor Proektor from IMEMO frankly lamented that 'Unfortunately our calls for an approach to European problems from a newly thought-out position have not met with sufficient echo on the part of West European Governments'.[87] Gorbachev also expressed surprise that 'Even in Western Europe voices are raised to the effect that it is difficult to part with American nuclear weapons, with American missiles'.[88] Nevertheless he clung to his new position, possibly not least because the package resulted from a compromise between various positions proposed within the Soviet apparatus. Shortly after the summit, on 7 November the Soviet delegation at Geneva optimistically submitted a draft on the entire range of issues discussed at Reykjavik. Once again an INF agreement was offered only as part of a larger package including a prohibition on research, testing and deployment of weapons in outer space. 'The sixth round of the negotiations, of which most was expected, ended in nothing' on 12 November.[89] Further disappointment came when the US delegation rejected the proposal that the seventh round open in December. Instead both sides agreed to hold an interim meeting early in December to settle the agenda for 15 January 1987, when round seven could begin. The interim meeting once more turned out to be 'Another blind alley'.[90]

7.6 THE ROAD TO WASHINGTON

Gorbachev was not deterred, though he was somewhat defensive about the results of the Reykjavik summit: 'It was not a failure; it was a breakthrough', he insisted.[91] On 8 January, with round seven in prospect and with every intention of making a 'decisive move forward at these talks',[92] he replaced Karpov at the head of the Geneva delegation with the more senior, the 'suave and talkative' First Deputy Foreign Minister Yuli Vorontsov, a confidant of Dobrynin's.[93] At Geneva Vorontsov accepted Kampelman's idea of codifying the differences that divided them. But the differences remained. 'Deadlock loomed once again'.[94] Finally Gorbachev accepted defeat. On 28 February he untied the strings of the Reykjavik package. With round seven due to close on 3 March and with the agreement of the Politburo, he issued a statement, via TASS, to the effect that 'the problem of medium-range missiles in Europe be singled out from the package of issues, and that a separate agreement on it be concluded, and without delay'. 'We were assured more than once that if the USSR singles out the issue of medium-range missiles from the Reykjavik package, there would be no difficulty in agreeing to their elimination from Europe. A good opportunity is now being offered to prove that in practice.'[95] Vorontsov called Kampelman that afternoon to convey the news.[96] Once again it was clear that the INF agreement was a means to an end and not merely an end in itself. Gorbachev's offer was, according to Vorontsov, 'also aimed at giving a positive impetus to work in other areas of the talks, namely on outer space and on strategic offensive armaments'.[97] The Russians needed to give the whole disarmament process another lease of life before the campaign for the presidential election in 1988 paralysed the presidency. 'The US delegation's attitude at the Geneva negotiations almost led to a deadlock. In view of the forthcoming elections in the United States, that situation could last', First Deputy Head of the Central Committee International Department Vadim Zagladin pointed out.[98]

Gorbachev had met the chief US objection. The US delegation swiftly presented a draft INF agreement at Geneva on 3–4 March 1987.[99] The Russians responded by accepting the principle of on-site inspection, thus remedying a grievance outstanding from the SALT treaties of the 1970s. 'Hitherto this question has been the result of a Western initiative against the Soviet Union', Vorontsov declared. 'This will change. We are very interested in this question and the West will have to get used to that fact . . . With regard to verification, the USSR will take the "offensive" ', Vorontsov threatened,[100] though as with other facets of the 'new thinking' words outpaced deeds. There were problems too. Reagan did not want his term to end without some success in the field of arms control. But as at Reykjavik the Americans, in haste to cement an INF agreement, had left some of their allies behind. The French were opposed to anything which weakened nuclear deterrence in Europe. The West Germans were divided: Foreign Minister Genscher was the most

sanguine, Chancellor Kohl uncertain, and Defence Minister Manfred
Wörner openly hostile. The compromise obtained between Washington and Bonn was that Soviet operational-tactical missiles should
be included within the agreement. The Russians had 82 SS-23 launchers deployed in the Soviet Union and East Germany; 115 SS-12
(model 2) launchers deployed in the Soviet Union, East Germany
and Czechoslovakia.[101] Gorbachev had said only that those launchers
and missiles would be removed from East Germany and Czechoslovakia at the conclusion of an INF agreement. Wörner insisted they
be liquidated within the terms of the agreement. The Germans also
insisted that even if the Pershing II were withdrawn, the infrastructure—launch pads, communications and command positions—should
remain in being in case of need for future deployment. They were
also interested in the conversion of the Pershing II into a shorter-
range Pershing 1B by the removal of one stage of the missile. Moreover with some US encouragement they insisted on the right to
maintain their own Pershing 1A missiles which were capped by US
nuclear warheads.[102] This the Russians strongly opposed on the
grounds that the Pershing 1A had a 740-kilometre range and was
therefore an operational-tactical missile[103] and because it could be
converted into a Pershing II in 48 hours.[104]

Soviet objections found form in a draft treaty tabled when negotiations re-opened on 23 April 1987. The draft 'Treaty between the
USSR and the United States on the Elimination of Soviet and US
Medium-Range Missiles in Europe and on Other Measures to Limit
and Reduce USSR and US Medium-Range Missiles' was presented
by Deputy Head of the Soviet delegation Alexei Obukhov on 27
April.[105] It followed the Reykjavik pattern in providing for the elimination of medium-range missiles in two stages over five years: a 50
per cent reduction in Europe and a reduction to 100 missiles in Asia
during the first stage and total elimination of all these missiles in the
second stage. The Russians insisted this be done simultaneously
on both sides (the Americans had argued the Russians go first).
Operational-tactical missiles would be reduced to a minimal level
(unspecified). Verification would include on-site inspection. And,
pressing home the expressed determination to take the offensive on
verification, Karpov announced in Moscow that 'These inspections
would be made both on the territory of the other side and the
territory of third countries where US medium-range missiles and
launch installations for such missiles are stationed. They would be
carried out on the sites of dismantling or destruction of medium-

range missiles or their launch installations, at test sites and military bases including those on the territory of third countries, and at warehouses, training centres, and manufacturing plants regardless of whether they are private or state-owned'.[106] In addition the Russians publicised their opposition to US attempts 'to switch cruise missiles from land bases to the sea and to deploy the remaining 100 warheads on medium-range missiles in Alaska, that is, within range of USSR territory'.[107] They also objected to attempts by the Americans to make their missiles and bases off-limits to verification and insisted that US Pershing 1A warheads be withdrawn to the United States.[108] Yet for all the differences remaining it was now clear that an INF agreement was very close to completion. First of all the US Government had to draw the West Germans into line, and given chronic West German dependence upon Washington for their own security this was merely a matter of time.

By the end of August the West Germans were persuaded to drop their opposition to the inclusion of all operational-tactical missiles in the forthcoming agreement.[109] Shevardnadze's visit to the United States on 15–17 September then saw the resolution of all 'the final issues of principle'.[110] NATO Europe was still uneasy, however. To reassure Bonn a meeting of NATO's Nuclear Planning Group on 3–4 November agreed that a number of US Sea-Launched Cruise missiles and more US dual-capable aircraft would be assigned to the alliance. The NPG also pressed for the deployment of the new Army Tactical Missile System with a range of 200 kilometres—a clear sign that at least some of the allies did not want tactical missile systems to be abolished in any future round of negotiations.[111] The Russians duly responded with an attempt to include a clause in the draft accord which would prohibit circumvention of the treaty by US augmentation of related nuclear arsenals. But Gorbachev was clearly not prepared to allow this to block the path to agreement due to be signed on his visit to Washington on 7–10 December. Thus when the Americans resisted, the Russians conceded. Similarly when the Russians made a last-ditch attempt to link the expected Reagan-Gorbachev summit to progress in negotiating limits on the SDI, US resistance once more caused the Russians to back down.[112]

Gorbachev arrived in Washington on 7 December to put his signature to the first treaty reducing the nuclear arsenals of the two Super-Powers. The 'Treaty Between the United States of America and the Union of Soviet Socialist Republics on the Elimination of their Intermediate-Range and Shorter-Range Missiles' was therefore signed on 8 December 1987. Both parties pledged to eliminate all their intermediate/medium-range missiles and launchers within three years of ratification and all shorter-range missiles and launchers within 18 months of ratification. This covered the SS-20s, SS-4s, SS-5s, SS-12s and SS-23s on the Soviet side; the Pershing II, 1A and Ground-Launched Cruise missiles on the American side. Replacement missiles were banned. On-site inspection was provided for at all operating bases and support facilities. And the treaty was of unlimited duration. The Soviet Government had thus reversed the policies of a decade or more in a bold move to halt a nuclear arms race which could only end to its disadvantage.

Clearly the elimination of the dreaded Pershing II was a welcome relief to many in the Soviet Union. Its hard-target capability and its short launching time made Moscow extremely nervous at this extension of a US counter-force capability to the very borders of the Soviet sphere. Along with the Pershing 1A its removal also meant the elimination of what was seen as an essential component of NATO's flexible response strategy. Gorbachev himself acknowledged this: 'I merely want to point out that this would deliver a perceptible blow to conceptions of limited use of nuclear weapons and the so-called "controlled escalation" of nuclear conflict'.[113] Boris Pyadyshev, Deputy Head of the Press Directorate of the Soviet Foreign Ministry, echoed this: 'Once medium- and shorter-range missiles are destroyed, Western strategists preferring the doctrine of the so-called controlled escalation of a nuclear conflict will have to reconsider their scenarios drastically . . . They will have to rely solely on . . . US forward-based weapons in Europe and Asia and . . . British and French nuclear capabilities. The reduced reliability of those variants must have a sobering effect and can eventually bring about their rejection'.[114] The new Defence Minister, Dimitrii Yazov, made a similar point to that of Gorbachev. He also stressed the importance of eliminating the Pershing II missiles which, he claimed, 'are capable of striking objects on the territory of the USSR and its allies with a flight-time to target of 8–10 minutes, which makes it unlikely that any kind of anti-missile defence could be effective'.[115]

All of this was perfectly true. Yet it had not been enough to prevent the Russians walking out of the INF talks in November 1983. It had not been enough to bring them back to the negotiating table in 1984. They had agreed to open a new round of the Geneva talks in January 1985, but only on condition that the talks cover the SDI.

During these talks they dropped their insistence on an SDI agreement as a direct precondition for an INF accord but this could scarcely have been due to anything new with respect to intermediate-range nuclear forces. They dropped this linkage only because they realised that it was playing into the hands of those in Washington who opposed any and all arms control or disarmament measures. At the 27th Party Congress Gorbachev pointed out: 'We must not let the "star wars" programme be used as a stimulus to a further arms race and as an obstacle on the road to radical disarmament. It would seriously help to overcome this obstacle if we could make tangible progress concerning a decisive reduction in nuclear capabilities. Therefore the Soviet Union is prepared to take a real step in this direction by resolving the question of medium-range missiles in the European zone separately—unconnected with the problems of strategic and space-based armaments'.[116]

Similarly Major-General Yuri Lebedev, Deputy Head of the General Staff Treaty and Legal Directorate, argued that 'in the circumstances it was extremely important to maintain the dynamism of resolving questions through negotiation, to anticipate' the activities of forces on the Right dreaming about dragging on the discussions at Geneva interminably'.[117] In this same article, which justified the agreement to the military, Lebedev emphasised the importance of the treaty as the necessary prelude to further disarmament which would ultimately forestall Reagan's SDI ambitions. In this respect the military substance of the INF accord was less important than its political aspect, and its political aspect in respect to US-Soviet relations was more significant than for Soviet policy towards Western Europe.

Lebedev wrote that 'in recent years a great deal has been said (and doubtless with justification) about the danger created by the deployment of new American medium-range missiles (MRMs) in Europe, about plans for first-use by the United States of nuclear weapons in Europe and other regions. But', he argued, 'the significance of coming to terms on the elimination of MRMs and operational-tactical missiles (OTMs) is, of course, not confined merely to military-strategic considerations . . . There is also the no less important political aspect, namely the MRM-OTM treaty may give impetus to progress in other directions for curbing the arms race, and above all it may become a good "prelude" to major 50% cuts in offensive strategic armaments, to an agreement reinforcing the ABM treaty regime.'[118] In Lebedev's opinion, and evidently the opinion of the Gorbachev leadership as a whole, 'the problem of eliminating MRMs and OTMs has, one might say, become the key to resolving other major problems in limiting the nuclear arms race, in disarmament, including such problems as forestalling an arms race in outer space'.[119]

Conclusions

A number of conclusions may be drawn from this study of the Soviet Union and the politics of nuclear weapons in Europe. First let us retrace the broad outline of the story. The problem of the SS-20 arose at a critical point. No substantial progress had been made towards complementing political *détente* in Europe with military *détente*. The Vienna negotiations on force reductions had not advanced an inch in reducing conventional weapons in Europe. The NATO Powers were not ready to place the array of US forward-based dual-capable aircraft on the table. Theatre nuclear weapons in Europe had been excluded from the agenda of both SALT I and SALT II. The Russians insisted they appear on the agenda of SALT III. It was clear that they lacked leverage. It thus appeared to make good sense to bolster their negotiating position by modernising their ageing theatre nuclear arsenal. These and other political and military exigencies merged to bring the SS-20 into being. This missile system would force the West to the negotiating table. It would also negate the unilateral advantage held by the United States in deploying forward-based systems in Europe. The trouble was that the FBS were also the mainstay of NATO Europe's defence against more powerful Soviet conventional land forces.

Despite political *détente* in Europe which settled the status of West Berlin and secured NATO recognition of post-war frontiers, Western Europe remained desperately concerned to retain a visible US nuclear as well as conventional military presence on the continent. In private the leading governments of Western Europe resolutely rejected any attempt by Washington to include the FBS or British and French nuclear forces on the SALT agenda. It was therefore highly unlikely that they would then sit back placidly when the USSR sought to offset NATO's long-standing theatre nuclear superiority while the Super-Powers were cementing parity in intercontinental weaponry.

West European concerns were rooted in the immediate postwar period when the Russians decided upon a unilateral solution to their security dilemma through the domination of Eastern Europe and the

175

forward deployment of Soviet conventional forces into the heart of Central Europe. It was felt in the West that without a counterbalance the continent of Europe would succumb to a *pax sovietica*. The West Europeans thus called in the New World to restore the balance of the Old. Without the pull from Western Europe the United States would find no secure foothold on the continent. It is West European insecurity that lies at the root of the problem. It is this insecurity which has produced periodic crises within NATO as well as between the alliance and the Soviet Union, of which the crisis over the SS-20 is a prime example.

The issue is whether the Russians have learnt a lesson from the SS-20 crisis; whether they have learnt that a unilateral solution to their security dilemma brings no real security at all; whether there can be a true accommodation between the legitimate security needs of both Western Europe and the Soviet Union. Thus far the signs are mixed. Retrospective criticism of SS-20 deployment from not only Soviet journalists but also a Deputy Minister of Foreign Affairs augurs well, as does Gorbachev's enunciation of the principle of 'reasonable sufficiency'—though precisely what this means is unclear. Recognition of the fact that Britain and France have a right to their own nuclear arsenals apart from the US-Soviet balance is undoubtedly a victory of sorts for Western Europe, though how long this can be sustained is still in question. Growing Soviet interest in Western Europe's potential as an independent political actor in the international system gives some cause for optimism though, once again, it is uncertain just how far this interest really goes. Indeed unless the West Europeans themselves pursue the goal of an integrated and autonomous defence structure and a co-ordinated foreign policy with more vigour and resolve it is unlikely to go much further. The signature of the INF treaty is arguably a success for the policy pursued by NATO from 1979; all the SS-20s are to be eliminated. Yet, as we have seen, it was the American SDI which proved crucial in bringing the Soviet Government to terms.

It is therefore scarcely surprising to find that the lessons learnt in Moscow from the SS-20 crisis are limited, and these lessons have been learnt more by some (notably a section of the Foreign Ministry and those in Gorbachev's inner circle) than by others (notably the Soviet military). One should therefore be cautious before racing to over-optimistic conclusions. The most we can say is that the chief lesson learnt by the Russians is that although Western Europe is still too weak and incoherent an entity to be treated as an effective actor in world politics, Western Europe has undeniably demonstrated that if its particular security interests are ignored by Moscow and Washington it is fully capable of upsetting the Super-Power apple-cart by mobilising US power to Soviet disadvantage.

But what does this lesson learnt tell us about Soviet foreign policy in general? Has the Soviet Union changed its overall objectives as a result of reordering its priorities in Europe? Any conclusions will of course be limited by the fact that this account covers only one side of Soviet policy—the politico-strategic dimension. And it does not attempt to treat this dimension in its totality. The focus is on Europe alone. But this is not an unimportant sphere of foreign and defence policy and although we must also look elsewhere at Soviet behaviour to test the assertion that fundamental changes are occurring, this is as good a starting-point as any.

The remarkable about-turn in Soviet policy on the SS-20 is perhaps the most significant sign so far of new thinking in Soviet foreign policy. It also represents a remarkable shift in the determination of Soviet strategic requirements. Here Gorbachev has broken with the policies of his immediate predecessors in redefining security as a political problem requiring a political rather than a military solution. This should not be taken to mean that the Russians no longer have any use for military power. There is no evidence for such an assertion. On the contrary the Soviet armed forces remain as powerful as ever. The modernisation of military equipment continues apace and arms supplies still reach client states in the Third World. It does, however, mean that where the deployment of military power is seen to have adverse political consequences, that power will be cut to meet diplomatic requirements. Diplomacy is thus displacing defence. A new spirit of realism has taken hold.

There appear to be several reasons for this. First, the secular slowdown in the growth of the Soviet economy has focused attention on the wastefulness of the arms race. Second, as a consequence of this arms race the excessive accumulation of Soviet nuclear weaponry seriously damaged *détente* in Europe as elsewhere. And, lastly, who can deny that diplomacy is cheaper than defence?

This is certainly not the first time that the focus of Soviet efforts has been redirected from defence to diplomacy to meet more pressing economic priorities. This happened under Lenin at the end of the civil war and allied war of intervention in 1920–21. It resulted in a major retreat from the Communist programme with the introduction of the New Economic Policy. It led to the demobilisation of the Red

Army to an absolutely minimal strength of a quarter of a million men. It happened again in 1929–32, this time with the implementation of the first five-year plan, the simultaneous suppression of the demands of the military and a renewed emphasis on the role of Soviet diplomacy. In both instances the Russians highlighted the importance of disarmament. In both cases they turned a smiling face to the West. On both occasions Western companies were encouraged to introduce their technology into Soviet Russia. Unfortunately in both instances these changes also proved all too temporary: a breathing-space to give time for economic reconstruction which ended with the unexpected intrusion of major threats to the security of the homeland.

The attainment of an INF accord thus raises several questions: what is the significance of this unprecedented agreement to reduce nuclear arms; how much deeper can one expect disarmament to go; and how long can we expect this process to continue?

It is clear from Soviet statements that Moscow hopes to follow through in Europe with further agreements. It is envisaged that these would sooner or later encompass not only conventional arms but also the reduction or liquidation of both US forward-based nuclear-capable aircraft and British and French nuclear systems. The Russians do not expect much progress on that front until an agreement is reached with the Americans reducing intercontinental weapons systems by about 50 per cent. They are also holding a comprehensive agreement on intercontinental systems hostage to a commitment by the United States to observe the provisions of the ABM treaty signed in 1972, which would prohibit the deployment of weapons in outer space. It is at present uncertain whether progress against the development of the SDI is likely to succeed; much depends upon the shifts in US domestic politics and the outcome of the Presidential elections in 1988.

The Russians are also interested in reducing conventional forces in Europe. They are moving towards a less provocative force posture on their side of the divide. It is, however, equally evident that they wish to retain forward-based troops in central Europe; there is certainly no sign of a Soviet withdrawal behind their own frontiers. The unilateral solution to Soviet security adopted under Stalin has yet to be challenged and changed. And it is unlikely that West Germany would permit a major reduction in NATO's conventional forces—particularly given that US forces would retreat across the Atlantic—if the Russians continue to possess such an advantage in the deployment of their forces on land. Great progress on conventional force reduction therefore seems improbable without major alterations in Soviet security policy towards Europe, and no signs of change are apparent.

Elsewhere in the world, Soviet policy is indeed more subtle and flexible, more realistic and oriented more to inter-state relations than relations with national liberation movements engaged in revolutionary struggle. But this retrenchment in support of Third World revolution has yet to be tested by a major upsurge in revolutionary conditions and by a deterioration in US-Soviet relations. The degree of Soviet support for revolutions beyond Soviet borders has always fluctuated over time, just as the degree of Soviet interest in co-operation with the West has been cyclical. In neither case have the fundamental tenets of Soviet foreign policy changed. For all the rhetoric and honeyed words, Gorbachev has given no sign of being other than a Marxist-Leninist. He is ultimately as committed to the long-term alteration in the correlation of world forces as were his predecessors; it is merely imprudent to talk about it. The intriguing question for the future of Soviet foreign policy in general, as it is in respect of Soviet policy towards Western Europe, is whether these short-term tactical adjustments necessitated by the mistakes of the 1970s, the appearance of the SDI and the secular decline in the Soviet economy, will acquire a dynamic of their own and ultimately undermine the traditional long-term goals of Soviet foreign policy; in other words, whether the Soviet Union will indeed be domesticated as a world Power and become a prop of the status quo across the globe. This may depend not only on the opportunities thrown up in the Third World and on Soviet domestic economic requirements but also on the incentives offered by the West to behave differently. And is the West really willing to take the risk of offering the Russians a place in the Third World without the certainty that Moscow will not then or in the future pocket these advantages and revert to past form? It is surely too early to say.

Notes

Preface

1. For the Soviet designation of the missile: treaty text in *New York Times*. 9 December 1987.
2. For the range and date of service of the missile: APN Military Bulletin—Foreign Broadcast Information Service (FBIS), *Daily Report: The Soviet Union*. 18 December 1987. For further data: *Jane's Weapons Systems 1987–88* (London, 1987) p. 9; B. Wright, *Soviet Missiles* (Lexington, Mass., 1986); testimony of former Secretary of Defense Harold Brown, 22 March 1982: *Overview of Nuclear Arms Control and Defense Strategy in NATO: Hearings before the Subcommittee on International Security and Scientific Affairs and on Europe and the Middle East of the Committee on Foreign Affairs, House of Representatives, 97th Congress, 2nd Session* (Washington DC, 1982) p. 181.
3. *Report of the Secretary of Defense Caspar W. Weinberger to the Congress on the FY 1986. FY 1987 Authorization Request and FY 1986–90 Defense Programs, February 4, 1985* (Washington DC, 1985) p. 50.
4. W. Hyland, 'The Struggle for Europe: An American View' in A. Pierre (ed.), *Nuclear Weapons in Europe* (New York, 1984) pp. 30–1. Similar views have been expressed in M. Tatu, *La bataille des euromissiles* (Paris, 1983).
5. A. Cockburn, *The Threat: Inside the Soviet Military Machine* (New York, 1983) pp. 14 and 200.
6. B. Hagelin, 'Swords into Daggers: The Origins of the SS-20 Missiles', *Bulletin of Peace Proposals*, vol. 15, no. 4, 1984, pp. 341–53.
7. Interview: 'Iskusstvo vozmozhnogo', *Novoe Vremya*, no. 46, 13 November 1987, p. 9.
8. Ibid.
9. R. Berman and J. Baker, *Soviet Strategic Forces: Requirements and Responses* (Washington DC, 1982) p. 67.
10. S. Meyer, 'Soviet Theatre Nuclear Forces. Part II: Capabilities and Implications', *Adelphi Paper 188* (London, 1984) pp. 26–8.
11. D. Holloway, *The Soviet Union and the Arms Race* (London, 1983) pp. 68–9.
12. R. Garthoff, 'The SS-20 Decision', *Survival*, vol. XV, no. 1, Jan./Feb. 1983, pp. 110–19. A slightly different version appears in Garthoff, *Detente and Confrontation: American-Soviet Relations from Nixon to Reagan* (Washington DC, 1985) p. 875. For a review of the various

interpretations of the origins of the SS-20: M. Evangelista, 'Why the Soviets Buy the Weapons They Do', *World Politics*, no. 4, July 1984, pp. 597–618.

Introduction

1. A. Bovin, 'Moscow: "We are serious" ', *Observer*, 28 October 1979.
2. 19 June 1975: (FBIS), *Daily Report: The Soviet Union*, vol. 3, no. 130, 6 July 1976.
3. Marshal S. Akhromeev, 'Velikaya pobeda i ee uroki', *Izvestiya*, 7 May 1985.
4. Rotterdam NRC HANDELSBLAD, 23 March 1984: FBIS, *Daily Report: The Soviet Union*, vol. 3, no. 061, 28 March 1984.
5. A. Bullock, *Ernest Bevin: Foreign Secretary 1945–1951*, (London, 1983) pp. 125, 151, 100–01. For the larger political significance of these moves, see M. Leffler, 'The American Conception of National Security and the Beginnings of the Cold War, 1945–48', *The American Historical Review*, vol. 89, no. 2, April 1984, pp. 346–81.
6. R. Futrell, *Ideas, Concepts, Doctrine: A History of Basic Thinking in the United States Air Force 1907–1964*, (Alabama, 1971) pp. 109–10.
7. D. Campbell, *The Unsinkable Aircraft Carrier: American Military Power in Britain* (London, 1984) p. 28.
8. Bill Yenne, *A Primer of Modern Strategic Airpower: SAC* (London, 1984) p. 60.
9. See D. Rosenberg, 'American Atomic Strategy and the Hydrogen Bomb Decision', *The Journal of American History*, vol. 66, June 1979, p. 62–87.
10. Quoted in M. Armitage and R. Mason, *Air Power in the Nuclear Age*, 2nd ed. (Urbana, 1985) p. 189. Air Marshal Sir Michael Armitage is a Deputy Chief of Defence Staff in the British Ministry of Defence. Air Commodore R. A. Mason is Deputy Air Secretary and Director of Personnel Management (Policy and Plans) for the Royal Air Force.
11. Yenne, *A Primer*, p. 62; Futrell, *Ideas, Concepts*, p. 121; Armitage and Mason, *Air Power*, p. 190.
12. Armitage and Mason, *Air Power*, p. 191; Rosenberg, 'American Atomic Strategy', p. 68.
13. Rosenberg, 'American Atomic Strategy', p 69.
14. C. Campbell, *Nuclear Weapons Fact Book* (London, 1984) p. 37.
15. Futrell, *Ideas, Concepts*, p. 172.
16. Armitage and Mason, *Air Power*, p. 196.
17. Futrell, *Ideas, Concepts*, p. 172.
18. For the size of Soviet conventional forces: M. Evangelista, 'Stalin's Postwar Army Reappraised', *International Security*, Winter 1982–83, vol. 7, no. 3, pp. 110–38. Also, see R. Berman and J. Baker, *Soviet Strategic Forces*, p. 39.
19. For more information: D. Holloway, *The Soviet Union*, chapter 2.
20. Two B-29s from the USA force-landed in the Soviet Far East in August and November 1944 respectively. They were taken apart and

copied by the Tupolev bureau in Kazan: Armitage and Mason, *Air Power*, p. 149.

21. V. Tolubko, *Nedelin* (Moscow, 1979) pp. 174–5.
22. G. Tokaty, 'Soviet Space Technology', *Spaceflight*, vol. 5 (1963) p. 62.
23. For further information: Holloway, *The Soviet Union*, chapter 2; also Armitage and Mason, *Air Power*, p. 147.
24. Tokaty, 'Soviet Space Technology', p. 61.
25. Tolubko, *Nedelin*, pp. 150–2.
26. *Soviet Military Power* (Washington DC, 1985) p. 39.
27. Tolubko, *Nedelin*, p. 175.
28. Tokaty, 'Soviet Space Technology', p. 62.
29. Ibid.
30. Ibid., p. 63.
31. *Kalendar' Voina na 1986 god*, ed. A. Shesternev (Moscow, 1985) p. 280.
32. Marshal P. Batitsky, 'The National Defense (PVO Strany) Troops,' *Voennaya Mysl'*, no. 11, November 1973, pp. 31–44: CIA, *Foreign Press Digest*.
33. M. Pervukhin, *Bratislavskaya Pravda*, 6 September 1975: FBIS, *Daily Report: The Soviet Union* no. 177, 11 September 1975.
34. S. Meyer, 'Soviet Theatre Nuclear Forces', p. 4.
35. Memorandum by the Acting Special Assistant to the Secretary of State for Intelligence (Howe) to the Acting Secretary of State, 1 March 1954: *Foreign Relations of the United States [FRUS], 1952–1954, Vol. II, National Security Affairs. Part I* (Washington DC, 1984) p. 634.
36. Draft statement of policy proposed by the National Security Council, 30 September 1953, *FRUS*, p. 491.
37. Futrell, *Ideas, Concepts*, p. 258.
38. Armitage and Mason, *Air Power*, pp. 149–50.
39. For the date: N. Pavlov and A. Sidorov, *Amerikanskii 'Evrorakety': Voennaya Ugroza i Politicheskii Shantazh* (Moscow, 1984) p. 30.
40. *Pravda*, 15 January 1960.
41. D. Rosenberg, 'American Postwar Air Doctrine and Organization: The Navy Experience', in *Air Power and Warfare: The Proceedings of the 8th Military History Symposium, United States Air Force Academy 18–20 October 1978*, ed. A. Hurley and R. Ehrhart (Washington DC, 1979) pp. 245–78.
42. N. Friedman, *Carrier Air Power* (London, 1981) p. 61.
43. Ibid., p. 42.
44. Ibid., p. 71.
45. Statement of Vice Admiral James Doyle, Jr., Deputy Chief of Naval Operations for Surface Warfare, 9 February 1977: *Hearings on Military Posture and H.R. 5068 (H.R. 5970) and H. R. 1755, Department of Defense Authorization for Appropriations for Fiscal Year 1978 Before the Committee on Armed Services, House of Representatives, Ninety-fifth Congress, First Session, Part 4* (Washington DC, 1977) p. 247.
46. Ibid., p. 241.

47. Ibid., p. 286.
48. U.S. *Security Issues in Europe: Burden Sharing and Offset, MBFR and Nuclear Weapons, September 1973, A Staff Report Prepared for the Use of the Subcommittee on US Security Agreements Abroad of the Committee on Foreign Relations, United States Senate, 2 December 1973* (Washington DC, 1973) p. 21.
49. Interview with Marshal P. F. Batitsky, 'Chistoe nebo nad rodinoi'. *Nedelya*, no. 51, 19 December 1974.
50. *Sovetskie Vooruzhennye Sily: Istoriya Stroitel'stva* (Moscow, 1978) p. 508.
51. *Voennyi Entsiklopedicheskii Slovar'*, ed. N. Ogarkov et al. (Moscow, 1983) pp. 198–9.
52. Colonel V. Vovk, 'Protivovozdushnaya oborona v sisteme zashchity Sovetskogo gosudarstva', *Vestnik Protivovozdushnoi Oborony*, no. 3, 1984.
53. *Sovetskie Vooruzhennye*, p. 386.
54. *Ordena Lenina Moskovskii Okrug PVO: Istoriya Ordena Lenina Moskovskogo Okruga Protivovozdushnoi Oborony* (Moscow, 1981) p. 177.
55. *Bakinskii Okrug Protivovozdushnoi Oborony: Istoricheskii Ocherk 1920–1947gg.* (Baku, 1974) pp. 194–5.
56. Vovk. 'Protivovozdushnaya . . .'
57. Reports of US reconnaissance flights over Soviet territory in 1949 and 1950 can be read in documents of the Soviet border forces: *Pogranichnye Voiska SSSR 1945–1950* (Moscow, 1975).
58. Vovk, 'Protivovozdushnaya . . .'
59. A. Gorokhov, 'Boevoe dezhurstvo', *Pravda*, 13 April 1986.
60. *Ordena Lenina*, pp. 184–5.
61. Armitage and Mason, *Air Power*, p. 157.
62. *Sovetskie Vooruzhennye*, p. 396.
63. *Voennyi Entsiklopedicheskii*, p. 199.
64. Ibid., p. 407.
65. Armitage and Mason, *Air Power*, pp. 157–8. As CIA chief Allen Dulles told the Senate Foreign Relations Committee in May 1960: 'We do . . . credit the Soviets with having a pretty good capability in ground-to-air missiles up to 60,000 feet and some capability between 60,000 and 70,000'. *Executive Sessions of the Senate Foreign Relations Committee (Historical Series), Vol. XII, 86th Congress, 2nd Session, 1960* (Washington DC, 1982) p. 349. This was a hearing on the U-2 affair (31 May 1960).
66. *Istoriya Ural'skogo Voennogo Okruga* (Moscow, 1970) p. 285.
67. For the story of the U-2 flights from Eisenhower's papers: S. Ambrose, *Eisenhower: Volume Two, The President* (New York, 1984) pp. 227–8, 258, 340–1, 374, 455–6, 476, 513–15, 563, 568–9, 571–9.

1. SALT I and Nuclear Weapons in Europe, 1969–72

1. *Department of Defense Authorization for Appropriations for Fiscal Year 1983: Hearings before the Committee on Armed Services, United*

184 Notes

States *Senate, Ninety-Seventh Congress, Second Session on S.2248. Pt. 7—Strategic and Theatre Nuclear Forces* (Washington DC, 1982) p. 4371.

2. See R. Garthoff, 'SALT I: An Evaluation', *World Politics*, vol. xxxi, no. 1, October 1978, pp. 1–3. Garthoff served as deputy head of the US delegation.

3. From the memoirs of the head of the US delegation: G. Smith, *Doubletalk: The Story of the Strategic Arms Limitation Talks* (New York, 1980) pp. 90–1.

4. Ibid., p. 184.

5. A. Shevchenko, *Breaking with Moscow* (New York, 1985) p. 202. This testimony is not always reliable, but the author's statements on this matter accord with other known evidence, including Western official sources speaking off the record (1985).

6. Col. M. Vetrov, 'Problems of War and Peace and the World Revolutionary Process', *Voennaya Mysl'*, no. 8, August 1971, p. 20. The text is unavailable in the original, having been declassified and released by the CIA in translation only, as *Foreign Press Digest: Selected Translations from 'Voennaya Mysl'*.

7. Speech delivered on the 26 November 1969: 'Vozrastanie roli, zadachi i otvetstvennosti molodykh ofitserov na sovremennom etape razvitya sovetskikh vooruzhennykh sil', *Krasnaya Zvezda*, 27 November 1969.

8. 'Third Annual Report to the Congress on United States Foreign Policy', 9 February 1972: *Public Papers of the Presidents of the United States: Richard Nixon 1971* (Washington DC, 1972) p. 309.

9. 'Second Annual Report to the Congress on United States Foreign Policy', 25 February 1971: *Public Papers of the Presidents of the United States: Richard Nixon 1971* (Washington DC, 1972) p. 231.

10. Yu. Arbatov, 'SShA: Bol'shie raketnye debaty', *Izvestiya*, 15 April 1969.

11. D. Tomashevskii, 'Leninskii printsip mirnogo sosushchestvovaniya i klassovaya bor'ba', *Kommunist*, no. 12, August 1970, pp. 101–13.

12. Smith, *Doubletalk*, p. 91.

13. Ibid., p. 127.

14. Ibid., p. 129.

15. Ibid., p. 179; also p. 183.

16. Ibid., p. 92.

17. Colonel V. Alexandrov, 'Dlya provedeniya agressivnoi politiki: udarnaya aviatsiya SShA', *Krasnaya Zvezda*, 13 May 1970.

18. Smith, *Doubletalk*, p. 91.

19. Major-General (aviation) A. Baranov, Colonel A. Orlov, 'Proval amerikanskoi vozdushnoi agressii protiv DRV', *Voenno-Istoricheskii Zhurnal*, no. 2, February 1970, pp. 28–9.

20. M. Skinner, *U.S.A.F.E.: A Primer of Modern Air Combat* (Novato, 1983) p. 56. For an excessively self-congratulatory account written from the North Vietnamese standpoint: Major-General Nguyen Suan Mau, 'Nadezhnyi shchit neba V'etnama', *Vestnik Protivovozdushnoi Oborony*, no. 7, July 1980, pp. 67–9.

21. Marshal (aviation) S. Krasovskii, 'Trends in the Use of Aircraft in a

Nuclear War', *Voennaya Mysl'*, no. 3, March 1967: *Selected Readings from Soviet 'Military Thought' (1963–1973)*, ed. J. Douglass and A. Hoeber (Virginia, 1980) pp. 227–39.

22. V. Nikolaev, 'Sredstva vozdushnogo napadeniya NATO v Tsentral'noi Evrope', *Vestnik Protivovozdushnoi Oborony*, no. 3, March 1979, p. 69.

23. Colonel S. Nikanorov, 'US Aviation in the War in Vietnam', ibid., no. 6, June 1967, pp. 69–78: CIA, *Foreign Press Digest: Selected Translations from 'Voennaya Mysl''*.

24. Interview given to the *Frankfurter Rundschau* published on the 1 October 1981: FBIS, *Daily Report: Eastern Europe*, vol. 3, no. 193.

25. B. Nalty, Office of Air Force History, United States Air Force, *Air Force and the Fight for Khe Sanh* (Washington DC, 1973) p. 105.

26. Ibid., p. 103.

27. Skinner, *U.S.A.F.E.*, pp. 57–8.

28. E. Ulsamer, 'Tac Air's Responsiveness', *Air Force Magazine*, vol. 15, no. 12, December 1972, p. 36.

29. Quoted in J. Hansen, 'The Development of Soviet Tactical Air Defense', *International Defense Review*, vol. 14. no. 5, 1981, p. 533.

30. *United States Military Posture for FY 1979 by Chairman of the Joint Chiefs of Staff, General George S. Brown, USAF* (Washington DC, 1978) p. 38.

31. Marshal P. Batitsky, 'The National Air Defense (PVO Strany) Troops', *Voennaya Mysl'*, no. 11, November 1973, pp. 31–44: CIA, *Foreign Press Digest*.

32. Colonel M. Yegorov, 'Raketnoe oruzhie protiv nizkoletayshuchikh tselei', *Vestnik Protivovozdushnoi Oborony*, no. 6, June 1974, p. 71.

33. Captain B. Agapov, 'V vozdukhe—nizkiletyashchaya tsel' ', ibid., no. 11, November 1983, p. 26.

34. *United States Military Posture FY 1985: The Organization of the Joint Chiefs of Staff* (Washington DC, 1984) p. 32; also, *Jane's Weapons Systems 1981–82* (London, 1981) p. 229.

35. Marshal Batitsky interview: 'Chistoe nebo nad rodinoi', *Nedelya*, no. 51, 19 December 1974, p. 4.

36. Colonel A. Barabanshchikov, 'Sovremennye trebovaniya k obucheniyu i vospitaniyu sovetskikh voinov', ibid., p. 55.

37. Colonel-General V. Sozinov, Chief of the General Staff of the Air Defence Forces, 'Slazhennost' i operativnost' v rabote shtaba', *Vestnik Protivovozdushnoi Oborony*, no. 4, April 1975, p. 23.

38. Barabanshchikov, 'Sovremennye . . .', p. 55.

39. See Major N. Vinogradov, 'O povyshenii deistvennosti trenirovok', ibid., no. 1, June 1975, p. 43; editorial, 'Krepit' voinskuyu ditsiplinu, i ustavnoi poryadok', ibid., no. 8, August 1975; editorial, 'Krepit' ditsiplinu i ustavnoi poryadok', ibid., no. 9 September 1976; also Colonel-General Soizinov, 'Bditel'no nesti boevoe dezshurstvo', ibid., no. 12, December 1976.

40. Sozinov, 'Slazhennost' . . .', p. 26.

41. Ibid.

42. Ibid., p. 23.

43. Colonel-General V. Sozinov, 'Vozdushnoe prostranstvo SSSR i zashchita ego neprikosnovennosti,' ibid., no. 1, January 1978, p. 4.
44. Colonel A. Krasnov (professor) and Colonel V. Koroteev (pilot), 'Taktika palubnoi aviatsii SShA', ibid., no. 8, August 1975, p. 82.
45. G. Borisov, 'Tendentsiya razvitiya samoletnogo parka i vooruzheniya takticheskoi i palubnoi aviatsii stran NATO', ibid., no. 9, September 1977, p. 74.
46. Interview: 'Vernye strazhi neba otchizny', *Pravda*, 9 April 1978. For the date of Batitsky's replacement: *Spravochnik Ofitsera Protivovozdushnoi Oborony* (Moscow, 1981), p. 15.
47. Testimony of Dr. Jack Vorona, 8 November 1979: *Soviet Defense Expenditure and Related Programs: Hearings Before the Subcommittee on General Procurement of the Committee on Armed Services, United States Senate, 96th Congress, 1st and 2nd Sessions, 1, 8 November 1979; 4 February 1980* (Washington DC, 1980) p. 63.
48. H. Brown, *Thinking About National Security: Defense and Foreign Policy in a Dangerous World* (Boulder, 1983) p. 63.
49. Skinner, *U.S.A.F.E.*, p. 67.
50. Ibid., p. 61.
51. Testimony, 25 May 1970: *United States Security Agreements and Commitments Abroad: Hearings Before the Subcommittee on United States Agreements and Commitments Abroad of the Committee on Foreign Relations United States Senate, 91st Congress*, vol. 11, Part 5–11 (Washington DC, 1971) pp. 2018–19.
52. This tortuous tale has been well told by Bill Gunston in his *F-111 General Dynamics: Modern Combat Aircraft 2* (London, 1978).
53. Skinner, *U.S.A.F.E..*, pp. 60–1.
54. 'USAFE—American Air Shield for Europe', *Air Force Magazine*, vol. 55, no. 5, May 1972, p. 67.
55. *United States Military Posture for FY 1979 by Chairman of The Joint Chiefs of Staff* (Washington DC, 1984) p. 32.
56. *United States Military Posture FY 1985: The Organization of the Joint Chiefs of Staff* (Washington DC, 1984) p. 32.
57. IISS, *Military Balance 1972–73* (London, 1972) p. 89; for an assessment of the balance—W. White, *U.S. Tactical Air Power: Missions, Forces, and Costs* (Washington DC, 1974) pp. 112–21.
58. US Department of Defense, *Soviet Military Power 1985* (Washington DC, 1985) p. 85.
59. Testimony, 5 March 1974: *Senate Hearings Before the Committee on Appropriations, Department of Defense Appropriations, 93rd Congress, 2nd Session, Fiscal Year 1975*, Part I (Washington DC, 1974) p. 286.
60. US Department of Defense, *Annual Report of Secretary of Defense Donald H. Rumsfeld* (Washington DC, 1976) p. 127.
61. US Department of Defense, *Annual Report of Secretary of Defense Harold Brown*, FY 1981 (Washington DC, 1980) p. 103.
62. US Department of Defense, *Soviet Military Power 1983* (Washington DC, 1983) p. 43.
63. Department of State, 'FBS and Other Non-Central Systems in SALT

TWO', Memorandum for the Verification Panel Working Groups, 20 October 1972, pp. 28–9: quoted in R. Garthoff, *Perspectives On The Strategic Balance* (Washington DC, 1983) p. 19–20.

64. Final Report, 21 December 1970: *United States Security Arrangements and Commitments Abroad: Hearings Before the Subcommittee on United States Security Arrangements and Commitments Abroad of the Committee on Foreign Relations United States Senate, 91st Congress*, vol. 1, Parts 5–11 (Washington DC, 1971) p. 2427.

65. 'NATO Ministerial Meeting, Final Communiqué (Brussels, December 1967) *NATO Letter*, January 1968, vol. 16, no. 1, p. 25.

66. 'NATO Council—5th December 1969, Final Communiqué', ibid., January 1970, vol. 18, p. 24.

67. *US Security Issues in Europe: Burden Sharing and Offset, MBFR and Nuclear Weapons, September 1973, A Staff Report Prepared for the Use of the Subcommittee on U.S. Security Agreements and Commitments Abroad of the Committee on Foreign Relations, United States Senate*, 2 December 1973 (Washington DC, 1973) p. 13.

68. *NATO Letter*, March-April 1971, vol. 19, no. 2, p. 13.

69. Colonel B. Samorukov, 'Combat Operations Involving Conventional Means of Destruction', *Voennaya Mysl'*, no. 8, August 1967: *Selected Readings*, pp. 259–78.

70. A. Grechko, 'V.I. Lenin i stroitel'stvo sovetskikh vooruzhennykh sil', *Kommunist*, no. 3, 1969, p. 23.

71. Major-General N. Vasendin and Colonel N. Kuznetsov, 'Modern Warfare and Surprise Attack', *Voennaya Mysl'*, no. 6, June 1968: *Selected Readings*, pp. 337–48.

72. Smith, *Doubletalk*, p. 127.

73. 'Second Annual Report to the Congress on United States Foreign Policy', 25 February 1971: *Public Papers of the Presidents of the United States: Richard Nixon 1971* (Washington DC, 1972) p. 231.

74. M. Debré, 'France's Global Strategy', *Foreign Affairs*, April 1971, vol. 49, no. 3, p. 403.

75. *Public Papers*, p. 238.

76. 'Third Annual Report to the Congress on United States Foreign Policy', 9 February 1972: *Public Papers of the Presidents of the United States: Richard Nixon 1972* (Washington DC, 1972) p. 200.

77. *Statement on the Defence Estimates 1968, Command 3540* (London, 1968) p. 4.

78. IISS, *The Military Balance 1970–71* (London, 1970) pp. 35–6.

79. Ibid., pp. 26–7; also *US Security Issues in Europe*, pp. 23–4.

80. Smith, *Doubletalk*, p. 145.

81. *US Security Issues in Europe*, p. 23.

82. Konstantin Sevakin, on Moscow radio in English to the US, 10 May 1982: FBIS, *Daily Report: The Soviet Union*, vol.3, 091.

83. 'Beseda A. A. Gromyko s politicheskimi obozrevatelyami', *Izvestiya*, 15 January 1985.

84. 'Press-konferentsiya A. A. Gromyko', 2 April 1983, *Pravda*, 3 April 1983.

85. Smith, *Doubletalk*, p. 189; R. Garthoff, 'SALT and the Soviet Mili-

tary'. *Problems of Communism*, January-February 1975, p. 31; Garthoff, 'The Soviet SS-20 Decision', *Survival*, no. 3, May-June 1983, p. 111. Garthoff was at that time deputy head of the US SALT delegation. For the treaty text: United States Arms Control and Disarmament Agency (USACDA), *Arms Control and Disarmament Agreements* (London, 1984) pp. 150–7.
86.	Ibid., p. 157.
87.	Ibid.
88.	M. Tatu in *Le Monde*, 5 February 1983; also his *La bataille des euromissiles*.

2 The Chinese Connexion, 1969–73

1.	H. Kissinger, *The White House Years* (London, 1979) p. 183.
2.	E. Hoxha, *Reflections on China 1: 1962–1972. Extracts from the Political Diary* (Tirana, 1979) pp. 438–9.
3.	Editorial, 'Vernost' voinskomu dolgu', *Krasnaya Zvezda*, 25 March 1969.
4.	Colonel L. Sytov, 'Voenno-politicheskii avantyurizm maoistov', *Kommunist Vooruzhennykh Sil*, no. 8, April 1969, p. 10.
5.	Smith, *Double Talk*, pp. 139–40.
6.	Ibid., p. 140.
7.	Ibid., p. 141.
8.	Ibid., pp. 142 and 295.
9.	O. Borisov and B. Koloskov, *Sovetsko-Kitaiskie Otnosheniya 1945–1977*, 2nd, revised ed. (Moscow, 1977) p. 480.
10.	*Pravda*, 23 June 1971; also, 'Moscou précise son projet de conférence des cinq puissances nucléaires', *Le Monde*, 24 June 1971. The former Soviet diplomat Shevchenko claims to be the author of the proposal: Shevchenko, *Breaking with Moscow*, pp. 162–3.
11.	I. Alexandrov, 'Po povodu kontaktov Pekina s Vashingtonom', *Pravda*, 25 June 1971.
12.	G. Arbatov, 'Voprosy, trebuyushchie prakticheskogo otveta: k plani-ruemoi amerikano-kitaiskoi vstreche v verkhakh', ibid., 10 August 1971.
13.	The following Soviet explanation is revealing: 'one section of the leading circle of Maoists headed by Lin Piao considered it possible and necessary to combine the struggle against the USSR with simultaneous opposition to the United States . . . The other section, headed by Mao Tse-tung and Chou En-lai, were determined to make use of anti-Sovietism for a 'volte-face' westwards, and for a reorientation of the CPR's foreign policy towards a rapprochement with the USA in particular'—Borisov and Koloskov, *Sovetsko-Kitaiskie Otnosheniya*, p. 461.
14.	'Reading the minutes of a talk with Chou En-lai', 17 December 1972: Hoxha, *Revelations*, p. 761.
15.	See note 13.
16.	Garthoff, *Detente and Confrontation*, p. 208.

17. Col. L. Sytov, 'Voenno-politicheskii avantyurizm maoistov', *Kommunist Vooruzhennykh Sil*, no. 8, April 1969, pp. 10 and 15.
18. Kissinger, *The White House Years*, p. 173.
19. Entry, 24 July 1970: Hoxha, *Reflections*, p. 504.
20. Ibid., p. 502.
21. Entry, 9 June 1972: ibid., p. 722.
22. Berman and Baker, *Soviet Strategic Forces*, p. 43.
23. C. Murphy, 'China's Nuclear Deterrent', *Air Force Magazine*, April 1972, vol. 55, no. 4, p. 24.
24. Berman and Baker, *Soviet Strategic Forces*, loc. cit.
25. US ACDA, *Arms Control and Disarmament Agreements* (London, 1984) pp. 159–60.
26. V. Akimov and A. Pamor, 'The Foreign Press on Military-Economic Preparations of the Chinese People's Republic', *Voennaya Mysl'*, no. 9, September 1973: CIA, *Foreign Press Digest*, 3 October 1974, pp. 99–108.
27. 'Studio 9', on Moscow television, 18 July 1975: FBIS, *Daily Report: The Soviet Union*, no. 146, 29 July 1975. I have corrected the translation.

3 SALT's Side-Effects, 1973–74

1. V. Kosovan and K. Semenov, 'International Situation—Questions and Answers', Moscow domestic service, 12 February 1982: FBIS, *Daily Report: The Soviet Union*, 17 February, 1982, no. 32.
2. *Financial Times*, 25 May 1972; also R. Garthoff, *Detente and Confrontation*, p. 100.
3. Editorial, 'Sily Sotsializma nesokrushimy', *Krasnaya Zvezda*, 22 June 1972.
4. O. Grinev, V. Pavlov, 'Vazhnyi shag k obuzdaniyu gonki vooruzhenii', *Pravda*, 22 June 1972.
5. H. Kissinger, *Years of Upheaval* (Boston, 1982) p. 267.
6. U. Alexis Johnson, *The Right Hand of Power* (New Jersey, 1984) p. 588.
7. H. Kissinger, *Years of Upheaval* p. 272.
8. Johnson, *The Right Hand* pp. 596–7.
9. Ibid., 589.
10. *Senate Hearings Before the Committee on Appropriations, Department of Defense Appropriations, 93rd Congress, Second Session, Fiscal Year 1975*, Part 1 (Washington DC, 1974) p. 268.
11. *Statement on the Defence Estimates 1975: Command 5976* (London, 1975) p. 8.
12. *Hearing Before the Subcommittee on Arms Control, International Law and Organization of the Committee on Foreign Relations, United States Senate, 93rd Congress, 2nd Session, 11 September 1974* (Washington DC, 1975) p. 43.
13. 'Observers' Roundtable', Moscow domestic service, 30 December 1973: FBIS, *Daily Report: The Soviet Union*, 2 January 1974, no. 1.
14. Speech in Warsaw, 17 October 1974: *Pravda*, 18 October 1974.

15. *US-USSR Strategic Policies: Hearing Before the Subcommittee on Arms Control, International Law and Organization of the Committee on Foreign Relations, United States Senate, 93rd Congress, 2nd Session on US and Soviet Strategic Doctrine and Military Policies*, 4 March 1974 (Washington DC, 1974) p. 50.
16. Ibid., p. 51.
17. *US-USSR Strategic Policies*, p. 8.
18. Page 62 of Schlesinger's report cited by Senator Symington: ibid., p. 18.
19. Ibid., p. 18.
20. *Hearing Before the Subcommittee*, p. 42.
21. *Military Implications of the Treaty of the Limitation of Strategic Offensive Arms and Protocol Thereto (SALT II Treaty). Hearings Before the Committee on Armed Services, United States Senate, 95th Congress, 1st Session*, Part 1 (Washington DC, 1979) p. 170.
22. *Full Committee Considerations of Overall National Security Programs and Related Budgeted Requirements: Committee on Armed Services, House of Representatives, 94th Congress, 1st Session* (Washington DC 1975) p. 157.
23. *The American Commitment to NATO: Report of the Special Subcommittee on North Atlantic Treaty Organization Commitments of the Committee on Armed Services, House of Representatives, 92nd Congress, 2nd Session, 17 August 1972* (Washington DC, 1972) p. 14947.
24. *US Security Issues*, p. 13.
25. Kissinger, *Years of Upheaval*, p. 136; see also Garthoff, *Detente and Confrontation*, pp. 321.
26. For the text: USACDA, *Arms Control and Disarmament*, pp. 159–60.
27. For the circumstances surrounding the agreement: Garthoff, *Detente and Confrontation*, pp. 334–44.
28. *US Security Issues*, p. 13.
29. Testimony of General Goodpastor, SACEUR, in the 4 March 1974: *US Military Commitments to Europe*, p. 153; Garthoff, *Detente and Confrontation*, pp. 401–5.
30. Ibid. p. 153.
31. 'Secretary Kissinger Interviewed for L'Express of France', *Department of State Bulletin*, 12 May 1975, p. 612.
32. Ibid., p. 609.
33. Alexander Druzhinin (All-Union Radio and TV), 'International Observers' Roundtable', Moscow Radio, 14 July 1974: FBIS, *Daily Report: The Soviet Union*, 15 July 1974, vol. 3, no. 136.
34. 'International Observers' Roundtable', Moscow radio, 10 March 1974: ibid., 11 March 1974, vol. 3, no. 48.
35. N. Polyanov, 'NATO: Krizis doveriya', *Izvestiya*, 24 April 1975.
36. Prof. N. Molchanov, 'Polemika: Novye Otkroveniya Bzhezinskogo', *Literaturnaya Gazeta*, 4 June 1975.
37. *United States Military Posture for FY 1976 by Chairman of the Joint Chiefs of Staff General George S. Brown, USAF* (Washington DC, 1975) pp. 124–8. For a balanced assessment of conventional forces in

Europe and a critique of worst-case approaches, see J. Dean, *Watershed in Europe: Dismantling the East-West Military Confrontation* (Lexington Mass., 1987) pp. 38–58.
38 J. Callaghan, *Time and Change* (London, 1987) p.552.

39. *US Security Issues in Europe. Burden Sharing and Offset, MBFR and Nuclear Weapons, September 1973. A Staff Report Prepared for the Use of the Subcommittee on US Security Agreements and Commitments Abroad of the Committee on Foreign Relations, United States Senate, 2 December 1973* (Washington DC 1973) pp. 9 and 12–13.

40. *Cmnd. 6201*, doc. 124.

41. Ibid., doc. 128.

42. Ibid., doc. 154.

43. Ibid., doc. 161.

44. *Pravda*, 31 March 1971.

45. *Materialy XXIV S''ezda KPSS* (Moscow, 1971) pp. 191–6, *XXV S''ezd Kommunisticheskoi Partii Sovetskogo Soyuza: Stenograficheskii Otchet* vol. 1 (Moscow, 1976) p. 464; *XXVI S''ezd Kommunisticheskoi Partii Sovetskogo Soyuza*, vol. 1 (Moscow, 1981) p. 375.

46. *Materialy XXIV S''ezd KPSS*, pp. 191–6.

47. Speech to voters of the Bauman electoral district, Moscow: *Pravda*, 12 June 1971,

48. For the inside story: J. Dean, *Watershed in Europe* pp. 99–110.

49. Ibid., also, Yu. Kostko, 'Voennaya konfrontatsiya i problema bezopasnosti v Evrope', *Mirovaya Ekonomika i Mezhdunarodnye Otnosheniya* No 9, 22 August 1972, pp. 20 and 21.

50. *Miscellaneous No 17 (1977): Selected Documents* doc. 34.

51. L. Mendelevich, 'Diplomaticheskie zametki o khel'sinskikh konsul'tatsiyakh 1972–1973 godov po podgotovke obshchestvennogo soveshchaniya', *Diplomaticheskii Vestnik: God 1982* (Moscow 1983) p. 210.

52. *The Times*, 16 January 1974.

53. K. Borisov, 'Chto tormozit peregovory v Vene', *Novoe Vremya*, no. 12, 22 March 1974, p. 7.

54. See M. MccGwire, *Military Objectives in Soviet Foreign Policy* (Washington DC, 1987) pp. 388–405 and N. Trulock, 'Weapons of Mass Destruction in Soviet Military Strategy' (unpublished manuscript), pp. 52–60, in particular. Trulock bases his study on lecture material from the Voroshilov General Staff Academy which may be taken as authoritative.

55. The senior analyst was Lt. Col. John Hines. The quotation is from an article by Hines, P. Petersen and N. Trulock: 'Soviet Military Theory from 1945–2000: Implications for NATO', *The Washington Quarterly*, vol. 9, no. 4, Autumn, 1986, p. 124.

56. Speech to the Prague garrison, 19 December 1973: *Bratislavska Pravda*, 20 December 1973: FBIS, *Daily Report: The Soviet Union* no. 2, 3 January 1974.

57. Quoted in Garthoff, *Detente and Confrontation*, p. 433.

58. Ibid.

59. Editorial, 'V interesakh bezopasnosti narodov', *Krasnaya Zvezda*, 31 July 1974.

60. Lt. Gen. P. Zhilin, 'Pouchitel'nye uroki istorii', *Pravda*, 1 August 1974.
61. A. Johnson, *At the Right Hand*, p. 600.
62. Kissinger, *Years of Upheaval*, p. 429.
63. Garthoff, *Detente and Confrontation*, p. 429.
64. A. Arbatov and G. Arbatov, 'Idei Dzh. Shlesindzhera po forme i soderzhaniyu'. *Novoe Vremya*, no. 30, 25 July 1975, p. 20.
65. Johnson, *At the Right Hand*, p. 604.
66. G. Ford, *A Time to Heal* (New York, 1979) p.216.

4 The SS-20 Decisions: from Testing to Deployment, 1974–77

1. *Kak ustranit' ugrozu Evrope* (Moscow 1983) p. 26.
2. V. Sobakin, *Ravnaya bezopasnost': printsip ravenstva i odinakovoi bezoposnosti v sovremennykh mezhdunarodnykh otnosheniyakh* (Moscow 1984) p. 131.
3. Interview: *Frankfurter Rundschau*, 1 October 1981.
4. R. Garthoff, *Detente and Confrontation* p. 875.
5. *APN Military Bulletin*—FBIS, *Daily Report: The Soviet Union*, 18 December 1987.
6. R. Kaufman, 'Causes of the Slowdown in Soviet Defense', *Survival* vol. XXVII, No. 4, July/August 1985, p. 185.
7. US Department of Defense, *Soviet Military Power* (Washington DC, 1983) p. 43.
8. D. Holloway, *The Soviet Union and the Arms Race* (London, 1983) pp. 151–2; Garthoff, 'The Soviet SS-20 Decision', *Survival*, vol XXV, no. 3. May/June 1983.
9. Berman and Baker, *Soviet Strategic Forces*, p. 66.
10. Holloway, *The Soviet Union*, p. 69; Garthoff, 'The Soviet SS-20 Decision', p. 112 and *Detente and Confrontation*, p. 875; S. Meyer, 'Soviet Theatre Nuclear Forces', p. 23; 'Sinnlos und gefährlich, gefährlich fur alle', *Der Spiegel*, no. 39, 26 September 1983, p. 173; *Jane's Weapons Systems 1985–86* (New York, 1986) p. 9.
11. 'Sinnlos und gefährlich . . .', pp. 173–4.
12. Entry: *Voennyi Entsiklopedicheskii Slovar'* (Moscow, 1983) pp. 812–13.
13. CIA, *The Soviet Weapons Industry: An Overview* (Washington DC, 1986) p. 21.
14. *New York Times*, 28 November 1987.
15. J. Thomson, 'The LRTNF Decision: Evolution of US Theatre Nuclear Policy 1975–9', *International Affairs*, vol. 60, no. 4, Autumn 1984, p. 602.
16. The spy referred to by the Russians was Emelda Therop, who worked in NATO's international secretariat: FBIS, *Daily Report: The Soviet Union*, no. 143, 25 July 1983.
17. Statement made on Moscow domestic television, 25 December 1981: FBIS, ibid., no. 249, 29 December 1981.
18. M. Legge, *Theater Nuclear Weapons and the NATO Strategy of Flexible Response* (Santa Monica, 1983) p. 29.

Notes 193

19. *International Defense Review*, vol. 10, no. 6, December 1977, p. 1027.
20. 'Defence Planning Committee Communiqué (Brussels, 22–23 May 1975)', *The NATO Review*, vol. 23, no. 3, 1975, p. 28.
21. R. Shearer, 'Nuclear Weapons and the Defence of Europe', ibid., no. 6, 1975, p. 14.
22. Secretary of Defense James Schlesinger, *The Theater Nuclear Force Posture in Europe: A Report to the United States Congress in Compliance with Public Law 93–365* (Washington DC, 1975) p. 15.
23. C. Paine, 'Pershing II: the Army's Strategic Weapon', *The Bulletin of the Atomic Scientists*, vol. 36, no. 8, October 1980, p. 25.
24. Ibid.; also *Report to the Congress Completed by the Comptroller General of the United States: Comparison of the Pershing II Program With the Acquisition Plan Recommended by the Commission of Government Procurement, Department of Defense* (Washington DC, 1977) p. 22.
25. Paine, 'Pershing II . . .', pp. 25–6.
26. *Senate Hearings Before the Committee on Appropriations, Department of Defense Appropriations, 93rd Congress, 2nd Session, Fiscal Year 1975, Part 2, Department of the Army: Hearings Before a Subcommittee of the Committee on Appropriations, United States Senate, 93rd Congress 2nd Session* (Washington DC, 1974) p. 565.
27. 'NATO Missile Standardization Pushed', *Aviation Week and Space Technology*, 2 June 1975, p. 63.
28. Ibid., 11 November 1974, p. 11.
29. *International Defense Review*, vol. 10, no. 1, February 1977, p. 19. For a Soviet evaluation published a year later: M. Shelekhov, 'Krylatye rakety SShA', *Vestnik Protivovozdushnoi Oborony*, no. 5, May 1978, pp. 84–7.
30. F. Kaplan, 'Warring Over New Missiles for NATO', *New York Times* (Magazine), 9 December 1979, p. 56. Kaplan exaggerates the significance of the group, at least according to one of its members in correspondence with the author.
31. Garthoff, *Detente and Confrontation*, pp. 446–7.
32. Thomson, 'The LRTNF decision . . .', p. 603.
33. The CIA disagreed with the original and faulty DIA assessment: M. Gordon, 'Pentagon Reassesses Soviet Bomber', *Washington Post*, 1 October 1985.
34. Garthoff, *Detente and Controntation*, pp. 540–1.
35. U. Alexis Johnson, *The Right Hand of Power* (New Jersey, 1984) p. 617. Johnson headed the US negotiating team to SALT II at this time. Also, Thomson, 'The LRTNF . . .', p. 603; and C. Vance, *Hard Choices: Critical Years in America's Foreign Policy* (New York, 1983) p. 47.
36. Thomson, 'The LRTNF decision . . .', p. 603.
37. R. Huiskon, 'The History of Modern Cruise Missile Programs', ed. R. Betts, *Cruise Missiles: Technology, Strategy, Politics* (Washington DC, 1981) p. 90.
38. *Department of Defense Appropriations for 1978: Hearings Before a Subcommittee of the Committee on Appropriations, House of*

Representatives 95th Congress, 1st Session, Part 1 (Washington DC, 1977) p. 573.
39. *International Defense Review*, vol. 10, no. 1, February 1977, p. 19.
40. *Financial Times*, 10 December 1974.
41. Ibid.
42. J. Sharp, 'Prospects for Limiting Nuclear Forces in Europe', eds M. Olive and J. Porro, *Nuclear Weapons in Europe: Modernization and Limitation* (Lexington, 1983) p. 76.
43. J. Keliher, *The Negotiations on Mutual and Balanced Force Reductions: The Search for Arms Control in Central Europe* (New York, 1980?) pp. 67–73.
44. *SALT AND THE NATO ALLIES: A Staff Report to the Subcommittee on European Affairs of the Committee on Foreign Relations, United States Senate* (Washington DC, 1979) p. 29.
45. Ibid., p. 30.
46. Ibid., p. 26.
47. Thomson, 'The LRTNF . . .', p. 603. General Haig, then SACEUR, recalls: 'It came as a great shock to me as a NATO Commander when I learned that American negotiators had indeed such a protocol [on Cruise] in their bilateral discussions with the Soviet Union without ever having coordinated such a position with me as the responsible commander in Europe . . . when that was revealed in Europe it was not only a shock to our allies, it was a great shock to me, because they came to me and said, "What in heavens name have you done to place in hostage systems which we might need for our defense and concurrently to let systems run free which are a direct threat to us?" ', statement to the Senate Armed Services Committee, 26 July 1979: *Military Implications of the Treaty on the Limitation of Strategic Offensive Arms and Protocol Thereto (SALT II Treaty): Hearings Before the Committee on Armed Services, US Senate, 96th Congress, 1st Session, Part 1* (Washington DC, 1979) pp. 357 and 361.
48. The American official was Paul Warnke, briefly head of the US Arms Control and Disarmament Agency, in 1977. The quotation appears in S. Talbott, *Endgame: The Inside Story of SALT II* (New York, 1979) p. 73.
49. *Senate Delegation Report on SALT Discussions in the Soviet Union, August 25–30, 1979: A Report to the Committee on Foreign Relations, United States Senate* (Washington DC, 1979) p. 8.
50. Colonel Alexei Leont'ev, 'Neft' pakhnet krov'yu: Zametki voennogo obozrevatelya', *Krasnaya Zvezda*, 1 December 1974.
51. *Pravda*, 17 April 1975; *Kommunisticheskaya Partiya Sovetskogo Soyuza v Rezolyutsiyakh i Resheniyakh S"ezdov, Konferentsii i Plenumov TsK*, vol. 12 (1975–77) (Moscow, 1977) p. 13.
52. Editorial, 'Kursom pravil'nym dal'novidnym', *Krasnaya Zvezda*, 27 April 1975.
53. Efimov, 'Problemy voennoi razryadki v Evrope': *Mezhdunarodnaya Zhizn'*, no. 11, 21 October 1975, p. 19.
54. K. Borisov, 'Venskie peregovory: chto dal'she', *Novoe Vremya*, no. 15, 9 April 1976, pp. 4–5.

55. *Miscellaneous No 17 (1977): Selected Documents Relating to Problems of Security and Cooperation in Europe, 1954–77*. *Cmnd 6932* (London, 1977) doc. 81.
56. Shevchenko, *Breaking With Moscow*, p. 264.
57. Ibid., p. 266.
58. Private information.
59. Report from 'Our Diplomatic Staff' entitled 'Soviet Slows Up SALT', *Daily Telegraph*, 13 November 1975.
60. A. Svetlov, 'Bor'ba Sovetskogo Soyuza za voennuyu razryadku', *Mezhdunarodnaya Zhizn'*, no. 1, 1976 (published 9 December 1975) p. 91.
61. Col. Dr Tyushkevich, 'Razvitie ucheniya o voine i armii na opyte velikoi otechestvennoi voiny', *Kommunist Vooruzhennykh Sil*, no. 22, 4 November 1975, p.14.
62. *Izvestiya* observer V. Osipov, 'Razryadka—inogo ne dano', *Novoe Vremya*, no. 7, 15 February 1974, p. 7.
63. FBIS, *Daily Report: The Soviet Union*, no. 188, 27 September 1976.
64. 'Topical Problems of International Life', Moscow domestic service, 30 November 1976: ibid., no. 233, 2 December 1976.
65. Albert Grigoryants, appearing on 'International Observers' Roundtable', Moscow television, 14 July 1974: ibid., no. 136, 15 July 1974.
66. Moscow radio in English broadcasting to Africa, 14 July 1976: ibid., no. 137, 15 July 1976.
67. V. Nekrasov, 'Razoruzhenie—neotlozhnaya zadacha', *Sovetskaya Rossiya*, 23 September 1976.
68. Prof. Major-General R. Simonyan, 'Kontseptsiya "vybora tseli"', *Krasnaya Zvezda*, 28 September 1976.
69. *Statement on the Defence Estimates 1975: Cmnd. 5976*, p. 28.
70. *White Paper 1973/1974: The Security of the Federal Republic of Germany and the Development of the Federal Armed Forces* (Bonn, 1973?) p. 16.
71. Ibid., p. 15.
72. *Statement on the Defence Estimates 1975*, p. 8.
73. *Statement on the Defence Estimates 1976: Cmnd. 6432*, p. 9.
74. US Department of Defense, *Annual Report of Secretary of Defense Donald H. Rumsfeld* (Washington DC, 1976) p. 106.
75. Ray Huffstutler, director, strategic research, CIA, 1 November 1979: *Soviet Defense Expenditures and Related Programs: Hearings Before the Subcommittee on General Procurement of the Committee on Armed Services, United States Senate, 96th Congress, 1st and 2nd Sessions* (Washington DC, 1980) p.43.
76. *United States Military Posture: An Overview By General David C. Jones, USAF, Chairman of the Joint Chiefs of Staff, For FY 1980* (Washington DC, 1979), p. 35.
77. *United States Military Posture For FY 1979 By Chairman of the Joint Chiefs of Staff General George S. Brown (USAF)* (Washington DC, 1978) p. 48.
78. Skinner, *U.S.A.F.E.*, p. 14.
79. *United States Military Posture: An Overview*, p. 35.

196 *Notes*

80. B. Gunston, *An Illustrated Guide to NATO Fighters and Attack Aircraft* (New York, 1983), p. 82.
81. Skinner, *U.S.A.F.E.* p. 64.
82. *United States Military Posture: An Overview*, p. 35.
83. Ibid.
84. D. Rumsfeld, *Annual Defense Report FY 1978* (Washington DC 1977), p. 211.
85. *Public Papers of the Presidents of the United States: Jimmy Carter 1977*, Book 1 (Washington DC, 1977) p. 3.
86. P. Nitze, 'Assuring Strategic Stability in an Era of Detente', *Foreign Affairs*, vol. 54, no. 2, January 1976, p. 207.
87. *New York Times*, 17 December 1976.
88. Ibid., 28 December 1976.
89. See Z. Brzezinski, *Power and Principle: Memoirs of the National Security Adviser 1977–1981* (London, 1983), pp. 157–63; C. Vance, *Hard Choices*, pp. 48–9.
90. Brzezinski, *Power and Principle*, p. 152; J. Carter, *Keeping Faith: Memoirs of a President* (London, 1982) p. 217.
91. *Public Papers of the Presidents of the United States: Jimmy Carter 1977, Book 1* (Washington DC, 1977) p. 447.
92. *Public Papers*, p. 498.
93. K. Georg'ev, 'Zadacha—ogranichenie strategicheskikh vooruzhenii', *Kazakhstanskaya Pravda*, 3 September 1976.
94. Brzezinski, *Power and Principle*, pp. 153–4; Carter, *Keeping Faith*, p. 218.
95. Ibid., pp. 154–5.
96. Vance, *Hard Choices*, p. 54.
97. Brzezinski, *Power and Principles*, p. 162.
98. Talbott, *Endgame*, pp. 73–4.
99. *Public Papers*, pp. 542–3.
100. 'Press-Konferentsiya A. A. Gromyko', *Pravda*, 1 April 1977.
101. *Senate Delegation Report on SALT Discussions*, p. 9.
102. J. Reifenberg, 'Mit Amerika nicht im reinen', *Frankfurter Allgemeine*, 21 March 1977.
103. *Stampa Sera*, 9 May 1977: FBIS, *Daily Report: Western Europe*, no. 94, 16 May 1977.
104. Vance, *Hard Choices*, p. 66.
105. Ibid., p. 53.
106. J. Callaghan, *Time and Change*, (London, 1987) p. 483.
107. See A. Vadarmis, 'German-American Military Fissures', *Foreign Policy*, no. 34, Spring 1979, pp. 91–2. Vadarmis was then serving as a colonel in the US Army; also D. Schwartz, *NATO's Nuclear Dilemmas* (Washington DC, 1983) p. 213.
108. Schmidt's speech to the Bundestag, 12 May 1977: FBIS, *Daily Report: Western Europe*, no. 93, 13 May 1977.
109. Brzezinski, *Power and Principle*, p. 293.
110. Vance, *Hard Choices*, p. 66.
111. Thomson, 'The LRTNF decision . . .', p. 604.
112. Kaplan, 'Warring Over New Missiles For NATO', p. 56.

113. Personal communication from Ambassador James Goodby.
114. Thomson, 'The LRTNF decision . . .', p. 604.

5 The Reaction in Western Europe 1977–79

1. J. Barry, 'Revealed: the Truth about Labour and Cruise', *The Sunday Times*, 6 February 1983.
2. Thomson, 'The LRTNF decision . . . ', p. 604.
3. On the creation of the HLG: P. Buteux, *Strategy, Doctrine and the Politics of Alliance: Theatre Nuclear Force Modernisation in NATO* (Boulder, 1983) p. 102. Buteux appears to overstate the degree of alarm at the SS-20 and its role in the foundations of the HLG. Legge describes the HLG's purpose as being 'to emphasize that the U.S. was still serious about theater nuclear forces'. The implication of this is that the creation of the HLG was meant as a gesture, not as a serious step towards confronting the threat emerging from the SS-20. See Legge, *Theater Nuclear Weapons*, p. 34.
4. H. Schmidt, 'If the Missiles Go, Peace May Stay', *New York Times*, 29 April 1987.
5. For the text: *Survival*, vol. XX, no. 1, Jan/Feb 1978, p. 4.
6. *Briefings on SALT Negotiations: Hearings Before the Committee on Foreign Relations, United States Senate, 95th Congress, 1st Session* (Washington DC, 1978) p. 32.
7. Private information.
8. Barry, 'Revealed . . .'.
9. Ibid.
10. Legge, *Theater Nuclear Weapons*, p 70.
11. 'U.S. Sale of Trident One Missiles to U.K.': A background briefing released by the White House, Tuesday 15 July 1980, quoting an 'Administrative Official' (unnamed)—*International Communication Agency, US Embassy, London, Official Text*, Thursday 17 July 1980.
12. The diplomat has not been identified: *SALT AND THE NATO ALLIES*, p. 20.
13. The journalist has not been identified: ibid., pp. 20–1.
14. Thomson, 'The LRTNF decision . . .'.
15. 'V Tsentral'nom Komitete KPSS', *Pravda*, 27 August 1978.
16. Vadim Nekrasov on Moscow radio in English to Britain, 7 April 1977: FBIS, *Daily Report: The Soviet Union*, no. 67, 9 April 1977.
17. 'International Observers' Roundtable', 10 April 1977: ibid., no. 69, 11 April 1977.
18. Shevchenko, *Breaking With Moscow*, pp. 168–9; also, the memoirs of another former Soviet diplomat: N. Polianski, *M.I.D.: Douze ans dans les services diplomatiques du Kremlin* (Paris, 1984) p. 35.
19. Polianski, *M.I.D.* p. 36.
20. Shevchenko, *Breaking With Moscow*, p. 111.
21. Ibid., pp. 265–6.
22. D. Ardamatsky, 'America is Now Trying to Involve Europe in the Strategic Arms Race', *Aktuelt* (Copenhagen) 10 June 1977: FBIS, *Daily Report: The Soviet Union*, no. 116, 16 June 1977.

23. V. Berezin and V. Vinogradov, 'Novye stavki Pentagona', *Krasnaya Zvezda*, 3 July 1977.
24. N. Lebedev (ed.) *XXVI S"ezd KPSS i Aktual'nye Problemy Mezhdunarodnykh Otnoshenii* (Moscow 1983), p. 178.
25. This much is evident from the testimony of Paul Warnke, head of the US Arms Control and Disarmament Agency on 29 November 1977: *Briefings on SALT Negotiations: Hearings Before the Committee on Foreign Relations, United States Senate, 95th Congress, 1st Session* (Washington DC, 1978) p. 51; also, interview with Ambassador Goodby.
26. A more official protest was issued by TASS on 31 July: *Pravda*, 31 July 1977.
27. 'WPC Calls for Worldwide Action Against Neutron Bomb. *Unite, say "No" to Horror-Bomb!'*, special issue of the World Peace Council newsletter, *Peace Courier*, August 1977.
28. Haslam, *Soviet Foreign Policy 1930–33: The Impact of the Depression* (London, 1983) pp. 91–2.
29. 'You and I have both fought against pacifism as a programme for the revolutionary proletarian party. That much is clear. But who has ever denied the use of pacifists by that party to soften up the enemy, the bourgeoisie?' – Lenin to Chicherin, 16 February 1922: V. Lenin, *Collected Works*, vol. 45 (Moscow, 1970) doc. 637.
30. Interview with Jakob Berman in T. Toranska, *'Them': Stalin's Polish Puppets* (New York, 1987) *Congrès Mondial des intellectuels pour la paix – Pologne, 25–28 août 1948*, p. 290, (Warsaw, 1948).
31. A useful summary of the story appears in the East German Peace Council newsletter: *Information*, no. 4, 1979.
32. *Vtoroi Vsemirnyi Kongress Storonnikov Mira, Varshava, 16–22 noyabrya 1950 goda* (Moscow, 1951) pp. 529–30.
33. Romesh Chandra, 'Okean, kotoryi vsegda v dvizhenii', *Novoe Vremya*, no. 28, 11 July 1975, p. 17.
34. See *Covert Action (The Forgery Offensive): Hearings Before the Subcommittee on Oversight of the Permanent Select Committee on Intelligence, House of Representatives, 96th Congress, 2nd Session* (Washington DC, 1980) p. 72; also J. Barron, *KGB Today: The Hidden Hand* (New York, 1985) p. 219, who appears to have access to US Intelligence sources; and *Soviet Active Measures: Hearings Before the Permanent Select Committee on Intelligence, House of Representatives, 97th Congress*, 2nd Session (Washington DC, 1982) pp. 58–9.
35. CIA, *Directory of Soviet Officials: National Organizations* (Washington DC, 1983) p. 13. Also, A. Alexiev, 'The Soviet Campaign Against INF: Strategy, Tactics, And Means', *Orbis*, vol. 29, no. 2, Summer 1985, p. 335.
36. *Soviet Active Measures*, pp. 6 and 35; Barron, *KGB Today*, p. 218.
37. V. Shaposhnikov, 'Dvizhenie obshchestvennykh sil za mir i razryadki mezhdunarodnoi napryazhennosti', *Obshchestvennost' i Problemy Voiny i Mira*, ed. G. Morozov *et al.* (Moscow, 1976) p. 23.
38. 'WPC Calls . . .'

39. *Peace Courier*, January 1978.
40. Yu. Zhukov, 'Neotdolimaya sila', *Kommunist*, no. 7, May 1983, p. 89.
41. Thomson, 'The LRTNF decision . . .'. pp. 605–6.
42. Entry in Brzezinski's diary, 17 August 1977: Brzezinski, *Power and Principle*, p. 302. For Carter's own account, which obfuscates rather than clarifies the position: Carter, *Keeping Faith*, pp. 226–8.
43. Brzezinski, *Power and Principle*, pp. 304–5.
44. Ibid., pp. 305–6.
45. Vance, *Hard Choices*, p. 96.
46. Thomson, 'The LRTNF decision . . .', p. 606.
47. *Peace Courier*, July 1978.
48. Carter, *Keeping Faith*, p. 235; Brzezinski, *Power and Principle*, p. 295; Schmidt, 'If the Missiles Go . . .'.
49. Brzezinski, *Power and Principle*, p. 295.
50. Carter recalls: 'Helmut was very contentious, insisting that he would permit the deployment of additional missiles on his soil only when other European nations agreed to similar arrangements. I replied that Helmut had initiated this entire discussion of a European nuclear imbalance' – Carter, *Keeping Faith*, p. 235; *Washington Post*, 31 October 1981; also Callaghan, *Time and Change*, p. 548.
51. Thomson, 'The LRTNF decision . . .'; also, Callaghan, *Time and Change*, p. 550.
52. Ibid., p. 611.
53. Lt. General M. Milshtein, 'Kuda natseleny amerikanskie rakety', *Izvestiya*, 19 July 1978.
54. *Information*, no. 7, 1979.
55. *Pravda*, 7 October 1979.
56. *Peace Courier*, November 1979.
57. *Keesing's Contemporary Archives*, 28 March 1980, p. 30160.
58. Ibid., p. 30159.
59. *Fiscal Year 1981 Arms Control Impact Statements: Statements Submitted to the Congress by the President Pursuant to Section 36 of the Arms Control and Disarmament Act* (Washington DC, 1980) p. 251.
60. Ibid., pp. 251–2.
61. *Peace Courier*, January 1980.

6 Negotiation from Weakness: The INF Talks, 1980–83

1. 'V Politburo TsK KPSS, Prezidiume Verkhovnogo Soveta SSSR, Sovete Ministrov SSSR Ob Itogakh Peregovorakh Rukovoditelei SSSR i FRG', *Pravda*, 5 July 1980.
2. *Pravda*, 23 September 1980.
3. Ibid., 24 September 1980.
4. Ibid. This position was duly reiterated in the assembly's resolutions, its 'charter': ibid., 28 September 1980.
5. Speech to the Sofia Peace Assembly, 24 September 1980: ibid., 25 September 1980.
6. Yu. Zhukov and A. Krushinskii, 'Ob"edinyaya usiliya', ibid.

7. *Peace Courier*, November 1980.
8. *Keesing's Contemporary Archives*, 20 February 1981, p. 30731. S.
Talbott, *Deadly Gambits: The Reagan Administration and the Stalemate in Nuclear Arms Control* (New York, 1984) pp. 41–2.
9. Letter to the *New York Times*, 18 November 1980.
10. The issue of the range of the Pershing II has long been a matter of
controversy. The official US position – that the missile cannot reach
Moscow – is belied by what is said in private, as well as what the
Russians themselves maintain.
11. *New York Times*, 6 January 1981.
12. Ibid., 7 January 1981.
13. *Pravda*, 24 February 1981.
14. *Facts on File, vol. 40, no. 2067, 20 June 1980, p. 451.* This elicited a
letter of protest from President Carter on 16 June.
15. *Keesing's Contemporary Archives*, 25 September 1981, p. 31099.
16. U. S. Arms Control and Disarmament Agency, *Soviet Propaganda
Campaign against NATO* (Washington DC, 1983), p. A4.
17. *New York Times*, 1 and 7 April 1981.
18. Talbott, *Deadly Gambits*, p. 49.
19. *New York Times*, 20 May 1981.
20. *Keesing's Contemporary Archives*, 25 September 1981, p. 31099.
21. *Soviet Active Measures*, p. 39.
22. *New York Times*, 13 September 1981.
23. *Keesing's Contemporary Archives*, 16 April 1982, p. 31429.
24. World Peace Council Bureau, meeting 6–8 January 1982: *Peace
Courier*, January-February 1982.
25. 'I could see where you could have the exchange of weapons against
troops in the field without it bringing either one of the major powers
to pushing the button' – press briefing, 16 October 1981: *Keesing's
Contemporary Archives*, 16 April 1982, p. 31430.
26. Ibid., p. 31429.
27. Speech to The National Press Club, Washington DC, 18 November
1981.
28. Schmidt, 'If the Missiles . . .'
29. *Keesing's Contemporary Archives*, 16 April 1982, p. 31429.
30. *New York Times*, 25 February 1986.
31. Speech in Bonn, 23 November 1981: *Pravda*, 24 November 1981.
32. 'V Politburo TsK KPSS, Prezidiume Verkhovnogo Soveta SSSR
Sovete Ministrov SSSR, Ob Itogakh Vizita General'nogo Sekretarya
TsK KPSS, Predsedatelya Prezidiuma Verkhovnogo Soveta SSSR L.
I. Brezhneva v Federativnuyu Respubliku Germanii': ibid., 1
December 1981.
33. Private information, plus *Diplomaticheskii Slovar'*, vol. 2, ed. A.
Gromyko (Moscow, 1985) p. 28, and E. Warner, *The Military in
Contemporary Soviet Politics: An Institutional Analysis* (New York,
1977) p. 225.
34. Private information, plus *Diplomaticheskii Slovar'*, vol. 3, ed. A.
Gromyko (Moscow, 1986) p. 507.
35. For more detail, Talbott, *Deadly Gambits*, pp. 81–4.

36. Vitaly Kobysh, 'Zheneva: proverka na iskrennost'', *Literaturnaya Gazeta* 2 December 1981. Kobysh was an official of the Central Committee International Information Department.
37. M. Binyon (Moscow), 'Russia fears arms talks will fail', *The Times*, 13 January 1982.
38. *Information*, no. 7, 1979.
39. V. Shaposhnikov, 'O nekotorykh problemakh sovremennogo antivoennogo dvizheniya', *Mirovaya Ekonomika i Mezhdunarodnye Otnosheniya*, no. 12, December 1981, p. 19.
40. Ibid., p. 21.
41. Ibid., p. 24.
42. Ibid., p. 25.
43. Yu. Krasin and B. Leibzon, 'Kommunisty i novye dvizheniya obshchestvennogo protesta', *Kommunist*, no. 5, March 1984, p. 115.
44. 'A Show for the European Theatre?' *Guardian*, 23 February 1981, reprinted in E. Thompson, *Beyond the Cold War: A New Approach to the Arms Race and Nuclear Annihilation* (New York, 1982) p. 112.
45. *Peace Courier*, January-February 1982. 'In recent years the effectiveness of the large well-established Communist international front organizations has been eroded in many areas because of their pronounced pro-Soviet bias on virtually every issue'. – *Soviet Active Measures*, p. 40. An attack on E. P. Thompson appears in V. Orel, 'Antivoennoe dvizhenie: ego druz'ya i protivniki', *Mezhdunarodnaya Zhizn'*, no. 3, 1983, pp. 40–8.
46. *Soviet Active Measures*, p. 51.
47. Krasin and Leibzon, 'Kommunisty . . .', p. 115.
48. 23 February 1982 – *Overview of Nuclear Arms Control and Defense Strategy in NATO: Hearings Before the Subcommittees on International Security and Scientific Affairs and on Europe and the Middle East of the Committee on Foreign Affairs, House of Representatives, 97th Congress, 2nd Session* (Washington DC, 1982) p. 51.
49. Ibid., p. 67.
50. *The Times*, 4 February 1982.
51. Brezhnev's statement to the leaders of the Socialist International was paraphrased in *Pravda*, 4 February 1982. Shaposhnikov attended the meeting as did Alexandrov (Brezhnev's personal aide) and Ponomarev.
52. *Overview*, p. 51.
53. TASS, 'Byt'' ili ne byt'' novomu vitku gonki vooruzhenii', *Pravda*, 10 February 1982.
54. *The Times*, 11 February 1982.
55. *Pravda*, 19 May 1982.
56. CIA, *The Soviet Weapons Industry: An Overview* (Washington DC, 1986) p. 1. The CIA calculates that from 1964 to 1974 Soviet defence expenditure 'grew at a real average annual rate of about 5 percent'. But expenditure dropped to an increase of 'an average of about 2 per cent annually from the mid–1970s until at least 1984' – ibid.
57. 'O prodovol'stvennoi programme SSSR na period do 1990 goda i merakh po ee realizatsii: Doklad General'nogo sekretarya TsK KPSS

tovarishcha L. I. Brezhneva na Plenume TsK KPSS, 24 maya 1982 goda', *Kommunist*, no. 9, June 1982, pp. 4–15.

58. Marshal Ustinov, 'Otvesti ugrozu yadernoi voiny', *Pravda*, 12 July 1982.

59. Talbott, *Deadly Gambits*, chapter 6. Talbott had originally obtained an inaccurate account of the episode from contacts in the US Government. He then approached Nitze. As Nitze recalls: 'When Strobe [Talbott] indicated to me what he had already been told by others about the "walk in the woods" I decided it would be better that he have the facts straight rather than having them wrong. I therefore did my best to help him get the sections dealing directly with me right. I tried not to add information on subjects [on] which he had not already been informed' – letter to *New York Times* (book review), 7 November 1984: *New York Times*, 16 December 1984. Talbott's account can therefore be equated with Nitze's account. But since Talbott had no equivalent access to Kvitsinsky, the account cannot be assumed to be completely accurate. No interpreter was present, so Talbott's account rests on Nitze's memory. 'I would write down notes in my car and then dictate as close to a verbatim memorandum of conversation as possible'—letter to *New York Times*, 19 November 1984: ibid. For Kvitsinsky's recollections—Yuli Kvitsinsky, 'Geneva: a month after', *Soviet News*, 18 January 1984.

60. Interview with a Novosti military correspondent: ibid., 29 September 1982.

61. Kvitsinsky, 'Geneva . . .'; Talbott, *Deadly Gambits*, pp. 144–50.

62. 'Soveshchanie voenachal'nikov v kremle', *Pravda*, 28 October 1982.

63. CIA, *Directory of Soviet Officials, National Organizations* (Washington DC, 1987) p. 16.

64. *Peace Courier*, November 1982.

65. *Pravda*, 23 November 1982.

66. Ibid., 1 February 1983.

67. *Diplomaticheskii Slovar'*, vol. 1, ed. A. Gromyko *et al.* (Moscow, 1984) p. 81; J. Steele and E. Abraham, *Andropov in Power: From Komsomol to Kremlin* (Oxford, 1983) chapters 3 to 7.

68. *The Times*, 4 November 1982.

69. 'Otvety ministra oborony SSSR Marshala Sovetskogo Soyuza D. F. Ustinova na voprosu korrespondenta TASS': *Pravda*, 7 December 1982.

70. Ibid., 22 December 1982.

71. Ibid., 31 December 1982. This was an interview with Kingsbury Smith.

72. *Daily Telegraph*, 22 December 1982.

73. Ibid., 24 December 1982.

74. *The Times*, 6 January 1983.

75. Ibid., 12 January 1983.

76. *Pravda*, 7 January 1983.

77. 'V Politburo TsK KPSS, Prezidiume Verkhovnogo Soveta SSSR i Sovete Ministrov SSSR', ibid., 8 January 1983.

78. 'Otvet Tovarishcha Yu. V. Andropova na vopros gazety "Rude pravo" ', *Pravda*, 6 January 1983.

79. *The Times*, 12 January 1983.
80. Ibid., 13 January 1983.
81. Ibid., 21 January 1983.
82. Ibid., 24 January 1983.
83. Ibid., 25 January 1983.
84. Ibid., 26 January 1983.
85. Quoted in Talbott, *Deadly Gambits*, p. 181.
86. Ibid., p. 182.
87. 'Press-konferentsiya A. A. Gromyko': *Pravda*, 3 April 1983.
88. Letter from T. Kozlovskaya (Moscow region), N. Chernousov (Baku) and others, 'Vopros. Otvet.'—*Argumenty i Fakty*, no. 8, 22 February 1983.
89. 'Miting druzhby', *Pravda*, 7 April 1983.
90. 'Kommyunike zasedaniya komiteta ministrov inostrannykh del gosudarstv-uchastnikov varshavskogo dogovora', 7 April 1983: ibid., 8 April 1983.
91. 'Otvety Yu. V. Andropova zhurnalu "Shpigel" (FRG)', 19 April 1983: *Izvestiya*, 25 April 1983.
92. *Neues Deutschland*, 3 March 1983.
93. Speech, 3 May 1983: Yu. V. Andropov, *Izbrannye rechi i stat'i*, 2nd ed. (Moscow, 1983) p. 275.
94. *Pravda*, 4 May 1983.
95. 'Sovmestnoe kommyunike ob itogakh ofitsial'nogo druzhestvennogo vizita v Sovetskii Soyuz partiino-gosudarstvennoi delegatsii GDR', ibid., 8 May 1983.
96. See, for example, 'Zheneva: pered ocherednym raundom', ibid., 13 May 1983.
97. 'Zayavlenie sovetskogo pravitel'stva', *Pravda*, 28 May 1983.
98. Richard Owen (Moscow), 'Andropov faces test of strength', *The Times*, 13 June 1983.
99. Ibid.
100. 15 June 1983: Andropov, *Izbrannye rechi i stat'i*, pp. 284–99.
101. Editorial, 'Edinstvo i splochennost' ', *Pravda*, 24 June 1983.
102. 'Na strazhe bezopasnosti otchizny: Priem v Kremle v chest' vypusnikov voennykh akademii': ibid., 28 June 1983.
103. Ibid., 29 June 1983; also see Owen, 'Warsaw Pact tread softly with West', *The Times*, 29 June 1983.
104. Novosti, 30 June 1983: FBIS *Daily Report: The Soviet Union*. vol. 3, no. 128, 1 July 1983.
105. For both speeches: *Pravda*, 21 July 1983.
106. 'Otvety ministra oborony SSSR Marshala Sovetskogo Soyuza D. F. Ustinova na voprosy korrespondenta TASS': ibid., 31 July 1983.
107. *Cmnd. 7979*.
108. Hansard, *Parliamentary Debates: House of Commons*, vol. 45, col. 746, 12 July 1983.
109. Ibid., vol. 42, col. 11, 3 May 1983.
110. 'Otvety Yu. V. Andropova na voprosy gazety "Pravda" ': *Pravda*, 27 August 1983.
111. 'Soveshchanie sekretarei tsentral'nykh komitetov bratskikh partii

204 Notes

sotsialisticheskikh stran', 20 September 1983: *Pravda*, 21 September 1983.
112. FBIS, *Daily Report: The Soviet Union*, no. 185, 22 September 1983.
113. 'V Politburo TsK KPSS': *Pravda*, 24 September 1983.
114. 'Mit Entsetzen', *Der Spiegel*, no. 47, 21 November 1983, p. 137.
115. 'Sovmestnoe sovetsko-chekhoslovatskoe kommyunike o vizite v Sovetskii Soyuz ministra inostrannykh del ChSSR', 27 September 1983: *Pravda*, 28 September 1983.
116. 'Kommyunike zasedaniya komiteta ministrov inostrannykh del gosudarstv-uchastnikov Varshavskogo Dogovora', 14 October 1983: ibid., 15 October 1983.
117. 'Kommyunike o vneocherednom zasedanii komiteta ministrov oborony gosudarstv-uchastnikov Varshavskogo Dogovora': ibid., 22 October 1983.
118. 'V Ministerstve oborony SSSR': ibid., 25 October 1983.
119. *Neues Deutschland*, 27 October 1983.
120. Editorial comment by Antonin Kostka—Prague Domestic Service, 25 October 1983: FBIS, *Daily Report: Eastern Europe*, no. 209, 27 October 1983.
121. *Rudé Právo*, 5 November 1983: FBIS, ibid., no. 217, 8 November 1983.
122. 'Otvety Yu. Andropova na voprosy gazety "Pravda" ': *Pravda*, 27 October 1983.
123. According to Kvitsinsky: 'During the last two rounds, that is, in the summer and in the autumn of 1983 Ambassador Nitze probed the problem of working out a form of "compensation" to the Soviet Union (a compensation acceptable to the USA) for the armaments of Britain and France and of the size of that "compensation". Nitze believed that this compensation should not be open. He tried to find a camouflaged solution to the problem to save the face of the USA and not to irritate the Thatcher and Mitterand governments. He was not consistent in his attempts. On all accounts, this reflected the internal struggle around this question in Washington and NATO'. (Kvitsinsky, 'Geneva . . .'). Nitze's version of events as related by Talbott refers to discussion of such ideas 'before' late October 1983 (Talbott, *Deadly Gambits*, p. 200) and Vice President George Bush told reporters on 28 September that British and French missiles would eventually have to be put on the bargaining table (*The Times*, 29 September 1983). So the idea certainly was in circulation on the American side. Kvitsinsky tells us that the Russians also left any increases in British and French arsenals to the strategic arms talks or some future forum. This differs from Talbott's account (see Talbott, *Deadly Gambits*, pp. 202–3). Right or wrong, Kvitsinsky's account is confirmed by a Soviet Foreign Ministry announcement on 22 November (*Krasnaya Zvezda* 22 November 1983) and was also confirmed by Pravda editor-in-chief Viktor Afanas'ev in an interview with *Volksstime* (Vienna) on 19 November 1983: FBIS, *Daily Report: The Soviet Union*, no. 225, 21 November 1983.
124. *Peace Courier*, December 1983.

125. *Pravda*, 24 November 1983.
126. Ibid., 25 November 1983.

7 Reversing from the Cul-de-Sac, 1984–87

1. Interview with *Volksstime* (Vienna), 19 November 1983: FBIS, *Daily Report: The Soviet Union*, no. 225, 21 November 1983.

2. This much was clear from Gromyko's speech at a luncheon in honour of Oskar Fischer, the East German Foreign Minister, on 4 January: 'To continue negotiations after the USA has begun to deploy its nuclear missile weapons would merely serve to help deceive the people'—*Pravda*, 5 January 1984. This was emphasised by other senior Soviet officials—'Moscú entiende que si la URSS hace concesiones ayudara a Ronald Reagan a ganar las elecciones', *El País*, 14 January 1984. For the French role in the origins of the Stockholm conference, see Dean, *Watershed in Europe*, pp. 187–8.

3. *Soviet Strategic Force Developments: Joint Hearing Before the Subcommittee on Strategic and Theater Nuclear Forces of the Committee on Armed Services and the Subcommittee on Defense of the Committee on Appropriations. United States Senate. 1st Session* (Washington DC, 1986) p. 9.

4. 'Meditsinskoe zaklyuchenie o bolezni i prichine smerti Andropova Yuria Vladimirovicha', *Pravda*, 11 February 1984.

5. Z. Mlynař, 'Il mio compagno di studi Mikhail Gorbaciov', *l'Unità*, 9 April 1985.

6. Speech delivered 23 March 1983: *New York Times*, 24 March 1983.

7. 'Zayavlenie sovetskogo pravitel'stva o nedopushchenii militarizatsii kosmicheskogo prostranstva', *Pravda*, 30 June 1984. For date of despatch to the US Government, see *Vneshnyaya Politika Sovetskogo Soyuza i Mezhdunarodnye Otnosheniya 1984 god: Sbornik Dokumentov* (Moscow, 1985) p. 255, note 27. From Moscow, *Washington Post* correspondent Dusko Doder reported that although the primary concern of the Russians 'was in stopping what they call the "militarization of outer space", they also were aware that the talks could provide an opening wedge to break the current deadlock in negotiations over medium-range and strategic nuclear weapons'—*Washington Post*, 4 August 1984.

8. *Washington Post*, 4 August 1984.

9. Ibid.

10. *The Times*, 23 August and 1 September 1984; also *The Sunday Times*, 2 September 1984.

11. TASS, 23 July 1984: FBIS, *Daily Report: The Soviet Union*. no. 143, 24 July 1984.

12. Doder, reporting from Moscow: *Washington Post*, 20 October 1984.

13. The last Central Committee plenum was referred to but not the General Secretary; a most unusual practice: editorial, 'Otchetno-vybornye partiinye sobraniya', *Pravda*, 4 September 1984.

14. See T. Colton, *The Dilemma of Reform in the Soviet Union* (New

York, 1986) p. 199; also. G. Weickhardt, 'Ustinov versus Ogarkov', *Problems of Communism*, Jan-Feb. 1985, pp. 77–82.

15. B. Evladov, 'Opushchennyi parus: Obzor pechati', *Pravda*, 10 September 1984.
16. *Washington Post*, 25 September 1984.
17. *Pravda*, 28 September 1984.
18. Reported from Moscow: *The Times*, 1 October 1984.
19. *The Times*, 1 October 1984.
20. *Pravda*, 18 October 1984.
21. Doder, reporting from Moscow: *Washington Post*, 20 October 1984.
22. This became apparent only later: *The Sunday Times*, 27 January 1985 and *The Times*, 26 February 1985. Gorbachev was chairing the Politburo in Chernenko's absence by the end of 1984: *Keesing's Contemporary Archives*, vol. XXXI, no. 4, p. 33537.
23. *Washington Post*, 9 and 15 November 1984.
24. Ibid., 21 November 1984.
25. *The Times*, 23 November 1984.
26. D. Hoffman, 'U.S. Firm in Pursuing "Star Wars": Reagan Rules Out Any Deal at Geneva To Limit Program', *Washington Post*, 4 January 1985; L. Gelb, 'Arms Role Reversed: Two Sides Switch Disarmament Aims', *New York Times*, 6 January 1985.
27. The discussion of the Soviet negotiating position was mentioned as the first item on the agenda in the usual summary of Politburo proceedings: 'V Politburo TsK KPSS', *Izvestiya*, 4 January 1985.
28. 'Beseda A. A. Gromyko s politicheskimi obozrevatelyami', ibid., 15 January 1985.
29. Joint communiqué: *Washington Post*, 9 January 1985.
30. 'V Politburo TsK KPSS', *Izvestiya*, 11 January 1985.
31. Moscow television on 13 January 1985: as recorded and translated by FBIS, *Daily Report: The Soviet Union*, no. 009, 14 January 1985. The version published in the Soviet press was heavily edited: *Izvestiya*, 15 January 1985.
32. 'V Politburo TsK KPSS', *Izvestiya*, 25 January 1985. For Obukhov's graduate education in the USA: *Washington Post*, 7 January 1985.
33. 'Meditsinskoe zaklyuchenie o bolezni i prichine smerti Chernenko Konstantina Ustinova', *Pravda*, 12 March 1985.
34. *The Times*, 13 March 1985.
35. *Kommunist*, no. 5, March 1985, p. 3.
36. Ibid., p. 7.
37. M. Gorbachev, *Perestroika i novoe myshlenie dlya nashei strany i dlya vsego mira* (Moscow, 1987) p. 163.
38. D. Doder, *Shadows and Whispers: Power Politics Inside the Kremlin from Brezhnev to Gorbachev* (New York, 1986) p. 287. The fact of Gorbachev's trip to Italy in 1971 came out during his visit to Washington DC in December 1987.
39. M. Gorbachev, *Perestroika i novoe myshlenie*, p. 18.
40. 'Kursom edinstva i splochennosti: Vstrecha izbiratelei s M. S. Gorbachevym', *Izvestiya*, 21 February 1985.

41. 'Beseda M. S. Gorbacheva s redaktorom gazety *Pravda*': ibid., 8 April 1985.
42. Ibid., 31 May 1985.
43. 'Zheneva: Chto pokazal pervyi raund peregovorov', *Pravda*, 27 May 1985.
44. Edward Rowny, special adviser on arms control to the President and Secretary of State noted: 'There has . . . been verbal jousting between Marshal Ogarkov and Gorbachev over high technology and perceptions of the threat. When Gen. Yepishev, the ideological watchdog over the armed forces, signaled early qualms about having the Geneva summit, he was swiftly removed from his key post. Immediately following the removal of Grigoriy Romanov as the CPSU secretary for military affairs, Gorbachev held an unprecedented meeting of high military officers in Minsk, where it is rumored he asserted his leadership. A number of key shifts in the top military leadership occurred immediately after this meeting'—Edward Rowny, 'On Arms Control, Gorbachev Knows Where He's Going', *Washington Post*, 8 May 1986.
45. A. Gromyko, *Pamyatnoe*, 2 (Moscow, 1988) p. 246.
46. Shevardnadze was a history teacher by profession, rising to become Party leader in Georgia in 1972, where he made some innovative economic reforms. He had visited such countries as Portugal, Brazil, India and Algeria in recent years but this appears to have been the sum total of his experience in international affairs: *The Times*, 3 July 1985.
47. 'Vstrecha s britanskimi parlamentariyami', *Izvestiya*, 11 July 1985.
48. M. Maksimova, 'Evropeiskoe soobshchestvo—realnost' nashego vremeni', *Mirovaya Ekonomika i Mezhdunarodnye Otnosheniya*, no. 8, 1986, p. 138. The book under review was *Zapadnoevropeiskaya integratsiya: politicheskie aspekty* ed. N. Kishilov (Moscow, 1985). Maclean wrote most of his work under the nom de plume S. P. Madzoevskii. Under this name he edited two other works: *Zapadnaya Evropa: ekonomika, politika, klassovaya bor'ba* (with V. Kuznetsov, Moscow, 1979), and *Velikobritaniya* (with E. Khesin, Moscow, 1981). *British Foreign Policy Since Suez* (London, 1971) was also published in Russian but under his own name: Maklein, D., *Vneshnyaya politika Anglii posle Sueza* (Moscow, 1972).
49. FBIS, *Daily Report: The Soviet Union* no. 064, 2 April 1984.
50. A. Bovin, 'Evropeiskoe napravlenie': ibid., 26 September 1985. Bovin was closely associated with the reformist element in the Khrushchev era, the so-called 'Kuusinen group', which later came under the patronage of Andropov. Others included Georgii Arbatov, now head of the Institute for the Study of the USA and Canada, and Fyodor Burlatsky, director of the Institute of Philosophy, a leading political sociologist.
51. Ibid., 3 October 1985.
52. Ibid., 4 October 1985.
53. Ibid., 6 October 1985.
54. 'Evropa—nash obshchii dom', *Pravda*, 13 November 1985. Too much

significance should not be attached to this slogan. Brezhnev used it during his visit to Bonn on 22–25 November 1981.

55. 'Press-konferentsiya M. S. Gorbacheva', 21 November 1985: *Izvestiya*, 22 November 1985.
56. Editorial, 'Gorizonty Zhenevy', ibid., 25 November 1985.
57. 'Sovmestnoe sovetsko-amerikanskoe zayavlenie', 21 November 1985: ibid., 22 November 1985; *New York Times*, 22 November 1985.
58. As note 55.
59. 'V Politburo TsK KPSS', *Izvestiya*, 27 November 1985.
60. *Pravda*, 16 January 1986. This appeared in the form of an advertisement paid for by the Soviet Government in *New York Times*, 5 February 1986. It is here that the text is dated 15 January, as it is in *Bor'ba SSSR protiv yadernoi opasnosti, gonki vooruzhenii, za razoruzhenie: Dokumenty i materialy*, ed. A. Gromyko *et al.* (Moscow, 1987) doc. 41.
61. N. Ashford, 'West Reacts to Kremlin Speech: Second Thoughts on Preconditions', *The Times*, 28 February 1986.
62. *New York Times*, 25 February 1986.
63. Quoted by J. Newhouse in 'The Diplomatic Round: Summiteering', *The New Yorker*, 8 September 1986, p. 50.
64. On 24 February Reagan put forward a counter-proposal: *The Times*, 25 February 1986.
65. Ibid., 11 March 1986.
66. Ibid., 13 February 1986.
67. Ibid., 11 March 1986.
68. *Izvestiya*, 26 February 1986; M. Gorbachev, *Izbrannye rechi i stat'i* vol. 3 (Moscow, 1987) pp. 243–58.
69. Programme on the INF agreement: Moscow Radio—FBIS, *Daily Report: The Soviet Union*, 28 December 1987.
70. P. Taubman, 'Soviet Diplomacy Given a New Look Under Gorbachev', *New York Times*, 10 August 1986.
71. *Diplomaticheskii Slovar'*, vol. 1, ed. A. Gromyko *et al.* (Moscow, 1984) p. 219.
72. Ibid., p. 14.
73. V. Zorin, *Osnovy diplomaticheskoi sluzhby* (Moscow, 1977) pp. 76–7.
74. As note 67.
75. A. Yakovlev, 'Mezhimperialisticheskie protivorechiya—sovremennyi kontekst', *Kommunist*, no. 17, 20 November 1986, p. 16.
76. Ibid.
77. *New York Times*, 10 October 1986.
78. See Gorbachev's press conference at Reykjavik, 12 October 1986: *Pravda*, 14 October 1986.
79. *Washington Post*, 23 September 1986.
80. *Pravda*, 14 October 1986.
81. Ibid.
82. *The Economist*, 25 October 1986.
83. Ibid.
84. *New York Times*, 17 October 1986.

85. 'Vystuplenie General'nogo sekretarya TsK KPSS M. S. Gorbacheva po sovetskomu televideniyu', *Izvestiya*, 24 October 1986.
86. *Dagens Nyheter*, 3 April 1987: FBIS, *Daily Report: The Soviet Union*, vol. III, no. 069, 10 April 1987.
87. Prof. D. Proektor, 'Puti Evropy', *Izvestiya*, 27 October 1986.
88. As note 84.
89. Viktor Levin on Moscow radio (domestic service), 15 January 1987: FBIS, *Daily Report: The Soviet Union*, vol. III, no. 011, 16 January 1987.
90. Ibid.; also Karpov's interview with *Komsomol'skaya Pravda*, 13 February 1987.
91. Speech delivered on 16 February 1987: *Pravda*, 17 February 1987.
92. Deputy Foreign Minister Vladimir Petrovsky at a press conference in Moscow at the Foreign Ministry on 13 January 1987: Moscow, TASS International Service, 13 January 1987—FBIS, *Daily Report: The Soviet Union*, vol. III, no. 009, 14 January 1987.
93. *New York Times*, 22 May 1987.
94. Deputy Foreign Minister Alexander Bessmertnykh at a press conference in the Soviet Foreign Ministry, 2 March 1987—Moscow radio (domestic service), 2 March 1987: FBIS, *Daily Report: The Soviet Union*, vol. III, no. 041, 3 March 1987.
95. *Pravda*, 1 March 1987.
96. Bovin in *Moscow News*, 8 March 1987.
97. TASS interview—Moscow International Service, 6 March 1987: FBIS, *Daily Report: The Soviet Union*, vol. III, 10 March 1987.
98. Interview with *Frankfurter Rundschau*, 2 April 1987.
99. *New York Times*, 5 March 1987.
100. *Le Figaro*, 7–8 March 1987: FBIS, *Daily Report: The Soviet Union*, vol. III, no. 047, 11 March 1987.
101. *New York Times*, 24 January 1988.
102. Ibid., 4 March 1988.
103. Obukhov was insistent on this point—Hamburg DPA (in German): FBIS, *Daily Report: The Soviet Union*, vol. III, no. 082, 29 april 1987.
104. Karpov interview with *Ya* (Madrid), 29 April 1987: FBIS, *Daily Report: The Soviet Union*, vol. III, no. 086, 5 May 1987.
105. *Pravda*, 29 April 1987.
106. Karpov in *Pravda*, 19 May 1987.
107. Interview with Obukhov, Bratislav *Smena*, 13 May 1987: FBIS, *Daily Report: The Soviet Union*, vol. III, no. 094, 15 May 1987.
108. 'We have said nothing about the missiles themselves', General Chervov emphasised—*NRC Handelsblad*, 27 May 1987: FBIS, *Daily Report: The Soviet Union*, 12 June 1987.
109. On the state of opinion in West Germany and elsewhere in Western Europe, see 'NATO on Arms Pact: Relief and Fear', *New York Times*, 25 September 1987.
110. 'An interview with Paul H. Nitze: The Final Steps to an INF Treaty', *Arms Control Today*, vol. 17, no. 8, October 1987.
111. *The Economist*, 7 November 1987.
112. 'The Soviet conception [of the summit] envisaged signature of the

treaty on medium and shorter range missiles and the preparation of key positions for an agreement on a 50% reduction in strategic offensive armaments'—V. Avakov, V. Ivanov and V. Shambert, 'Tekushchie problemy mirovoi politiki', *Mirovaya Ekonomika i Mezhdunarodnye Otnosheniya*, no. 1, 1988 (15 December 1987) p. 61. The Russians did not succeed in this but went ahead with the treaty and the summit anyway. For more on this, see *New York Times*, 4 March 1988.

113. 'Realnost' i garantii bezopasnogo mira', *Pravda*, 17 September 1987.
114. B. Pyadyshev 'Breakthrough. On a World with Medium- and Shorter-Range Missiles', *Moscow News*, 27 September 1987.
115. Speech to the Supreme Soviet on ratification of the INF accord, 10 march 1988: *Krasnaya Zvezda*, 11 March 1988. This is a more complete account than that given in *Pravda* of the same date.
116. Gorbachev, *Izbrannye rechi i stat'i*, vol. 3, p. 248.
117. Maj. Gen. Yu. Lebedev and A. Podberezkin, 'Unikal'nyi shans dlya Evropy, dlya vsei planety', *Kommunist Vooruzhennykh Sil*, no. 22, 6 November 1987, p. 94.
118. Ibid., p. 91.
119. Ibid., p. 94.

Bibliography

BIBLIOGRAPHICAL NOTE

The reader should note that there is little distinction between Soviet primary and secondary sources. Tight censorship has until very recently been exercised over all Soviet comment on international relations and defence. Second, the Soviet press provides the bulk of the raw material for the analysis of Soviet foreign and defence policy. As those with access to classified sources know, there is a close relationship between Soviet secret and open sources on these matters. Third, because the United States enjoys greater freedom of official information than any other Power of importance and because its government devotes an extraordinary degree of attention to Soviet behaviour, US documents represent a source of major significance. Finally, the secondary sources listed are confined to those of immediate use in the research on this book: essentially those which offered something unobtainable elsewhere. Many other works have also been consulted. But there is little to be gained from listing all of them; such a list is unlikely to impress the attentive and informed reader.

PRIMARY SOURCES

Soviet/Communist

Andropov, Y. *Izbrannye rechi i stat'i* (2nd ed., Moscow 1983).
Congrès Mondial des intellectuels pour la paix—Pologne. 25–28 août 1948 (Warsaw, 1948).
Diplomaticheskii Vestnik (published each year: Moscow, 1984–86).
Foreign Ministry of the USSR, *Bor'ba SSSR protiv yadernoi opasnosti, gonki vooruzhenii, za razoruzhenie: dokumenty i materialy* (Moscow, 1987).
Gorbachev, M. *Perestroika i novoe myshlenie dlya nashei strany i dlya vsego mira* (Moscow, 1987).
Izbrannye rechi i stat'i vols. 1–3 (Moscow, 1987).
Kak ustranit' ugrozu Evrope (Moscow, 1983).
Kommunisticheskaya Partiya Sovetskogo Soyuza v rezolyutsiyakh i resheniyakh s"ezdov, konferentsii i plenumov TsK, vol. 12 (1975–77) (Moscow, 1977).
Lenin, V., *Collected Works*, vol. 45 (Moscow, 1970).
Otkuda iskhodit ugroza miru (Moscow, 1984).
Pogranichnye voiska SSSR 1945–50 (Moscow, 1975).
Vneshnyaya Politika Sovetskogo Soyuza i Mezhdunarodnye Otnosheniya: sbornik dokumentov (also published each year: Moscow, 1970–87).

211

212 *Bibliography*

Vtoroi vsemirnyi kongress storonnikov mira, Varshava, 16–22 noyabrya 1950 goda (Moscow, 1951).
Who Wrecked the Geneva Talks and Why? (Moscow, 1983).

Miscellaneous

White Paper 1973–1974: The Security of the Federal Republic of Germany and the Development of the Federal Armed Forces (Bonn, 1973?).
Statement on the Defence Estimates 1968: Cmnd. 3540 (London, 1968).
Statement on the Defence Estimates 1975: Cmnd. 5976 (London, 1975).
Statement on the Defence Estimates 1976: Cmnd. 6432 (London, 1976).
Statement on the Defence Estimates 1977: Cmnd. 7979 (London, 1977).
Miscellaneous No. 17 (1977): Selected Documents Relating to Problems of Security and Cooperation in Europe 1954–77: Cmnd. 6932 (London, 1977).
Hansard, *Parliamentary Debates: House of Commons*, vol. 45 (London, 1983).

United States

United States Security Agreements and Commitments Abroad: Hearings Before the Subcommittee on United States Agreements and Commitments Abroad of the Committee on Foreign Relations, United States Senate, 91st Congress. Volume 2, Part 5–11 (Washington DC, 1971).
Public Papers of the Presidents of the United States: Richard Nixon 1972 (Washington DC, 1972).
U.S. Security Issues in Europe: Burden Sharing and Offset. MBFR and Nuclear Weapons, September 1973. A Staff Report Prepared for the Use of the Subcommittee on U.S. Security Agreements Abroad of the Committee on Foreign Relations, United States Senate, 2 December 1973 (Washington DC, 1973).
Senate Hearings Before the Committee on Appropriations, Department of Defense Appropriations, 93rd Congress, 2nd Session, Fiscal Year 1975. Part 2. Department of the Army: Hearings Before a Subcommittee of the Committee on Appropriations, United States Senate, 93rd Congress, 2nd Session (Washington DC, 1974).
Senate Hearings Before the Committee on Appropriations, Department of Defense Appropriations, 93rd Congress, 2nd Session, Fiscal Year 1975, Part 1 (Washington DC, 1974).
Secretary of Defense James Schlesinger, The Theater Nuclear Force Posture in Europe: A Report to the United States Congress in Compliance with Public Law 93–365 (Washington DC, 1975).
US Department of Defense, *Annual Report of Secretary of Defense Donald H. Rumsfeld* (Washington DC, 1976).
Department of Defense Appropriations for 1978: Hearings Before a Subcommittee of the Committee on Appropriations, House of Representatives, 95th Congress, 1st Session, Part 1 (Washington DC, 1977).
Public Papers of the Presidents of the United States: Jimmy Carter 1977, Book 1 (Washington DC, 1977).
Report to the Congress Completed by the Comptroller General of the United

States: Comparison of the Pershing II Program With the Acquisition Plan Recommended by the Commission on Government Procurement Department of Defense (Washington DC, 1977).

D. Rumsfeld, *Annual Defense Report FY 1978* (Washington DC, 1977).

United States Military Posture for FY 1979 By Chairman of the Joint Chiefs of Staff, General George S. Brown, USAF (Washington DC, 1978).

Briefings on the SALT Negotiations: Hearings Before the Committee on Foreign Relations, United States Senate, 95th Congress, 1st Session (Washington DC, 1978).

SALT AND THE NATO ALLIES: A Staff Report to the Subcommittee on European Affairs of the Committee on Foreign Relations, United States Senate, October 1979 (Washington DC, 1979).

Senate Delegation Report on SALT Discussions in the Soviet Union, August 25–30, 1979: A Report to the Committee on Foreign Relations, United States Senate (Washington DC, 1979).

Military Implications of the Treaty on the Limitation of Strategic Offensive Arms and Protocol Thereto (SALT II Treaty): Hearings Before the Committee on Armed Services, US Senate, 96th Congress, 1st Session, Part 1 (Washington DC, 1979).

Fiscal Year 1981 Arms Control Impact Statements: Statements Submitted to the Congress by the President Pursuant to Section 36 of the Arms Control and Disarmament Act (Washington DC, 1980).

Soviet Defense Expenditure and Related Programs: Hearings Before the Subcommittee on General Procurement of the Committee on Armed Services, United States Senate, 96th Congress, 1st and 2nd Sessions, November 1, 8, 1979; February 4, 1980 (Washington DC, 1980).

Covert Action (The Forgery Offensive): Hearings Before the Subcommittee on Oversight of the Permanent Select Committee on Intelligence, House of Representatives, 96th Congress, 2nd Session (Washington DC, 1980).

US Department of Defense, *Annual Report of Secretary of Defense Harold Brown, FY 1981* (Washington DC, 1980).

Department of Defense Authorization for Appropriations for Fiscal Year 1983: Hearings Before the Committee on Armed Services, United States Senate, 97th Congress, 2nd Session, on S. 2248. Part 7—Strategic and Theater Nuclear Forces (Washington DC, 1982).

Soviet Active Measures: Hearings Before the Permanent Select Committee on Intelligence, House of Representatives, 97th Congress, 2nd Session (Washington DC, 1982).

Overview of Nuclear Arms Control and Defense Strategy in NATO: Hearings Before the Subcommittees on International Security and Scientific Affairs and on Europe and the Middle East of the Committee on Foreign Affairs, House of Representatives, 97th Congress, 2nd Session (Washington DC, 1982).

Executive Sessions of the Senate Foreign Relations Committee (Historical Series), Volume XII, 86th Congress, 2nd Session 1960 (Washington DC, 1982).

US Department of Defense, *Soviet Military Power 1983* (Washington DC, 1983).

United States Military Posture FY 1985: The Organization of the Joint Chiefs of Staff (Washington DC, 1984).

Foreign Relations of the United States, 1952–54, Volume II, National Security Affairs, Part 1 (Washington DC, 1984).

United States Arms Control and Disarmament Agency, *Arms Control and Disarmament Agreements* (New Jersey, 1984).

US Department of Defense, *Soviet Military Power 1985* (Washington DC, 1985).

Central Intelligence Agency, The Soviet Weapons Industry: An Overview (Washington DC, 1986).

Central Intelligence Agency, *Directory of Soviet Officials, National Organizations* (Washington DC, 1987)

Treaty Between the United States of America and the Union of Soviet Socialist Republics on the Elimination of their Intermediate-Range and Shorter-Range Missiles, December 1987.

Memoirs

Brzezinski, Z., *Power and Principle: Memoirs of the National Security Adviser 1977–81* (London, 1983).

Callaghan, J., *Time and Change* (London, 1987).

Carter, J., *Keeping Faith: Memoirs of a President* (London, 1982).

Charlton, M. (ed.), *From Deterrence to Defense: The Inside Story of Strategic Policy* (Cambridge, Mass., 1987).

Dean, J., *Watershed in Europe* (Lexington, Mass., 1987).

Doder, D., *Shadows and Whispers: Power Politics Inside the Kremlin from Brezhnev to Gorbachev* (New York, 1986).

Ford, G., *A Time to Heal* (New York, 1979).

'The Vladivostok Negotiations and Other Events', *IGCC Policy Papers*, no. 2 (San Diego, 1986).

Gladwyn, *The Memoirs of Lord Gladwyn* (London, 1972).

Gromyko, A., *Pamyatnoe*, 1–2 (Moscow, 1988).

Hoxha, E., *Reflections on China 1: 1962–1972. Extracts from the Political Diary* (Tirana, 1979).

Johnson, A., *The Right Hand of Power* (New Jersey, 1984).

Kissinger, H., *White House Years* (Boston, 1979).

Kissinger, H., *Years of Upheaval* (Boston, 1982).

Kvitsinsky, Yu., 'Geneva: a month after', *Soviet News*, 18 January 1984.

Mendelevich, L., 'Diplomaticheskie zametki o khel'sinskikh konsul'tatsiyakh 1972–1973 godov po podgotovke obshchestvennogo soveshchaniya', *Diplomaticheskii Vestnik: God 1982* (Moscow, 1983).

Mlynář, Z., 'Il mio compagno di studi Mikhail Gorbachev', *l'Unità*, 9 April 1985.

Polanski, N., *M. I. D.: Douze ans dans les services diplomatiques du Kremlin* (Paris, 1984).

Schmidt, H., 'If the Missiles Go, Peace May Stay', *New York Times*, 29 April 1987.

Shevchenko, A., *Breaking with Moscow* (New York, 1985).

Smith G., *Doubletalk: The Story of the Strategic Arms Limitation Talks* (New York, 1980).
Thomson, J., 'The LRTNF decision: evolution of US theatre nuclear policy 1975–79', *International Affairs*, vol. 60, no. 4, Autumn 1984.
Tokaty, G., 'Soviet Space Technology', *Spaceflight*, vol. 5 (1963).
Toranska, T. (ed.), *'Them': Stalin's Polish Puppets* (New York, 1987).

Periodicals

Soviet
Argumenty i Fakty
Izvestiya
Kazakhstanskaya Pravda
Kommunist
Kommunist Vooruzhennykh Sil
Krasnaya Zvezda
Literaturnaya Gazeta
Mezhdunarodnaya Zhizn'
Mirovaya Ekonomika i Mezhdunarodnye Otnosheniya
Nedelya
Novoe Vremya
Peace Courier (Helsinki)
Pravda
Sovetskaya Rossiya
Soviet News (London)
Vestnik Protivovozdushnoi Oborony
Voennaya Mysl' (in US translation)
Voenno-Istoricheskii Zhurnal

Other
Air Force Magazine
Aviation Week and Space Technology
Bulletin of the Atomic Scientists
Bulletin of Peace Proposals
Daily Telegraph
The Economist
Facts on File
Foreign Affairs
Foreign Broadcast Information Service: Daily Report
Foreign Policy
Frankfurter Allgemeine
Frankfurter Rundschau
Information
International Affairs (London)
International Defense Review
Keesing's Contemporary Archives
Le Matin
Le Monde
The NATO Review

Neues Deutschland
New York Times
Observer
Orbis
El Pais
Der Spiegel
The Sunday Times
Survival
The Times
l'Unità
Washington Post
World Politics

MONOGRAPHS

Alexiev, A., 'The Soviet Campaign Against INF: Strategy, Tactics, Means', *A Rand Note* (Santa Monica, 1985).
Ambrose, S., *Eisenhower: Volume 2. The President* (New York, 1984).
Armitage, M. and Mason, R., *Air Power in the Nuclear Age*, 2nd ed. (Urbana, 1985).
Babakov, A., *Vooruzhennye sily SSSR posle voiny* (Moscow, 1987).
Bakinskii okrug protivovozdushnoi oborony: istoricheskii ocherk 1920–1947 (Baku, 1974).
Barron, J., *KGB Today: The Hidden Hand* (New York, 1985).
Berman, R., *Soviet Air Power in Transition* (Washington DC, 1978).
Berman, R. and Baker, J., *Soviet Strategic Forces: Requirements and Responses* (Washington DC, 1983).
Best, K. *et al.*, *Playing at Peace: A Study of the 'Peace Movement' in Great Britain and the Federal Republic of Germany* (London, 1983).
Betts, R. (ed.), *Cruise Missiles: Technology, Strategy, Politics* (Washington DC, 1981).
Bialer, S., *The Soviet Paradox: External; Expansion, Internal Decline* (New York, 1986).
Blechman, B. and Luttwak, E., *International Security Yearbook 1984/85* (Boulder, 1985).
Bol'shakov, V. *et al.*, *Zheneva: kak eto bylo* (Moscow, 1986).
Borisov, O., Koloskov, B., *Sovetsko-kitaiskie otnosheniya 1945–1977*, 2nd, revised ed. (Moscow, 1977).
Bovin, A., 'Moscow: "We are serious" ' *Observer*, 28 October 1979.
Bovin, A., *Pogovorim po sushchestvu . . .* (Moscow, 1985).
Brown, H., *Thinking About National Security: Defense and Foreign Policy in a Dangerous World* (Boulder, 1983).
Bullock, A., *Ernest Bevin: Foreign Secretary 1945–51* (London, 1983).
Buteux, P., *Strategy, Doctrine and the Politics of Alliance: Theatre Nuclear Force Modernisation in NATO* (Boulder, 1983).
Campbell, D., *The Unsinkable Aircraft Carrier: American Military Power in Britain* (London, 1984).

Cockburn, A., *The Threat: Inside the Soviet Military Machine* (New York, 1983).

Colton, T., *The Dilemma of Reform in the Soviet Union* (New York, 1986).

Cordesman, A., 'Deterrence in the 1980's: Part 1. American Strategic Forces and Extended Deterrence', *Adelphi Paper* 175 (London, 1982).

Evangelista, M., 'Why the Soviets Buy the Weapons They Do', *World Politics*, no. 4, July 1984.

Freedman, L., *Britain and Nuclear Weapons* (London, 1980).

Friedman, N., *Carrier Air Power* (London, 1981).

Futrell, R., *Ideas, Concepts, Doctrine: A History of Basic Thinking in the United States Air Force 1907–1964* (Alabama, 1971).

Gareev, M., *M. V. Frunze—voennyi teoretik: vzglyady M. V. Frunze i sovremennaya voennaya teoriya* (Moscow, 1985).

Garthoff, R., 'SALT and the Soviet Military', *Problems of Communism* January-February 1975.

Garthoff, R., 'SALT I: An Evaluation', *World Politics*, vol. XXXI, no. 1, October 1978.

Garthoff, R., 'The SS-20 Decision', *Survival*, vol. XV, no. 1, Jan./Feb. 1983.

Garthoff, R., *Perspectives on the Strategic Balance* (Washington DC, 1983).

Garthoff, R., *Detente and Confrontation: American-Soviet Relations from Nixon to Reagan* (Washington DC, 1985).

Gervasi, T., *The Myth of Soviet Military Supremacy* (New York, 1986).

Gunston, B., *F-111 General Dynamics: Modern Combat Aircraft 2* (London, 1978).

Hagelin, B., 'Swords into Daggers: The Origins of the SS-20 Missiles', *Bulletin of Peace Proposals*, vol. 15, no. 4, 1984.

Haslam, J., *Soviet Foreign Policy 1930–33: The Impact of the Depression* (London/New York, 1983).

Hewitt, E., *Reforming the Soviet Economy: Equality versus Efficiency* (Washington DC, 1988).

Hines, J., Petersen, P. and Trulock, N. 'Soviet Military Theory from 1945–2000: Implications for NATO', *The Washington Quarterly*, vol. 9, no. 4, 1986, pp. 117–37.

Holloway, D., *The Soviet Union and the Arms Race* (London, 1983).

Hurley, A. and Ehrhart, R., *Air Power and Warfare: The Proceedings of the 8th Military History Symposium, United States Air Force Academy 18–20 October 1978* (Washington DC, 1979).

Istoriya ural'skogo voennogo okruga (Moscow, 1970).

Kaplan, F., 'Warring Over New Missiles for NATO', *New York Times* (magazine) 9 December 1979.

Kaufman, R., 'Causes of the Slowdown in Soviet Defense', *Survival*, vol. XXVII, no. 4, July/August 1985.

Keliher, J., *The Negotiations on Mutual and Balanced Force Reductions: The Search for Arms Control in Central Europe* (New York, 1980?).

Knyazhinskii, V. (ed.), *Zapadno-evropeiskaya integratsiya: proekty i real'-nost'* (Moscow, 1986).

Kortunov, V., *Strategiya mira protiv yadernogo bezumiya* (Moscow, 1984).

Lambeth, B., *Moscow's Lessons From the 1982 Lebanon Air War* (Santa Monica, 1984).
Lebedev, N. (ed.), *XXVI S"ezd KPSS i aktual'nye problemy mezhdunarodnykh otnoshenii* (Moscow, 1983).
Leffler, M., 'The American Conception of National Security and the Beginnings of the Cold War 1945–48', *The American Historical Review*, vo. 89, no. 2, April 1984.
Legge, M., *Theater Nuclear Weapons and the NATO Strategy of Flexible Response* (Santa Monica, 1983).
MccGwire, M., *Military Objectives in Soviet Foreign Policy* (Washington DC, 1987).
Meyer, S., 'Soviet Theatre Nuclear Forces' *Adelphi Paper* 187 (London, 1984).
Morozov, G. *et al.*, *Obshchestvennost' i problemy voiny i mira* (Moscow, 1976).
Murphy, C., 'China's Nuclear Deterrent', *Air Force Magazine*, April 1972.
Nalty, B., *Air Force and the Fight for Khe Sanh* (Washington DC, 1973).
National Security Issues 1981 Symposium: Strategic Nuclear Policies, Weapons and the C Connection (Washington DC, 1981).
Newhouse, J., 'The Diplomatic Round: Summiteering', *The New Yorker*, 8 September 1986.
Nikonov, A. (ed.), *Gonka vooruzhenii: prichiny tendentsii puti prekrashcheniya* (Moscow, 1986).
Nordeen, L., *Air Warfare in the Missile Age* (Washington DC, 1985).
Olive, M. and Porro, J., *Nuclear Weapons in Europe: Modernization and Limitation* (Lexington, 1983).
Ordena Lenina moskovskii okrug PVO: istoriya ordena Lenina moskovskogo okruga protivovozdushnoi oborony (Moscow, 1981).
Paine, C.,'Pershing II: the Army's strategic weapon', *Bulletin of the Atomic Scientists*, vol. 36, no. 8, October 1980.
Pavlov, N. and Sidorov, A., *Amerikanskii 'Evrorakety': voennaya ugroza i politicheskii shantazh* (Moscow, 1984).
Pierre, A. (ed.), *Nuclear Weapons in Europe* (New York, 1984).
Ponomarev, A., *Aviatsiya nastoyashchego i budushchego* (Moscow, 1984).
Robinson, A., *Soviet Air Power* (New York, 1985).
Rosenberg, D., 'American Atomic Strategy and the Hydrogen Bomb Decision' *The Journal of American History*, vol. 66, June 1979.
Schwartz, D., *NATO's Nuclear Dilemmas* (Washington DC, 1983).
Sigal, L., *Nuclear Forces in Europe: Enduring Dilemmas, Present Prospects* (Washington DC, 1984).
Skinner, M., *U.S.A.F.: A Primer of Modern Air Combat* (Novato, 1983).
Sobakin, V., *Ravnaya bezopasnost': printsip ravenstva i odinakovoi bezopasnosti v sovremennykh mezhdunarodnykh otnosheniyakh* (Moscow, 1984).
Sovetskie vooruzhennye sily: istoriya stroitel'stva (Moscow, 1978).
Soviet Armed Forces Review Annual. Volume 9 (Florida, 1986).
Steele, J. and Abraham, E., *Andropov in Power: From Komsomol to Kremlin* (Oxford, 1983).
Talbott, S., *Endgame: The Inside Story of SALT II* (New York, 1979).

Talbott, S., *Deadly Gambits: The Reagan Administration and the Stalemate in Nuclear Arms Control* (New York, 1984).

Tatu, M., *La bataille des euromissiles* (Paris, 1983).

Thompson, E., *Beyond the Cold War: A New Approach to the Arms Race and Nuclear Annihilation* (New York, 1982).

Tolubko, V., *Nedelin* (Moscow, 1979).

Trulock, N., *Weapons of Mass Destruction in Soviet Military Strategy* (unpublished manuscript).

Vadarmis, A., 'German-American Military Fissures', *Foreign Policy*, no. 34, Spring 1979.

Warner, E., *The Military in Contemporary Soviet Politics: An Institutional Analysis* (New York, 1977).

Weickhardt, G., 'Ustinov versus Ogarkov', *Problems of Communism* Jan./Feb. 1985.

Wettig, G., 'Die sowjetischen INF-Daten kritisch beleuchtet', *Aussen Politik*, 1, 1983.

White, W., *U.S. Tactical Air Power: Missions, Forces and Costs* (Washington DC, 1974).

Wright, B., *Soviet Missiles* (Lexington, Mass., 1986).

Yakovlev, A., *Sovetskie samolety: kratkii ocherk*, 3rd ed. (Moscow, 1979).

Yenne, B., *A Primer of Modern Strategic Airpower: S.A.C.* (London, 1984).

Yost, D., 'France's Deterrent Posture and Security in Europe. Part 1: Capabilities and Doctrine', *Adelphi Paper* 194 (London, 1984).

Zuckerman, *Europe and America and The Nuclear Shadow* (London, 1983).

Index

A3D (Skywarrior), 11
A-6, 11
A9/10, 7
A-10, 78
ABM, 15, 42, 173, 177
ACDA, 80, 108
Adamishin, Anatoly, 163
Afanas'ev, Viktor, 141, 205
Afghanistan, 91, 106
Africa, 45
Agapov, 22
Agreement on Prevention of
    Nuclear War (1973), 40, 48
Air defence (Soviet), 11–13, 20,
    22–8, 59, 65, 109, 165
Akhromeev, Sergei, 85
Alaska, 171
Albania, 35, 39
ALCMs, 66
Alexandrov, 201
Alexandrov, I, 38
Algeria, 207
Amsterdam-Pleyel Conference, 97
Andropov, Yuri, 125–8, 131–3, 135,
    139, 141–2, 145, 152, 163
Angola, 91
Apel, Hans, 116
Arab oil embargo, 49
Arbatov, Georgii, 38, 70, 208
Ardamatsky, Dimitry, 95
Army Tactical Missile System, 171
Asia, 71, 119, 123, 129, 136, 166,
    170 (see also individual
    countries)
ASPAC, 45
ASU, 24, 25
Atomic bomb (Soviet), 6, 8
Azores, 4, 6

B-29, 5, 9, 12, 181

B-36, 6, 8, 9
B-45, 6
B-47, 9, 12
B-52, 9, 12, 20
B-70, 26
Backfire (see Tu-22M)
Baker, John, xi
Baltic, 51
Barabanshchikov, 23–4
Bari, 89
Batitsky, Pavel, 12, 22–3, 26
Belgium, 50
Berlin crisis, 5, 6
Berlin settlement, 114
Berlinguer, Enrico, 49, 131
Berman, Robert, xi
Bessmertnykh, Alexander, xi
Bevin, Ernest, 4, 5
Blaker, Peter, 135
Borejsza, Jerzy, 97
Borisov, G., 25
Bovin, Alexander, ix, 1, 41, 155–7,
    168, 208
Bradley, Senator, 70
Brandt, Willy, 31, 53, 94
von Braun, Werner, 7
Brazil, 207
Brezhnev, Leonid, 42–3, 45, 48, 53,
    55–8, 70–1, 74, 82–3, 102–3,
    106–7, 110, 113, 118, 120–21,
    123–6, 128, 141–2, 152, 163,
    165, 201, 208
Britain, x, 1, 4, 5, 6, 9, 32–3, 37–8,
    41, 44, 48, 50, 52, 57, 59, 65,
    69, 76, 78, 87, 90–1, 104, 108,
    113, 118–19, 122–4, 126–7,
    129, 131–2, 135, 139–40, 149,
    151–2, 157–62, 165–7, 175–7,
    204–5
Brosio, Manlio, 62

Brown, General, 51-2
Brown, Harold, 22, 26, 90, 95, 109
Brzezinski, Zbigniew, 79-81, 83, 86, 101
Budapest, 39
Bukin, 13
Bulgaria, 137
Burchinal, General, 26
Burlatsky, Fyodor, 208
Burov, V., 23
Burt, Richard, 65, 118
Bush, George, 204
Byrnes, James, 4

C-47s, 5
Callaghan, James, 52, 86, 99
Canada, 52, 132, 151-2
Cape Verde, 4
Carrington, Lord, 162, 167
Carter, Jimmy, 79-87, 89, 99, 105-6, 108, 111, 117, 121, 156, 161, 167, 199
Ceausescu, Nicolae, 137
CENTO, 45
Central Committee, 71-2, 75, 95, 103, 121, 123-5, 133, 142, 144, 146, 151, 163-4, 166
Chandra, Romesh, 97, 107, 117
Chernenko, Konstantin, 142-6, 150-2
Chernyshev, Vladimir, 163
Chevaline, 135
Chervov, Col. Gen. Nikolai, 61-2, 126, 210
Chile, 49
China, xii, 32, 34-41, 57, 59, 103, 119, 129, 136, 188
Chou En-lai, 35-6, 188
Christian Democrats, 127
CIA, 183, 193, 202
CMEA, 133
Cockburn, Andrew, xi
Committee in Defence of Peace (Soviet), 97-8
Committee on the Present Danger, 80, 114
Communist International, 97
Congress, 31, 52, 62-4, 105, 128

Council of Ministers (Soviet), 107, 113, 128
CPSU Congresses, 53, 95, 110, 162, 164-5, 173
Craxi, Bettino, 152
Cruise, 60, 65-7, 70, 73, 76, 78-9, 81-4, 87-92, 94-6, 97, 100-2, 104-5, 108-10, 114, 118, 123-5, 126-9, 132-5, 137-9, 141, 146, 148-9, 152, 156, 160-61, 165 (see also ALCMs, GLCMs, SLCMs)
CSCE (see ESC)
CSU, 129
Cuba, 16, 28, 44
Cyprus, 50-2
Czechoslovakia, 15, 31, 39, 42, 52-3, 137-8, 142, 170

Damansky/Chenpao, 35-6
Dawes Plan, 5
Debré, Michel, 31
Defence Ministry (Soviet), 166
Defence Council, 58
Department of Defense (Pentagon), 22, 28-9, 58, 62, 65-7, 70-1, 78, 87, 92, 95, 109, 126, 144, 152
Department of State, 87, 92, 100, 118-19, 144, 150
de Gaulle, Charles, 9
Denmark, 50
DIA, 26, 65, 193
Djerdap, 39
Dobrynin, Anatoly, 43, 81, 146, 163, 168-9
Dolgov, 127
Dual-track decision, 101, 104-6, 112
Dutch (see Netherlands)

East Germany, 39, 52, 68, 86, 102-3, 114-15, 130-32, 137-8, 170, 205
ECMS, 21-2, 26
EEC, 31, 39, 152, 154, 158-9
Eisenhower, Dwight D., 8
ERW (neutron bomb), 93, 96-100, 102

ESC (CSCE), x, 72, 75, 95, 163
Ethiopia, 91, 145
European-American Workshop,
    65–6
European Parliament, 127
European Recovery Plan, 3, 5
F-4, 68, 78
F-15, 78
F-16, 78-9
F-84, 6
F-111, 26, 30, 69, 77, 108
F-111A, 27
Falin, Valentin, 94, 114
Far East, xii, 35, 113, 136, 151, 181
    (see also Asia, and individual
    countries)
FB-111, 26, 66, 108, 119
FBS (US), xii, 4–6, 8–11, 13–14,
    16, 18–19, 25–33, 42–4, 47, 49,
    51–2, 55–9, 61, 63–4, 68–72,
    77–9, 85, 87–96, 100–01,
    104–15, 118–19, 122–4, 126–9,
    132–4, 137–9, 141, 146, 148,
    152, 156, 159–61, 164–66,
    170–75, 178
Fischer, Oskar, 205
Flexible response, xii, 29, 55, 64,
    172
Ford, Gerald, 57, 66, 80
Foreign Ministry (Soviet), 71, 94–5,
    103, 114, 125, 144, 163, 165–7,
    172, 205
Foreign Office, 127, 152
France, xii, 1, 6, 9, 31–3, 37–8, 48,
    57, 59, 69, 108, 113, 118–19,
    122–4, 126–9, 131–2, 135, 138,
    140, 149, 152, 155–63, 165–7,
    169, 175–7, 204–5
Free Democrats, 127
French Communist Party, 49
French Socialist Party, 49

Gagarin Air Force Academy, 20
Gal'finger, A., 23
Garthoff, Raymond, xi, 39, 60
Gelb, Leslie, 87
General Staff (Soviet), 21, 58, 61,
    126
Geneva, 86–7, 106, 108, 114, 118,

121, 123–9, 132, 134–5, 143,
    147–9, 152, 158, 166, 168–9
Genscher, Hans-Dietrich, 106, 127,
    139, 169
Georg'ev, K., 81
Gerasimov, Gennadi, 167
Germany, 1, 2, 4, 6–7, 12, 40, 43,
    86
GLCMs, ix, x, 65–7, 70, 87–8, 92,
    94–7, 100–2, 104–5, 107–111,
    115, 123, 126–7, 129, 132–5,
    137–9, 141, 148, 156, 160–1,
    165, 172
Gleneagles, 113, 167
Glitman, Maynard, 150
Goodby, James, 87
Goodpaster, General, 29, 48
Gorbachev, Mikhail, 121, 142, 146,
    150–3, 156–9, 161–71, 173–4,
    176–7, 179, 207
Govorov, Leonid, 13
Grechko, Andrei, 16, 17, 24, 30, 43,
    56, 71, 73, 145
Greece, 50–1, 138
Greenland, 6
Greenleaf, Maj. Gen. Abbott, 67
Gromyko, Andrei, 33, 60, 66, 72,
    83–4, 86–7, 94, 102–3, 106–7,
    112, 123, 128–30, 142–52, 205
Guadeloupe, 100, 102

Hagelin, Bjorn, xi
Haig, Alexander, 112, 194
Haiphong harbour, 42
Half Moon, 5
Hamburg, 89
Hartman, Arthur, 146
Heseltine, Michael, 135
Helsinki, 15, 95, 98, 105
Helsinki Final Act, 72, 95
High Level Group (NATO), 65, 89,
    91–2, 104, 197
Hines, Lt. Col. John, 55
Holloway, David, xi–xii
Holst, 65
Hönecker, Erich, 131–2, 138
House Armed Services Committee,
    47

House Committee on Appropriations, 67
Hoxha, Enver, 39
Hungary, 125, 134–5
Hyland, William, x, xi, xii

ICBMs, 10, 16, 17, 28, 33, 61
Iceland, 4, 5, 6, 166
IMEMO (see institute of World Economy and International Relations)
India, 163, 207
INF talks, 106–39, 141, 144–5, 147–53, 156–73
INF treaty, 170–3
Institute of the USA and Canada, 38, 152, 208
Institute of World Economy and International Relations, 116, 153–4, 168
International Department, 46, 97, 107, 115, 125, 152, 163, 169
International Information Department, 94, 114, 154
International Institute of Strategic Studies, 89
International Liaison Department, 125
International Liaison for Disarmament and Peace, 117
Iran, 91
IRBMs, 10, 16, 28, 32–3, 39–40, 46, 123
Israel, 22, 48
Italian Communist Party (PCI), 49, 131
Italy, 49, 104, 112, 132

Jackson, Senator Henry, 80
Japan, 1, 32, 40, 103, 132, 136, 164
Jaruzelski, Marshal, 137
Johnson, Alexis, 43–4, 56
Joint Chiefs of Staff (US), 5, 6, 11, 28, 44, 46, 51, 78
Jones, General, 46
Jordan, Amos, 47

Kadar, Janos, 134–5
Kampelman, Max, 150, 169

Karpov, Viktor, 108, 128, 149, 167–8, 170
Kaverznev, Alexander, 75
Keeny, Spuregon, 108
Kennedy, Edward, 162
KGB, 35, 72, 97, 126
Khe Sanh, 21
Khlestov, Oleg, 54
Khrushchev, Nikita, 10, 208
Kissinger, Henry, 15, 35, 38, 44, 48–50, 56–7, 60, 66–8, 79–80, 83, 87
Kohl, Helmut, 127, 129, 133, 170
Koldunov, Marshal Alexander, 26
Korea, 6, 12, 91
Korean War, 6, 12
Kornienko, Georgii, 70
Korolev, Sergei, 7
Korshunov, Yevgeny, 45
Kosygin, Alexei, 35, 43
Kovalev, Anatoly, 94–5, 163
Krasovskii, Marshal, 20
Krushinskii, 107
Kulikov, Marshal, 123, 136
Kuusinen group, 207
Kvitsinsky, Yuli, 114–15, 118, 122–4, 128–9, 131, 136, 138, 149–50, 160, 202, 204

Lance missiles, 75, 78
Lebedev, Nikolai, 95
Lebedev, Maj. Gen. Yuri, 3, 173
Leber, George, 62, 68
Legge, Michael, 90–1
Lenin, V. I., 1, 17, 97, 125, 164, 177
Leont'ev, Colonel, 71
Lin Piao, 35, 38, 188
Limited nuclear options, 45, 55, 64
Linebaugh, David, 108
Litvinov, 153
Lomeiko, Vladimir, 144, 146–7
London summit, 86
Louis, Viktor, 35
Luns, NATO Secretary-General, 50

von Mack, General, 167
Maclean, Donald, 152
McNamara, Robert, 15

Maksimova, M., 154
Malenkov, Georgii, 7
Mao Tse-tung, 35–6, 188
Martin, Laurence, 65
Martin Marietta, 64
Mediterranean, 56–7, 149
MGIMO, 95, 114
Meyer, Stephen, xi
Middle East, 22, 25, 48, 74, 77, 163
MiG-9, 12
MiG-15, 12
MiG-19, 13
MiG-21, 13
MiG-23, 27
MiG-31, 23, 27
Military doctrine, 29, 44–7, 52–3,
    59, 78, 109, 162, 172
MIRVs, ix, 33, 44, 57, 60, 84
MIT (NATO), 62
Mitterand, François, 128–9, 204
Mlynař, Zdenek, 142
Molotov, V. M., 150, 153
Moorer, Admiral Thomas, 28, 44
Morocco, 6
Moscow Treaty (1970), 31, 53
MRBMs, 10, 28, 33, 39, 107
Mulley, 90
Münzenberg, Willi, 97
Myasishchev-4, 10

Nadiradze Bureau, 61
NSC, 8, 91, 92, 99–101
NATO, 11, 20, 26–34, 44, 47–55,
    58–65, 68, 70–1, 75–80, 84,
    88–92, 95–6, 99–106, 108–9,
    111, 113, 116–17, 119, 122,
    127–30, 132–3, 135, 137,
    140–1, 149, 152, 155, 158,
    160–2, 164, 167, 171–2, 175–6,
    178, 194, 204
Nebraska, 80
Nedelin, Mitrofan, 7
Nekrasov, Vadim, 75–6, 93
NEP, 177
Nerlich, Uwe, 65
Netherands, 50, 68, 72, 101, 104,
    157, 161
Neutron Bomb (see ERW)
Nike Hercules, 68

Nitze, Paul, 79–80, 114–15, 117,
    122–4, 129, 136, 138–9, 160–2,
    165, 202, 204
Nixon, Richard, 15, 17, 31, 38,
    42–3, 47–9, 57, 79, 80
Non-aggression pact, 37
North Atlantic Council, 86
North Vietnam, 13, 20–21, 26, 42,
    74
Norway, 65
NPG (NATO), 6, 77, 89–90, 95,
    104, 113, 171
NPOs, 61, 63
NPT, 53, 69

Obukhov, Alexei, 149, 170
Ogarkov, Nikolai, 136, 145, 207
Okeanskaya (see Vladivostok)
Okinawa, 6, 71
Operation Niagara, 21
Operational-tactical missiles
    (Soviet), 137–8, 142, 166–7,
    170, 173–4
OSD (US), 66–7, 87
Ottawa, 90, 95
Outer Mongolia, 38

Pacific, 57, 129
Peenemünde, 7
Peled, Major-General, 22, 80
Pentagon (see Department of
    Defense)
Perle, Richard, 15, 109, 115, 118,
    148
Pershing 1, 11, 68
Pershing 1A, 64, 68, 104, 170–2
Pershing 1-B, 170
Pershing 2, ix, x, 61, 64, 76, 78, 90,
    96, 100–2, 104–5, 107–11, 115,
    118, 125, 127–9, 132–5, 137–9,
    141, 146, 148–9, 152, 156,
    160–1, 164, 166, 170, 172
Philippines, 71
Pilsudski, Jósef, 114
Pincus, Walter, 96
PIT (NATO), 63
Poland, 31, 39–40, 53, 86, 114–15,
    117, 121, 133
Polaris, 32, 135

Politburo, 9, 12, 42–3, 46, 57–8, 60, 71, 107, 113, 121–2, 128, 133, 136, 142, 145, 147–50, 152, 158–9, 164, 166, 169
Polyanov, Nikolai, 50
Ponomarev, Boris, 46, 107, 152, 157–8, 201
Portugal, 49, 50, 207
Poseidon, 63, 69, 78
Powers, Gary, 13
Presidium (Supreme Soviet), 107, 113, 128, 152
Proektor, Professor, 168
Pyadyshev, Boris, 172
Pym, Francis, 127, 129
R-1, 7
R-2, 8
Reagan, Ronald, 80, 107, 109–13, 123, 126, 129–30, 135-6, 138, 143–7, 158, 165–7, 169, 171, 173
Red Army, 3, 177–8
Republican Party, 110
Reykjavik summit, 164, 166–70
Rogers, General Bernard, 116
Romania, 39, 86, 137
Romanov, Grigorii, 145, 150, 152, 207
Rowny, Edward, 207
Rumsfeld, Donald, 27, 78–9

SACEUR, 11, 90, 116, 194
Sakharov, Andrei, 82
SALT I, xii, 15–34, 30–5, 37–8, 42–3, 53, 56, 58–60, 63, 65, 69, 74, 79, 92–3, 112, 119, 149–50, 159, 169, 175
SALT II, 33, 42–3, 55–60, 69–74, 78–84, 86–93, 96, 100, 102–4, 106, 108, 110, 112, 119, 145, 149–50, 159, 161, 169, 175
Samorukov, 29
SAMs, 20–2, 78
SAM-1, 13
SAM-2, 13, 68
SAM-6, 22
SAM-10, 23
Scandinavia, 51

Schlesinger, James, 44–6, 55, 59, 63–4, 68–9, 78
Schmidt, Helmut, 2, 65, 86, 89, 99, 101, 106, 111–12, 199
Scotland, 11, 113, 167
Scud, 68
SDI, 143, 147–50, 152, 156, 158, 160–2, 164–8, 172–3, 176–7, 179
SDP, 160
SEATO, 45
Second Fleet, 119
Second (Socialist) International, 118, 201
SED, 131
Semenov, Vladimir, 16, 19, 36–7, 56–7, 94
Senate, 66, 90–91
Senate Armed Services Committee, 46, 110
Senate Foreign Relations Committee, 28, 46, 48
Serov, Colonel-General, 7
Seventh Fleet, 57, 61
Shabanov, Col. Gen. Vitaly, 61
Shaposhnikov, Vitaly, 97–8, 115–17, 125
Shearer, Richard, 63
Shelepin, Alexander, 71
Shelest, 42–3
Shevardnadze, Eduard, 152, 165, 171, 207
Shevchenko, Arkady, 16, 72
Shishlin, Nikolai, 75, 154
Shultz, George, 124, 142, 146–8, 161
Silin, 2
Simonyan, Professor, 76
Sixth Fleet, 57, 61, 119
SLBMs, 32, 34, 90–1
SLCMs, 66–7, 70, 87–8
Smith, Gerard, 18–19, 32, 36–7, 43
Socialist International (see Second International)
Sokolov, Marshal Sergei, 147
Soviet Peace Fund, 97
Soviet Union (see under particular headings)
Sozinov, Colonel General, 24–5

Spadolini, Giovanni, 112
SPD, 110–11, 127–8
Sputnik, 10, 13
SS-3, 10
SS-4 (R-12), 10, 33, 39, 60, 103,
    108, 119–20, 157, 160, 172
SS-5 (R-14), 10, 33, 39, 60, 103,
    108, 119–20, 157, 172
SS-6, 10
SS-11, xii, 33, 39
SS-12, 142, 166, 170, 172
SS-14, xii, 61
SS-15, xii, 61
SS-16 (RS-14), xii, 61
SS-18 (RS-20), 81, 84
SS-19 (RS-18), 81, 84
SS-20 (RSD-10), pp, ix-x, 57–61,
    69–70, 82, 85, 88–90, 92–4, 96,
    102–3, 108–9, 113, 119–20,
    123, 127–9, 131, 135–6, 142,
    148, 152, 156–8, 160, 162, 172,
    175–7
SS-23, 142, 166, 170, 172
SS-N-6, xii
Stalin, 3, 5, 6, 7, 117, 142, 151–2,
    178
Starodubov, Major-General Viktor,
    21, 60
START, 121, 128, 141, 149–50
Stockholm conference, 141
Stockholm Peace Appeal, 97, 116
Strategic Air Command (US), 5, 9,
    29
Strategic Rocket Forces (Soviet), 7,
    9
Strauss, Franz-Josef, 129
Stutzle, Walter, 65
Su-17, 68
Su-24, 27
Supreme Soviet, 10, 152
Sweeney, Walter, 9

Tactical Air Command (US), 6, 21,
    64
Tactical Nuclear Weapons, 8
Taiwan, 91
Tandecki, Peter, 65
Thailand, 71

Thatcher, Margaret, 127, 135, 151,
    160, 162, 204
Therop, Emelda, 192
Third World, 70, 74, 92, 103–4, 111,
    176, 179 (see also individual
    countries)
Thompson, E. P., 117
Thompson, Llewellyn, 15
Thomson, James, 66–7, 70, 87, 91,
    99–101
Tito, 39
Tokaev, Tokaty, 7
Tomahawk, 67 (see also SLCMs)
Tower, Senator John, 150
Treaties (see under specific
    headings)
Trident, 91
Truman, Harry S., 6, 7
Tu-4, 6, 8, 9
Tu-16, 9, 60
Tu-20 (Tu-95), 10
Tu-22, 60
Tu-22M, 60, 66, 69, 81–2, 84, 104
Tukhachevsky, Marshal, 114
Turkey, 50–1
Tyushkevich, Colonel, 73

Urdmurtiya. 61
U-2, 12, 13, 183
UN Disarmament Week, 108
UN General Assembly, 81, 107,
    145–6
UN Security Council, 38
United States (see under specific
    headings)
USAF, 5, 10, 21–2, 64, 67
USAFE, 6, 27, 78
USSR (see under specific headings)
Ustinov, Marshal Dimitrii, 121–2,
    124, 126, 130, 134, 145–7
V-1, 7
V-2, 6, 7
Vance, Cyrus, 80–7, 90–1, 97, 99
Vasendin, Major-General, 30
Vetrov, Colonel M., 16
Vienna talks, 48, 52–6, 59, 68–72,
    114, 175
Vietnam War, 10, 13, 17, 20–1,

25–6, 30, 32, 38, 42, 47, 59, 71, 74, 78, 80
Vladivostok summit, 56–7, 65–6, 70–1, 79–85
Vogel, Hans-Jochen, 128
Voigt, Karsten, 110
Vorontsov, Yuli, 163, 168–9
Voroshilov Academy, 191
Votkinsk, 61
VRBMs, 39
Vulcan, 32, 135

War of intervention, 1, 12
Warnke, Paul, 80
Warsaw Pact, 27–8, 39, 47, 51–2, 63, 123, 127–8, 130–4, 136–7, 140, 161
Washington summit, 168, 171–2
Watergate, 47, 80
Weinberger, Caspar, x, xii, 110, 148
West Germany, 31, 43, 48, 52, 62–3, 65, 68–70, 72, 75–7, 79, 85–91, 93–5, 97–9, 101, 104, 106–7, 109–13, 116, 120, 122, 127–9, 131, 133, 136, 139–40, 163, 165, 167, 169–71, 178
Westmoreland, General, 21
WEU, 69, 154

Williamsburg, 132
Wohlstetter, A., 65
World Conference of Peace Supporters, 97
World Congress of Intellectuals for Peace, 97
World Parliament of Peoples for Peace, 105, 107–8
World Peace Council, 97–8, 100, 102–3, 105, 107, 111–12, 115–17, 125, 139
World War II, 1, 2, 3, 20–1, 43, 123, 136
Wörner, Manfred, 129, 170
Wroclaw, 97
Yak-15, 12
Yak-25, 12
Yakovlev, Alexander, 152, 164
Yazov, Dimitrii, 172
Yepishev, General, 56, 153, 207
Yugoslavia, 5

Zagladin, Vadim, 169
Zamyatin, Leonid, 94, 114
Zero-option, 113, 118, 122–3, 127, 129
Zhilin, Lt-General, 56
Zhukov, Yuri, 2, 98, 107
Zhurkin, Vitalii, 154